T0213070

Communications in Computer and Information Science   677

Commenced Publication in 2007
Founding and Former Series Editors:
Alfredo Cuzzocrea, Dominik Ślęzak, and Xiaokang Yang

Fernando Koch · Andrew Koster
Tiago Primo · Christian Guttmann (Eds.)

Advances in Social Computing and Digital Education

7th International Workshop on Collaborative Agents Research
and Development, CARE 2016, Singapore, May 9, 2016
and Second International Workshop on Social Computing
in Digital Education, SocialEdu 2016, Zagreb, Croatia, June 6, 2016
Revised Selected Papers

Springer

Editors
Fernando Koch
Korea University
Seoul
Korea (Republic of)

and

School of Design
The University of Melbourne
Melbourne
Australia

Andrew Koster
IIIA-CSIC
Bellaterra, Barcelona
Spain

Tiago Primo
Samsung Research Institute
Campinas
Brazil

Christian Guttmann
University of New South Wales
Sydney, NSW
Australia

and

Department of Learning, Informatics,
 Management and Ethics
Karolinska Institute
Stockholm
Sweden

ISSN 1865-0929   ISSN 1865-0937   (electronic)
Communications in Computer and Information Science
ISBN 978-3-319-52038-4   ISBN 978-3-319-52039-1   (eBook)
DOI 10.1007/978-3-319-52039-1

Library of Congress Control Number: 2017930214

Printed on acid-free paper

This Springer imprint is published by Springer Nature
The registered company is Springer International Publishing AG
The registered company address is: Gewerbestrasse 11, 6330 Cham, Switzerland

Preface

Humans are largely "collectively driven": One can understand how much human behavior is socially learned and peer influenced. That is, people are collectively rational, not individually rational. This aspect of human behavior reflects in any human endeavor, including education, where students are largely influenced by their peers, teachers, family, and society. Thus, in order to understand and improve education, we need to promote technologies that allows us to better understand the education environment as a social setting. These include techniques of continuous monitoring, human behavior analysis, recommendation systems, adjustment of education activities, intelligent content placement, and others.

In this context, we promoted the Second International Workshop on Social Computing in Digital Education (SOCIALEDU), organized in conjunction with the International Conference on Intelligent Tutoring Systems, on June 6, 2016, in Zagreb, Croatia, and the 7th International Workshop on Collaborative Agents Research & Development — CARE for Digital Education, hosted as a special session together with the COIN workshop, in conjunction with the International Conference on Autonomous Agents and Multi-Agent Systems (AAMAS) on May 9, 2016, in Singapore.

The objective of these workshops was to discuss models of social computing and computational intelligence applied to digital education. This is a growing field of research concerned with bringing interactive technology to teaching and learning in the classroom. We fomented the discussion around new forms of assessment, and models to understand the impact of social behavior, learning context, and individual profile upon learning performance. Some of the leading research questions revolved around:

- How to apply techniques of computational intelligence and social computing for the next-generation digital education scenarios?
- How to construct computational intelligence models to advance the elements of the digital education environment, namely, adaptive content, tutoring systems, intelligent composition systems, learning analytics, and others?
- How to apply computational intelligence and social computing to evolve adaptive learning and adjustable content reactive to social behavior?
- How to build an effective monitoring–recognition–intervention framework in digital education?
- How can we support/guide collaborative teams. How can we offer flexibility in how teams execute plans? How can we make team members follow agreed procedures? Incentives? Or more fundamental, by designing a new market?

This volume includes extended and revised versions of a set of selected works from two different workshops in the area of technology-enhanced learning. The volume is further complemented by a chapter by invited researchers in this field of research. The workshops promoted international discussion forums with submissions and Program Committee members from many countries in Europe (Germany, France, The Netherlands,

Portugal, Romania, Spain, Sweden), Asia and Oceania (Australia, Japan, Korea, New Zealand), Africa (Algeria), and the Americas (Argentina, Brazil, Colombia).

The CARE workshop received seven submissions through the workshop website, from which we selected four for presentation at the workshop. The SOCIALEDU workshop also received seven submissions through the workshop website, from which we selected six for presentation. Nine extended versions of these contributions are published as chapters of the current volume, together with one further chapter by invited researchers. All the submissions were reviewed by at least three different reviewers, and the works selected for this volume are representative of research projects around the aforementioned methods. The selections highlight the innovation and contribution to the state of the art, suggesting solutions to real-world problems and applications built upon the proposed technology.

In the first chapter, "SCALA Web System on the Internet of Things: An Exploratory Research in Social Computing," Lima et al. describe recent developments in the SCALA system, which is a computational system for improving literacy in people with autism. In particular, the paper proposes a roadmap for how to use Internet-of-Things technologies for this purpose and discusses how enhanced sensing capabilities and novel modes of interaction can help to better include students with autism in the teaching–learning process.

The second chapter, "A Link Between Worlds: Towards a Conceptual Framework for Bridging Player and Learner Roles in Gamified Collaborative Learning Contexts" by Borges et al., focuses on the use of gamification techniques for collaborative learning. Their work focuses on relating psychological game player profiles from the game design and gamification literature to roles in collaborative learning contexts. They discuss how to form groups of learners and how to use gamification techniques to support learning in these groups.

The third chapter, "Group Recommendation System for E-Learning Communities: A Multi-Agent Approach", by Irvan and Terano, deals with another aspect of collaborative learning: how to recommend content for a group of learners. They propose a multi-agent system to consider the different preferences of the students, and thus optimise the content recommendation.

In the fourth chapter, "The Impact of Social Similarities and Event Detection on Ranking Retrieved Resources in Collaborative E-learning Systems," Beldjoudi, Seridi, and Benzine propose methods for improving tags, and tag-based retrieval, in folksonomies, in particular for learning object repositories. They propose methods for reducing ambiguity in folksonomies by taking into account the user profile, social interactions, and other contextual information, both when creating the tag, and when searching in a learning object repository.

In the fifth chapter, "Using Semantic Web Technologies to Describe an Educational Domain," Primo, Behr and Vicari present a three-layered ontology for describing learning objects. They propose the use of various semantic web technologies to formalize and reason about learning objects. The aim is to use this approach for automated knowledge discovery in the educational domain.

The sixth chapter, "Forming Tests from Questions with Different Theoretical and Practical Degree" by Popescu and Bold, uses metadata about questions to automatically create tests in a dynamic model of assessment. They test the viability of their approach in a trial with 20 students, to compare predicted and actual degrees of difficulty.

In the seventh chapter, "Collaborative Assessments in On-Line Classrooms," Osman et al. describe their work on peer assessment for massive online open courses (MOOCs). They propose two complementary methods for leveraging the power of students in an MOOC assessing each other while not losing the specificity and expertise of a teacher performing the assessment. Evaluation in a classroom setting and using simulated data indicate that the methods outperform other commonly used algorithms.

The eighth chapter, "Argumentation Support Tool with Modularization Function and Its Evaluation" by Katsura et al. presents a tool for teaching students discussion skills. Their tool converts the statements that students propose into arguments in a formal argumentation framework and helps the students reason about the logical structure. An evaluation among students indicates that the argumentation tool allows students to better reason about the pros and cons of a statement.

In the ninth chapter, "Gamification Design Framework to Support Multi-Agent Systems Theory Classes," Baldeon et al. describe their experiences in using gamification techniques in a university course. They evaluate the effect of these gamification techniques on learning performance, student satisfaction, and motivation, and found that the gamified experience offered improvements on all three fronts.

Finally, the chapter "The Role of Agent-Based Simulation in Education" by Koster et al. discusses the possibility of using agent-based modelling and simulation to obtain insights into the classroom dynamics between students, teacher, and material. They describe how such a model can be calibrated and validated and its possible uses in better tailoring education for students and teachers in a classroom setting.

We would like to thank all the volunteers who made the workshops possible by helping to organize and peer review the submissions, and to EasyChair for the conference and proceedings management system. We appreciate the help and enormous dedication of the members of the CARE and SOCIALEDU research communities, who continuously participate in our activities as Technical Program Committee, submitting contributions, and helping us put the pieces together to promote this publication.

We are also grateful to Springer for the continuous support and for publishing the printed proceedings after our workshops. This is an invaluable contribution to further promoting the research around computation intelligence and social computing in education, helping to improve the education process and aiming at providing the best education for all.

Dr. Koch, Dr. Primo, and Dr. Koster were working with Samsung Research Institute Brazil during the time of the implementation of this project. We thank Samsung Research for providing the space and research grant to conduct the study and field tests.

Dr. Koch is the beneficiary of a CNPq Productivity in Technology and Innovation Award (Grant: CNPq 307275/2015-9). He is currently engaged as an invited professor with Korea University, South Korea, and is Honorary Senior Fellow with The University of Melbourne, Australia.

Dr. Koster is currently a Marie Sklodowska-Curie COFUND Fellow in the P-Sphere project, funded by the European Union's Horizon 2020 research and innovation program under grant agreement No. 665919. Andrew Koster also thanks the Generalitat de Catalunya (Grant: 2014 SGR 118).

October 2016

Fernando Koch
Andrew Koster
Tiago Primo
Christian Guttmann

Organization

Program Committee

Sergio Alvarez-Napagao	Universitat Politècnica de Catalunya, Spain
Raimundo Barreto	Federal University of Amazonas, Brazil
Ig Bittencourt	Federal University of Alagoas, Brazil
Daniel Cabrera-Paniagua	Universidad de Valparaiso, Chile
Carlos Cardonha	IBM Research, Brazil
Néstor Darío Duque Méndez	Universidad Nacional de Colombia, Colombia
Maira Gatti de Bayser	IBM Research, Brazil
Christian Guttmann	Karolinska Institute, Sweden and University of New South Wales (UNSW), Australia
Seiji Isotani	University of Sao Paulo, Brazil
Fernando Koch	Korea University, South Korea
Andrew Koster	IIIA-CSIC, Spain
Eduardo Oliveira	The University of Melbourne, Australia
Hugo Paredes	INESC TEC and UTAD, Portugal
Tiago Primo	Samsung Research Institute, Brazil
Alexandre Ribeiro	University of Caxias do Sul, Brazil
Jordi Sabater Mir	IIIA-CSIC, Spain
Joao Luis Silva	Instituto Communitas, Brazil
Jose Viterbo	Fluminense Federal University, Brazil
Leandro Krug Wives	Federal University of Rio Grande do Sul, Brazil

Contents

SCALA Web System on the Internet of Things: An Exploratory Research in Social Computing

Roceli P. Lima[1](✉), Magda Bercht[1], Liliana M. Passerino[1], Rosa M. Vicari[1], and João C. Gluz[2]

[1] Interdisciplinary Center for Educational Technologies (CINTED),
UFRGS, Porto Alegre, Brazil
rocelilima@gmail.com, {bercht,rosa}@inf.ufrgs.br,
liliana@cinted.ufrgs.br
[2] Post-Graduation Program in Applied Computer Science (PIPCA),
UNISINOS, São Leopoldo, Brazil
jcgluz@unisinos.br

Abstract. SCALA system is an effort to integrate Internet of Things (IoT) and Social Computing to provide an alternative communication system to improve literacy of people with autism. After introducing SCALA, this work presents a review on the state of the art about the application of IoT technologies to Autism, carried out in five international scientific databases. Based on this study, it is proposed a model for integrating SCALA to IoT with a focus on questions about the literacy process for children with autism. SCALA currently operates on web, desktop and tablet platforms. The proposed technological integration with IoT aims to bring additional functionalities for SCALA, which will enable mediation with its subjects by means of physical objects. Results can be of use for developers of similar systems.

Keywords: Social computing · Internet of Things · Autism · Alternative communication · SCALA system

1 Introduction

From 2009 onwards, the SCALA system, which is an alternative communication system to improve the literacy of people with autism [20], is being developed by our research group. During this period SCALA has been adapted to operate on several digital platforms, starting from a web system aimed to operate with desktop and laptop computers, which was eventually redesigned to work with tablets and, more recently, is evolving to a full HTML5 responsive multi platform interface [20]. The next challenge is to integrate this system with the Internet of Things.

The expression *Internet of Things* (IoT) was coined in 1999 at a lecture by researcher Kevin Ashton for P&G executives, focused on the idea of embedding electronic devices in physical objects, allowing this objects to established communication links to the Internet [3, 8]. A follow up on this idea, resulted in the creation of *Radio-Frequency Identification* (RFID) standard [26]. The concept of an Internet of "things" refers to objects (things) and representation of these objects that can share

© Springer International Publishing AG 2016
F. Koch et al. (Eds.): CARE 2016/SocialEdu 2016, CCIS 677, pp. 1–18, 2016.
DOI: 10.1007/978-3-319-52039-1_1

information with other objects and/or communicate over the networks (wired/wireless) often using the *Internet Protocol* (IP). The main idea about IoT is that data enables to recognize events and changes in the surrounding environments and "things" can act and react autonomously [16], for instance.

The use of *Information and Communication Technologies* (ICTs) with people on the *Autism Spectrum Disorder* (ASD) has gained importance and been considered on most part a valuable resource [13]. This disorder has two domains: social/communication deficits, as well as fixed interests and repetitive behaviors (see DSM-5 [9]). Among the ICTs used with children with ASD, we highlight the use of robots [2, 18, 23], alternative communication systems on computers [20], on the web [6, 7], on tablets [11], games, applications ("apps") for mobile platforms, tables with tangible user interface, as well as virtual platforms with 2D and 3D animations [10, 12, 19].

These results give support to the main research hypothesis of this work, that IoT and ICT technology can productively work together applied to ASD. As a consequence is important to define a clear road map on how to evolve SCALA to work on the IoT. This is important because today there is no established way on how to integrate IoT technology to alternative communication systems based on web.

To establish the base of the road map and to understand better the complex set of applications and technologies, which forms the context of the integration of SCALA with IoT, we did a systematic exploratory search over five international scientific databases, to find recent works about the integrated application of IoT technology to work with Autism cases.

This allowed us to define the main research goals of the road map. To evaluate the feasibility of these goals we focused on the integration of the Visual Narratives module of the SCALA on the Internet of Things (IoT). This work show how this integration scenario is being conceived.

2   The SCALA System

SCALA is an alternative communication system for the literacy of children with autism spectrum disorders (ASD) and no oral skills or with severe motor handicap [20]. The system was initially focused on children aged from 3 to 5.

ASD is a disorder affecting neurological development and it must be present since childhood or early childhood. According to the *American Psychiatric Association*, DSM-5, autism included in the diagnosis category for neurodevelopment disorders, under the sub-category of Autism Spectrum Disorders, which includes autism, Asperger's syndrome, *Childhood Disintegrative Disorder* (CDD) and *Pervasive Developmental Disorder Not Otherwise Specified* (PDD-NOS) [9].

The SCALA desktop system [4] was designed as a tool to build and use *communication boards*, which can be used as alternative communication devices with children with Autism. SCALA communication boards support the use of communication resources such as pictographs, voice synthesizing, audio recording, subtitles and animation.

Lately, SCALA was evolved to support web and tablet platforms [7], differently with the other system, for example, Vox4All [17] and Livox [24], appeared later in the Brazilian market as proprietary apps running on either iOS or Android.

New functionalities also were incorporated in the system: the Visual Narratives module, the prototype for a free communicator device, and a scanning system for the communication board module. Throughout the development process, several studies were developed involving children between 3 and 5 years with autism, their families and teachers of the schools. SCALA was entirely designed and developed using the Context-Centered Design of Usage principles [20], which allowed us to identify points to be improved and re-engineered.

The development of the web version of the SCALA system (http://scala.ufrgs.br/ Scalaweb/) begins in 2011 with the proposal to consider a cross-platform solution specially designed to meet the demands of applications for tablets. All development was accompanied and marked with a study case with three 3–4 years old children with Autism over two years. This study was developed in three different contexts: school, family and lab at the University. The SCALA has three modules: Communication Board (Fig. 1), Visual Narratives (Figs. 2, 3 and 4), Communication Free (Figs. 5 and 6) and was developed under GNU and Creative Commons licenses to ensure its open content.

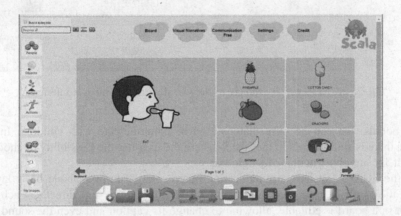

Fig. 1. The communication board module of SCALA system [7].

The pictographs used in the system were mostly developed by ARASAAC (http:// arasaac.org/) group and are available under Creative Commons licenses. With the use of ARASAAC images and with the users' own pictures, SCALA currently has more than four thousand images, divided into the categories: People, Objects, Nature, Action, Food, Feelings, Qualities and My Pictures, where the user has the option inserting his own images in the system. The images have a unique identification number that are associated with the respective physical file address, for example, the Duck and Cat objects are 14271 and 14544 numbers.

The modules differ in some ways that allow greater flexibility, depending on the objectives, strategies and degree of difficulty to be proposed for use. The Communication Board module has a user-friendly interface that integrates into single screen facilities to edit and use *communication boards*, allowing teachers, tutors or parents to

Fig. 2. SCALA web – example of the visual narratives module interface.

create boards that can be immediately used to communicate with children. In this module there is static space on the screen where the user has the possibility of choosing a layout for the construction of single boards.

In the SCALA system communication boards start from a scalable basic layout, which allows every user to create their own boards simply and directly. Each pictograph in a board is editable, allowing to change its caption and even the sound of it from a context-sensitive menu. The boards can be stored privately or in public spaces.

The Visual Narratives module will be used to implement the results of this research, proposing a project for this module and similar with IoT. This module is free to insert multiple images and textual elements (Fig. 2).

The Communication Board module consists of an editor of communication boards and viewer for these boards with a built-in voice synthesizer. Communication boards are assistive technology resources to facilitate communication between people with deficits in communication and other participants from the signaling or choice of images previously organized in the boards. Also, allows building stories with flexible preparing conditions. This module has diverse layouts that provide a variable degree of complexity. The screen has a blank space where it is possible to insert and edit images, which can be overlapped, increased or decreased in size, inverted or deleted.

There is the possibility to define the color background and insert and edit conversation balloons with small dialogues. The story then can be saved for posterior use.

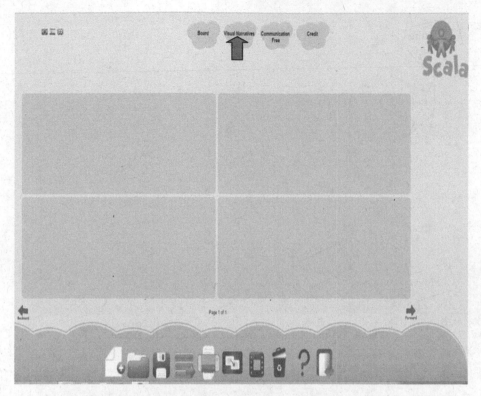

Fig. 3. Visual Narratives module interface.

It also can be played by the tablet's voice synthesizer which will read what was typed, otherwise the recorded sounds will be played.

To access the module "Visual Narratives" you must click on the corresponding cloud from the top menu (Fig. 3). Its differential compared to the module "Board", that can be inserted several figures for comics, as well as scenarios.

To start building your story, click on one of the layout frames. You will be redirected to a page to create a frame (scene) (Fig. 4).

The edit screen shows, on the left side, the categories of pictures and dialogue balloons. The top there is the image search field. In the center is the editing area in which images and dialog balloons can be inserted. The top of the editing area is an icon represented by a book. Clicking on this will open a field for entering the narration of the story, after this, you have to click "Finish". Also is possible change the comic scene. Click the "Scenario", represented by a color palette on the bottom menu.

The Communication Free is a module similar to the chat system, however makes use of assistive technology and alternative communication in order to offer to autistic child one tool for improve their literacy and have a better contact with people who have developed the same difficulty [7]. In this module, the children built phrases and text with the help of images and sounds [8].

Fig. 4. Visual Narratives module interface - edit screen.

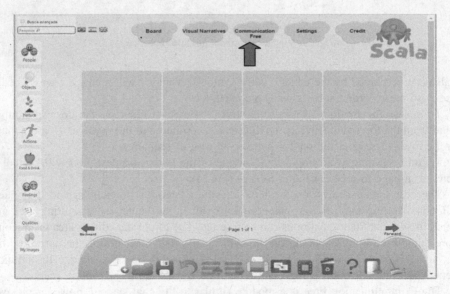

Fig. 5. Communication free module interface.

Current research on SCALA, besides the integration with IoT, includes, among other works, the development of a formal ontological support for the semantics of the alternative communication system, the integration and use of ARASAAC pictographs

Fig. 6. Communication free module interface: the children built phrases and text with the help of images and sounds.

(http://catedu.es/arasaac/) into SCALA, in My Pictures options the user has the option inserting his own images in the system. Also, support of a scanning mode in order to include individuals with physical disabilities. The past, present and future of SCALA system in a graphical perspective (Fig. 7).

This evolution system will going to resolve the problems when a same concept has many pictograms associated and to make additional functions for behaves semantically with this kind of situations [21]. Likewise, to implement advanced search to find in remotely picture data base, for instance, using ARASAAC API [14].

- SCALA IoT (new research)	2016
- SCALA with Advanced search engine (under construction)	2014 / 2015
- SCALA integrated to Siesta-Cloud - SCALA integrated to ARASAAC	2013
- SCALA WEB, SCALA TABLET, Visual Narratives Module, Scanning Module, Communication Free	2012
- SCALA Desktop	2011
- SCALA Prototype	2009

Fig. 7. Technological evolution of SCALA system.

3   Review of the State of Art on IoT and Autism

The review of the state of the art started with a systematic literature review based on the exploratory research method devised in [26], which aims to develop, clarify and change concepts and ideas, especially with the purpose to specify more accurately problems and hypotheses for subsequent studies.

The exploratory research method starts with the choice of the national and international scientific databases to be searched (see Sect. 3.1), follows to the definition of the descriptors to be used on the search of these databases (see Sect. 3.2) and to the execution of the search and the selection of works and papers (see Sect. 3.2). Detailed results about the most representative papers found about the application of IoT to Autism are presented in Sect. 3.3.

3.1   Scientific Databases

For the execution of the systematic research, five international scientific databases were initially analyzed, two of which pertaining to the field of Exact and Earth Sciences, and the three other pertaining to Multi-Disciplinary fields, ranging from 1999 to 2015. This period was chosen because in 1999 coined the term IoT.

3.2   Descriptors of the Exploratory Research

The exploration criteria defined for the research was to select papers from the databases that meet a query descriptor including the terms Internet of Things and Autism. The bibliographical research found 13 papers based on this descriptor, from 1999 to 2015, 5 of which obtained from the IEEE database, 1 from the SCOPUS database, 7 from the SPRINGER database and zero in ACM and SCIENCE DIRECT.

However, only three papers were considered for the detailed analysis, being considered the most representative of current works on the application of IoT technology to Autism. The contents of 2 papers were already included in other papers extracted from the databases. Other 8 papers did not present an integrated solution in terms of Internet of Things and Autism and were not considered.

3.3   Results of the Exploratory Research

The only work to make use of a machine learning algorithm was [5], which presented a web information retrieval filter, a visual interface system for presenting multimodal contents, and wireless sensors. The goal of this work was to personalize learning materials for children with special needs. Figures 8(a) and 10(b) present, respectively, the overall architecture and the multimodal interface of the system described in [5].

The control of IoT sensors was built on a Raspberry Pi board (Fig. 9) using a Linux-based operating system.

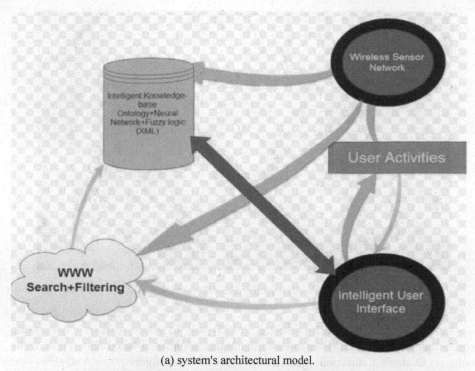

(a) system's architectural model.

(b) multimodal visual interface

Fig. 8. Architecture (a) and multimodal (b) interface of system presented in [5].

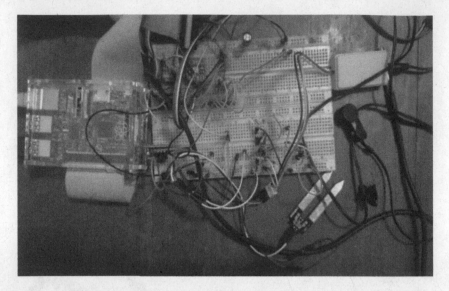

Fig. 9. Raspberry Pi board for controlling sensors (source [5])

The purpose of the work presented in [25] was to create a smart environment combining the IoT, P2P (Peer-to-Peer) communication, web-based and sensor technologies to monitor and control health status, and to assist children with ASD (Fig. 10).

The P2P system is based on a *JXTA-Overlay Platform,* responsible for communications between users. The SmartBox (Fig. 11) is a hardware built to manage children's monitoring sensors, among which we can highlight the sensor for hand and body moves, for detecting chair vibrations, for controlling ambient lighting, for controlling

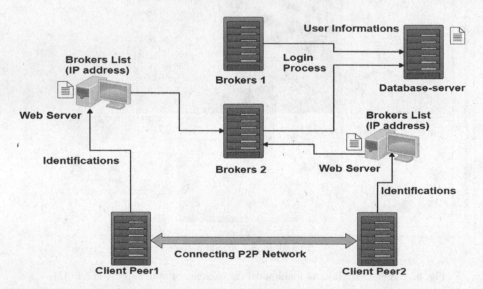

Fig. 10. Architectural model for the system presented in [25].

Fig. 11. SmartBox (source [25]).

ambient odors and for reproducing audio. Moreover, by means of the Heuristic Diagnostic Teaching (HDT), this smart environment was used to identify mathematical learning skills and creative characteristics for students that are diagnosed with autism.

The last paper found in the search [22], proposes a gesture and object recognition system for mobile platforms with the Android operating system, named MOBIS, which can assist autistic children to recognize objects when doing learning activities (Fig. 12).

Fig. 12. MOBIS system for visual object recognition (source [22]).

This system captures images by means of a cell phone or tablet camera and processes them by using visual support techniques. The system uses a vision-based object recognition algorithm to associate visual and oral markers to the object that is being captured and recognized. It associates the images of the objects to other textual and sound elements, in addition to other equivalent images found on the Internet.

Table 1 shows a summary of the main technologies used in the selected papers. These technologies were classified in software, hardware and communication technologies. Hardware technologies are mostly related to the sensors, actuators and devices identified in the selected papers. It was the base how IoT can change the current assistive technologies for children with autism. In the next section discussed the use each of these technologies.

Table 1. Technologies used in the papers about IoT and Autism

Software	Hardware	Communication
- Machine learning algorithm - Web information retrieval filter - Visual interface system for presenting multimodal contents - Monitoring sensors (temperature, vibration, motion) - Image processing and visual computing	- Audio generation - Sensor for controlling odors - Sensor for controlling lighting - Movement sensors - Raspberry Pi board - Mobile devices (cell phones and tablets) - Use of RFID tags	- P2P Communication protocol - Internet - Wireless - RFID

4   SCALA IoT: The SCALA Web System on Internet of Things

This section shows an innovative proposal on how to integrate IoT technologies with the SCALA Web System. The proposal is based on the idea to integrate several different types of real hand puppets to SCALA web system, allowing to create a concrete dimension to alternative communication narratives. Thus, the initial module to support IoT in SCALA is the Visual Narrative module. However, it is important to note that this integration strategy can be used for other modules and similar systems.

The state of art review helped to identify critical elements and functionalities of SCALA web system in respect to IoT. Table 2 shows elements and functionalities list of the Visual Narrative module of SCALA and the most important technologies identified in the exploratory research.

There are 17 functionalities in the SCALA web system and 15 main technologies identified on papers about IoT and Autism. In general, the SCALA web system already has similar features of web systems that provide alternative communication for people with autism. For example, the Communication Board module already incorporated a visual interface, audio generation, support for the Internet and for mobile devices technologies. Figure 13 show the methodology strategy to roadmap web system for

Table 2. SCALA web system functionalities and IoT technologies applied with Autism.

SCALA web system functionalities	IoT technologies applied with Autism
1. Board layout options	1. Machine learning algorithm
2. Create board	2. Web information retrieval filter
3. View board	3. Visual interface system
4. Undo command	4. Monitoring sensors
5. Image	5. Audio
6. Find image	6. Odor sensors
7. Save board	7. Lighting sensors
8. Open board	8. Raspberry Pi board
9. Add pages to board and clear board	9. Communication protocol
10. Export board	10. P2P
11. Import images	11. Internet
12. Print board	12. Wireless
13. Board Scanning module	13. Mobile device
14. Free Communication module	14. Visual computing
15. Editing story	15. Tags and RFID
16. Scenario	
17. IP communication protocol	

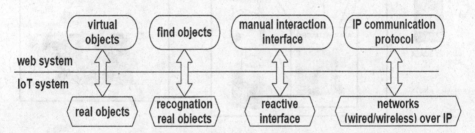

Fig. 13. Rodmap web systems for IoT.

IoT. The strategies define the next goals with respect to the evolution of SCALA web system on the IoT. As a starting point for the research the exact order of the tasks is not important now. However, as the research and development evolves, this ordering will be considered because these task are related and there are dependencies between them.

However, in order to properly integrate IoT on SCALA a road map composed of several different goals was conceived: (1) To incorporate the identification of RFID tags in abstract (scenario and actions) and physical (people, animal, things) objects; (2) To implement visual recognition algorithms for physical objects; (3) To adapt the Free Communication module in order to use pictographs represented by physical objects; (4) To elaborate a mapping strategy, between physical objects with virtual objects (pictographs). Web information retrieval systems and semantic technologies may be used to identify possible models of equivalent pictographs; (5) Encapsulate sensors in physical objects to identify approximation, location and touch, to execute audio, to show lights, for vibration, among other features; (6) Develop a routing protocol for a local network of physical objects, supporting on information security. In this case, a protocol like SPTP [1], which uses a secure P2P communication technology, can be used.

We expect that the fulfilling of these goals will make the experience to use the SCALA alternative communication system more productive and fun, bringing positive pedagogical results. The project of the Visual Narrative with IoT support, nicknamed SCALA IoT is shown in Fig. 14. This project is the initial step of the roadmap to IoT delineated below. Specifically, the goals (1), (3), (4) and (5) of this roadmap, are addressed by Puppet SCALA IoT project.

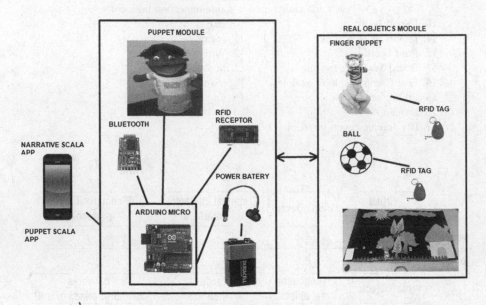

Fig. 14. Project SCALA IoT (Visual Narrative with IoT support).

The project is in the initial stage of implementation and has three modules: the implementation of the Puppet SCALA App for Android mobile platform, the insert of sensor on the Puppet Module and Real Objects Module.

Figure 14 shows the Puppet mobile app (left), the embedded RFID tag sensors on the hand puppet (center), and the RFID tags on the abstract scenarios and actions, and physical objects, like the puppet finger or a ball (right). These tags allow the hand puppet, in combination with the mobile app, to identify approximation, location and touch of objects, to execute audio, to show lights, for vibration, among other features (see Fig. 15). The Bluetooth module is used to communicate between the android mobile phone and the Puppet Module, also is possible to use Wifi. There are differences between two such data exchange protocols Wi-Fi and Bluetooth, for example IEEE Standards, Frequency, Devices Connected and Security. Moreover, Bluetooth until 7 devices can be connected to each other, while in Wi-Fi can accommodate 1 to several communicating devices at a time. If implement in HTML5 platform is recommended to use Wifi module.

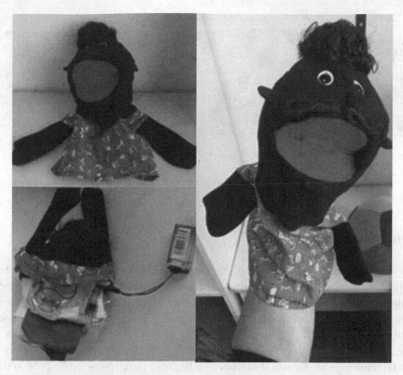

Fig. 15. Puppet Module with Arduino Micro, Bluetooth, RFID receptor (inside the nose) and power battery.

The mapping strategy between virtual (pictographs) and real objects is based on a mapping table, which associates the unique identification number of the pictographs with the RFID tag. The Table 3 shows an example of the mapping table for Puppet SCALA App.

Table 3. Mapping table for Puppet SCALA App

Unique identification number of the pictographs	tag RFID	Object
14271	73 32 6C 00	Scenario
14544	04 53 F1 6E	Ball

Puppet SCALA app automatically displays if some object (Fig. 16, for example) come close to the hand Puppet Module.

Fig. 16. Ball with RFID tag (real object) comes close to a scenario (abstract object) also with RFID tag.

5   Final Remarks

The project proposal constitutes an important initiative that seeks to enable the development of innovations in product and process technologies in digital learning environments, articulated with IoT technology into account the broad understanding of the complex processes that involve teaching-learning process and inclusion of people with autism.

The exploratory research methodology used to find works that apply Internet of Things technologies to Autism was effective because descriptors limited the scope of the research. The individual analysis of each of the 13 papers initially found, allowed us to identify three recent works with good ideas on how to proceed with the integration of IoT with SCALA. The detailed analysis of these works resulted on 15 examples of technologies that could then be compared to the functional characteristics already present on the SCALA system. The entire analysis and comparing process allowed us to propose a set of six new technological features to be incrementally developed and added to SCALA, resulting, in the end, in a system able to handle and transparently relate virtual and physical objects for a more productive alternative communication experience. This work requires a team of scientists because it involves the relationship between psychological, education and engineering. This knowledge gives support to studies with autism, development of educational strategies and building electronic circuits. One difficulty was the configuration of electronic circuits because it had different components and had not been tested to work together. Also, it was necessary to plan and control the road map of the real object to virtual for does not have index problem. This road map can be implemented in similar systems, for instance Vox4All and Livox because do not have integrated IoT technology.

It differs by the applicability and potential in the context of inclusive education in the public and private educational systems, which can generate products and replicable methodologies to cities whose educational policies are intended to ensure curricula, methods, techniques and educational resources that promote educational development of all students.

Acknowledgements. The authors are grateful to Foundation for Research Support of the State of Amazonas - FAPEAM (by means of RH-DOUTORADO Scholarships), Federal Education Institute of Amazonas (IFAM), Federal University of Rio Grande do Sul (UFRGS) and University of Vale do Rio dos Sinos the financial support given to this research.

References

1. Addo, I.D., Yang, J.-J., Ahamed, S.I.: SPTP: a trust management protocol for online and ubiquitous systems. In: Proceedings of Computer Software and Applications Conference (COMPSAC) 2014, IEEE 38th Annual, pp. 590–595. IEEE (2014)
2. Albo-Canals, J., Sans-Cope, O., Barco, A., Diaz C., Angulo, M.: Robotics@Montserrat: a case of learning through robotics community in a primary and secondary school. In: Proceedings of Child-Robot Interaction Workshop at Interaction Design and Children Conference (IDC) (2014)
3. Ashton, K.: That 'internet of things' thing. RFID J. (2009) http://www.rfidjournal.com/articles/view?4986
4. Avila, B.G.: Comunicação aumentativa e alternativa para o desenvolvimento da oralidade de pessoas com autismo. Dissertation, School of Education, Graduate Program in Education, UFRGS, Porto Alegre (2011)
5. Banik, L., Bhuiyan, M., Jahan, A.: Personalized learning materials for children with special needs using machine learning. In: Proceedings of Internet Technologies and Applications (ITA) 2015, pp. 169–174. IEEE (2015)
6. Bez, M.R.: Sistema de Comunicação Alternativa Para Processos de Inclusão em Autismo: uma proposta integrada de desenvolvimento em contextos para aplicações móveis e web. Thesis, Graduate Program in Education, UFRGS, Porto Alegre (2014)
7. Bez, M.R., Charao, P.S., Andriotti, I.C.C., Passerino, L.M.: Relato experiência: uso do SCALA em turma inclusiva. In: Anais do Congresso brasileiro de Comunicação Alternativa 2013, Gramado/RS, vol. 1, pp. 1–16 (2013)
8. Conti, J.P.: The Internet of Things. Commun. Eng. IET J. Mag. 20–25 (2006)
9. DSM-5. American Psychiatric Association. Diagnostic and Statistical Manual of Mental Disorders - DSM 5 (2013)
10. Eckhardt, M.R.: StoryScape: fun technology for supporting learning, language and social engagement through story craft. Thesis, Program in Media Arts and Sciences, School of Architecture and Planning, MIT, June 2015
11. Fage, C., et al.: Tablet-based activity schedule for children with autism in mainstream environment. In: ACM (2014)
12. Falcão, T.P., Gomes, A.S.: Interfaces Tangíveis para a Educação. Anais do Simpósio Brasileiro de Informática na Educação (SBIE) (2007)
13. Fletcher-Watson, Sue. Technology and autism: guidelines for parents (2013). http://www.dart.ed.ac.uk/wp-content/uploads/2013/09/Guidelines-v3-booklet.pdf. Accessed Nov 2014
14. Franciscatto, R., Perez, C.C.C., Bez, M.R., Passerino, L.M., Volpatto, D.R.: Scala - Sistema de Comunicação Alternativa para Letramento de Pessoas com Autismo: implementação de um sistema de busca avançada. In: Congreso de Tecnología en Educación y Educación en Tecnología - TE&ET, Buenos Aires. XI Congreso de Tecnología en Educación y Educación en Tecnología: Libro de Actas TE&ET 2016, vol. 1, pp. 384–393 (2016)
15. Gil, A.C.: Metodologia do ensino superior. Editora Atlas SA, 5th edn. (2010)

16. Höller, J., Tsiatsis, V., Mulligan, C., Karnouskos, S., Avesand, S., Boyle, D.: From Machine-to-Machine to the Internet of Things: Introduction to a New Age of Intelligence. Elsevier, Amsterdam (2014). ISBN 978-0-12-407684-6
17. Imagina. VOX4ALL (2016). http://vox4all.imagina.pt/faqs. Accessed Nov 2016
18. Lancheros, D.J.: Diseño e Implementación de un Módulo Didáctico para el Aprendizaje en la Construcción, Implementación y Manipulación de Robots. Formación universitaria 3(5), 3–8 (2010)
19. Marco, J., Baldassarri, S., Cerezo, E.: ToyVision: a toolkit to support the creation of innovative board-games with tangible interaction. In: Proceedings of 7th International Conference on Tangible, Embedded and Embodied Interaction, Barcelona, Spain, TEI (2013)
20. Passerino, L.M., Bez, M.R.: Building an alternative communication system for literacy of children with autism (SCALA) with context-centered design of usage. In: Fitzgerald, M. (ed.) Recent Advances in Autism Spectrum Disorders - Volume I. InTech, Rijeka (2013). doi:10.5772/54547
21. Perez, C.C.C., Passerino, L.M., Gluz, J.C.: Perspectivas para Busca Semântica para Comunicação Alternativa: o caso SCALA. In: 16th Biennial Conference of the International Society for Augmentative and Alternative Communication (ISAAC), Lisboa (2014)
22. Quintana, E., Ibarra, C., Escobedo, L., Tentori, M., Favela, J.: Object and gesture recognition to assist children with autism during the discrimination training. In: Alvarez, L., Mejail, M., Gomez, L., Jacobo, J. (eds.) CIARP 2012. LNCS, vol. 7441, pp. 877–884. Springer, Heidelberg (2012). doi:10.1007/978-3-642-33275-3_108
23. Ruiz-Velasco, S.E.: Educatrónica. Innovación en el aprendizaje de las ciencias y la tecnología. Díaz de Santos-UNAM. Madrid (2007)
24. Software Tela do software Livox® 2016. http://www.agoraeuconsigo.org/livox/. Accessed Nov 2016
25. Sula, A., et al.: A smart environment and heuristic diagnostic teaching principle-based system for supporting children with autism during learning. In: 28th International Conference on Proceedings of Advanced Information Networking and Applications Workshops (WAINA) 2014, pp. 31–36. IEEE (2014)
26. Thompson, C.: Smart devices and soft controllers. IEEE Comput. Soc. 82–85 (2005)

A Link Between Worlds: Towards a Conceptual Framework for Bridging Player and Learner Roles in Gamified Collaborative Learning Contexts

Simone S. Borges[1]([⊠]), Riichiro Mizoguchi[3], Vinicius H.S. Durelli[1],
Ig. I. Bittencourt[2], and Seiji Isotani[1]

[1] University of São Paulo, ICMC, São Carlos, SP, Brazil
{sborges,durelli,sisotani}@icmc.usp.br
[2] Federal University of Alagoas, Maceió, AL, Brazil
ig.ibert@ic.ufal.br
[3] Japan Advanced Institute of Science and Technology, Nomi, Ishikawa, Japan
mizo@jaist.ac.jp

Abstract. Gamification has been widely used in education with mixed results. Some empirical findings indicate that gamification can increase motivation and engagement in students; other findings highlight that gamification can be a distraction to students; and therefore it may end up hindering learning. To deal with this problem, it is necessary to design gamification to fit properly in individual and collaborative learning contexts. Unfortunately, there is a lack of studies on frameworks mapping game elements and learning theories to support the adequate design and application of gamification in education. Moreover, most proposed solutions do not take into account the need for personalized gamification. To bridge this gap, we set out to create models and a vocabulary to represent learner-player roles interactions in gamified collaborative learning contexts. We developed a conceptual framework using these models and the vocabulary. To demonstrate the framework's viability to design theory-based gamified collaborative learning scenarios, we describe a case study using the theory Peer Tutoring. Our conceptual framework is an effort to support the development of social software tailored towards improving the learners' interactions, providing rich and systematic new ways to learn and to explore the knowledge.

Keywords: Gamification · CSCL · Collaborative learning · Group formation · Framework · Social computing · Roles

1 Introduction

The term gamification originated in the digital media industry, however, such term only gained widespread acceptance after the end of 2010 [1]. Gamification refers to the use of game design elements like mechanics, aesthetics, and game thinking to non-game contexts that aim to engage people, motivate action, improve learning, and foster problem solving [2]. In gamification approaches, these game design techniques are not

© Springer International Publishing AG 2016
F. Koch et al. (Eds.): CARE 2016/SocialEdu 2016, CCIS 677, pp. 19–34, 2016.
DOI: 10.1007/978-3-319-52039-1_2

the center of the system, rather, the goal of these gamification approaches is to improve the user experience. Given that applying game elements to education has the potential to maximize the engagement of students and motivate them [2], there has been a growing interest in applying gamification to education [3].

However, simply inserting game elements in a system and hoping for the best will not improve the user experience [4, 5]. The same applies to gamification efforts that rely only on distributing points and badges (e.g., *pointfication*, *exploitationware*, shallow gamification) [6, 7]. Therefore, building sound educational systems that capitalize on gamification techniques require a careful analysis of the most suitable game design elements that will help to achieve the desired learning outcomes [2]. In this sense, the representation of learner roles and player roles, which rely on sound pedagogical basis, is highly desirable.

Despite the well-known benefits of Computer-Supported Collaborative Learning (CSCL), collaboration in education only has a positive influence on the learning process if its design and utilization take place in a proper way [8] since CSCL is not per se beneficial [9]. Consequently, the carefully design of CSCL environments and collaborative learning (CL) activities is a vital task; otherwise, there is no guarantee that the learning outcomes will meet the desired expectations. In this context, the role played by group formation is fundamental: it influences how students perceive the environment, interact with peers, use available didactic materials, and take part in learning activities and processes [10]. Group formation in CSCL refers to strategies, algorithms, techniques, and methods to cluster individuals according to several criteria with the objective of creating well-thought-out groups that will lead students to better interact with each other and maximize their learning gains. Thus, when a group is properly created, every student brings something relevant to the table, adding improvements to the group learning experience. To proper select students to create effective groups, characteristics such as, knowledge, learning style, performance in previous learning activities, and language barriers, to name a few, have to be considered in hopes of improving learning interactions and benefits [10].

Several researchers have been investigating how to design effective group formation methods that support collaborative learning sessions. However, as pointed out in [7], when scripts designed to support CL tasks are used, there are situations in which these scripts may interfere, at least to some degree, with the students' motivation. The interplay of motivation and cognition when students undertake collaborative group work is a research area that has not been fully investigated [11]. Still, it can be a promising area, because the success of both individual and group learning is closely related to the motivation of the students [12]. There are numerous different motivation construct analyses in the literature [13]. Usually, those analyses share a common distinction between two factors: intrinsic and extrinsic motivation. Briefly, extrinsic motivators are external factors to the person that can influence his/her interest and attitudes, while intrinsic motivation are internal mental states that can influence person's predisposition towards interests and attitudes [14].

As a result, many researchers and practitioners have been investigating gamification-based alternatives to motivate students in CL scenarios [2, 15]. However, since gamification is highly context-dependent, ill-designed gamification solutions can lead to harmful effects instead of the expected benefits [4, 5]. In addition, learners have different player styles, so it is important to understand such styles and adapt the reward system appropriately, since the customization of incentives, rewards, and the way they are presented to the individual can benefit learners [16]. Therefore, the construction of sound gamified CL sessions requires not only a careful analysis of appropriate gamified activities (e.g., environment's design) and meaningful rewards (e.g., suitable game elements) but also the ability to assign appropriate player roles for each learner.

As a first step towards these objectives, we set out to create *models* and a *vocabulary* to represent learner-player roles interactions. The vocabulary and models were organized as a conceptual framework that represents the interactions between learner-player roles in gamified CL contexts. This conceptual framework was designed in hopes of supporting the development of social software, improving learners' interactions and providing systematic new ways to learn and explore the knowledge [17].

2 Related Work

There is a large amount of research on motivation and learning coming from different backgrounds; all demonstrating that motivation plays a vital role in individual learning. However, in the case of CSCL, learning is a more complex process, and despite this, research in this field has not been completely explored yet [9]. In [18] for instance, a meta-analysis of 41 studies investigated the effects of having choice (related to autonomy) and possible intrinsic motivation outcomes. These studies investigated both children and adults samples in different environments. The meta-analysis shows evidence that backs up the idea that enabling learners to choose from different learning alternatives enhanced not only intrinsic motivation, but also: task performance, effort, and perceived competence. However, in [9], they raised some concerns with regards to manipulate students' motivation. In this study, an experiment was performed and the students' competence was evaluated (if appropriate) after completing specific collaborative tasks. The exploratory analyses presented evidence that the appraisal of one partner may have played an unexpected role increasing a freeride behavior on the other partners that did not receive an appraisal. The authors assumed that the freeride effect indicates that part of the participants lost their motivation, thus suggesting the influence of motivation also during CSCL.

Currently, to the best of our knowledge, no research effort has proposed a link between player roles to learner roles in CL and gamification. In [19], they present an e-learning environment wherein generic mechanics and player types found in the gamification literature were incorporated. They also investigated the effects of such mechanics into different learning activities aimed to observe the learning effectiveness of the selected mechanics and the relationship between the mechanics and player types. In [20], a gamified collaborative learning environment was built to foster group collaboration: the authors applied gamification techniques to motivate a group of learners while they performed a task in a collaborative fashion. During this investigation, the authors employed visible progress of task completion as feedback. Groups that used such feature demonstrated high levels of collaboration compared with groups that did not used any visible progress indicator. In [7], an ontology to gamify CL scenarios is described, although the focus of the study is the formalization of concepts concerned to gamification as a persuasive tool in CL, and the relationship between player roles and suitable learner roles is not taken into account. Furthermore, despite many attempts to unify players' behaviors and, as a result, to establish an ultimate taxonomy of players types, few studies have investigated players types from the standpoint of educational theories [15]. There is a lack of studies investigating what kind of player role a learner should play to trigger the desired behaviors in gamified CL settings.

3 Method

Firstly, in order to develop the framework, we designed a protocol to collect and analyze the literature on **group formation in CSCL**. More specifically, we carried out a systematic mapping study by following the guidelines proposed by [21]. Initially, we collected 3571 papers about CSCL that had the potential to provide valuable information about research on group formation. After a careful analysis of each paper, only 106 met the necessary requirements/criteria defined in our protocol. As a result, each of the 106 papers was categorized according to their contributions using information extracted from this systematic mapping.

Secondly, we performed another systematic mapping study to investigate the state of the art on how **gamification** has been applied in educational settings [15]. The information extracted from both mapping studies gave us a useful overview of the state of the art of both domains, such as new methods, algorithms or criteria for group formation; the rationale (or the absence of one) behind the group formation strategy; and also possible advantages, drawbacks and pitfalls when using gamification in learning environments.

Thirdly, we investigated the previous efforts developed by [10, 22–24], all based on sound instructional and learning theories, these studies provide significant contributions on how to model learner roles, and how to conduct CL activities in intelligent learning environments. Finally, we devised our definition of player roles crossing information extracted from **Motivations to Play** [25], **Self-determination Theory** (SDT) [13], and **players types** found in the gamification literature [26].

Motivations to play is an approach that differs from most available player models. Instead of using psychological archetypes in an effort to fit a player in one kind of dominant personality type, the proposed approach tries to identify not only the reasons that can motivate an individual to play a video game, but also their relationship and overlaps. In this way, the scale developed by [25] does not attempt to identify in which archetype one individual must fit, but rather to understand *what can motivate such an individual to play*. In addition, by identifying the reasons that may arouse motivation to play, by analyzing the results of the scoring system developed, one can also identify what can be deemed less attractive for such an individual.

To understand the psychological needs that drive motivations to play, we rely on SDT concepts. SDT seeks to explain how *intrinsic* and *extrinsic* motivators influence human behavior and the development of individuals. According to this theory, the three basic psychological needs considered fundamental to influence motivation are *autonomy*, *relatedness*, and *competence*. Therefore, by promoting the internalization of these psychological needs, individuals have the potential to carry out their activities with improved performance, persistence, and creativity, for instance.

Considering that our main goal was not to come up with a new player typology, we decided to keep things simple, by initially limiting the number of player types to five (Achiever, Killer, Socializer, Creator and Explorer). Although this is not an exhaustive set of players, we believe that this granularity can cover a reasonable scope of the most common player types found in the gamification literature, therefore fulfilling the purpose of the definition of our player roles [25, 26].

Next, we compared each selected player type with motivations to play and the psychological needs (extracted from SDT). As shown in Table 1, we linked the components *Achievement*, *Social*, and *Immersion*, with the following psychological needs: *Competence*, *Relatedness*, and *Autonomy*, respectively. The component Achievement has the subcomponents: Advancement, Mechanics, and Competition. In order to keep things simple, as shown in Table 1, some subcomponents and psychological needs were grouped together according to their synergies. We related the subcomponents Advancement and Mechanics to the psychological need Competence. We decided to join them because we consider that they are associated with the player type: Achiever. To support this decision we checked many player typologies [26–29] looking for information that could help us devise appropriate player roles for each subcomponent. We found, for example, that in the gamification literature, Achievers enjoy not only beating a game but also being the most successful player, accumulating rewards in the process. To do this, achievers strive to understand the game mechanics and/or they scrutinize the game to reach their goals. In other words, the achiever behavior is goal-oriented, and people experiencing this behavior will spend a lot of time to reach their goals. We used the same approach to connect the remaining components, subcomponents, psychological needs and player types.

In Table 1, both Achievers and Killers belong to the component Achievement, however, while Achievers are more interested in increasing their in-game reputation by completing different tasks, Killers are more interested in tasks that involve besting other people in some sense. In other words, Killers are people-oriented, and they score high in the subcomponent Competition. Killers, in game design literature, are the type

Table 1. Motivations to play X self-determination theory X player types

Motivations to play [25]		Self-determination theory [13]			Player types [26]
Component	*Subcomponent*	Psychological needs			*Common in*
		Competence	*Relatedness*	*Autonomy*	*the literature*
Achievement	Advancement	●			Achiever
	Mechanics	●			
	Competition	●			Killer
Social	Socializing		●		Socializer
	Relationship		●		
	Teamwork		●		
Immersion	Discovery			●	Explorer
	Customization			●	Creator

of players highly motivated by Competition. They find zero-sum game mechanics appealing [26, 30], so they enjoy rushing and competing against other people.

Next, we grouped all social subcomponents in a single player type, Socializer. Socializers are motivated mainly by interacting with people (e.g., being in groups and teams, forming partnerships, and playing collaborative games). Like Killers, Socializers are also people-oriented, however, instead of emphasizing defeating other players, they value socializing, sharing experiences, building relationships, and performing shared tasks. Finally, Explorers are associated with the subcomponent Discovery. Explorers are system-oriented players, and exploration is mainly what motivates these players: Explorers enjoy investigating the system's ins-and-outs (e.g., hidden or remote places, finding loopholes, knowing the rules that govern a space). Creators were linked to Customization: these players are also system-oriented, but they are more interested in customizing the system or modifying the virtual world (e.g., backgrounds, fonts, buildings, characters, weapons, and vehicles).

Once we gathered all information in Table 1, we devised the five **player roles** shown in Fig. 1 and described in Table 2. Although we borrow all names from the gamification literature, it is important to note that, instead of player types, we are looking for the creation of a set of player roles. According to [31], although there is no consensus about the definition of roles, it is possible to assume that a role is an entity that is played by another entity in a context. In this sense, "context" can be understood as something as a whole, including a relation in which the former "entity" is defined.

Conqueror   Achiever   Explorer   Humanist   Creator

Fig. 1. Player roles [6–8]

Moreover, considering that these player roles are meant to be used in educational environments, we carefully chose these labels, among several labels found in the literature, to avoid possible negative connotations (e.g. killer, exploiter). As pointed by [30, 32], to avoid the externalization of bad and/or undesirably behaviors, it is important not to provide the system with the kind of game design element that can lead to harmful behavior. As an example, Blizzard's electronic card game Hearthstone® does not allow players to chat with each other. There are pre-selected emotes that can vary slightly depending on the character. However, there is no way to send your custom text message to your opponent. The company recognizes the huge tradeoffs involved in such decision, however, since the game can be very competitive, they stated that this was the right decision to keep Hearthstone® fun, safe, and appealing to most players [33]. By substituting the chat system to pre-selected emotes, Blizzard tailored their game in order to restrain inappropriate vocabulary and harassment.

Nevertheless, although one can argue, since the research focus is on collaborative learning activities, why players such as *Achiever* and *Conqueror* should be considered, given that their specific nature is not collaborative at all. The answer is that it all

Table 2. Player roles description

Player role	Description	Source
Achiever (goal-oriented)	They enjoy not only completing a game, but also being the best winner, accumulating all rewards the game can offer. They are motivated by receiving glory (points, titles, medals, trophies, achievements); gathering (virtual currency and goods); and collecting rare or all in-game items (equipment, weapons, armor, vehicles, mounts, pets)	[25–27, 29, 30]
Conqueror (people-oriented)	They enjoy rushing and competing against other people. Usually, they enjoy testing their skills and seeing how they stack up against other people. They find external ranking systems and zero-sum game mechanics appealing	[25, 27, 29, 30]
Humanist (people-oriented)	They enjoy socializing with people (e.g., being part of groups and teams, forming partnerships, and playing collaborative games). They value socializing, sharing learning, and relationship building via shared tasks	[25, 27, 29, 30]
Explorer (system-oriented)	They enjoy exploring the system by discovering the ins-and-outs (e.g., hidden or remote places, finding loopholes, knowing the rules that govern a space)	[25, 27, 29, 30]
Creator (system-oriented)	They enjoy customizing the system (e.g., backgrounds, fonts, buildings, characters, armor, weapons, and vehicles)	[25–27, 29, 30]

depends on the context. The structure of the interaction between players is a choice to be decided early in any game project (or gamified project). Although the most well-known interaction pattern is the *player-vs-player*, there are other patterns to be considered [34]. *Community collaboration* pattern, for example, can be used to pose challenges to the users while working against the system in a collaborative fashion (e.g., tasks related to time limit or tasks that have to be performed against an Artificial Intelligence).

4   Vocabulary to Represent Interactions in Gamified Collaborative Learning

In Table 3, we present a non-exhaustive compilation of behaviors and player types. It is important to remember that, as stated before, there is no guarantee that all behaviors can be useful or appropriate for an educational environment, therefore behaviors should be carefully chosen to avoid triggering undesirable interactions. The information shown in Table 3 should be read as, for example: "The *Achiever* is *acting* on the *System* by *Comparing* his *Progress* (e.g., on the leaderboard)".

We used such information as a starting point to devise appropriate behaviors that one can use in a gamified CL environment to foster learning. By appropriate we mean behavior that is able to motivate learners to play and at the same time satisfies their respective psychological needs as established by SDT. As any model, the scheme presented in Table 3 is a simplification of the reality and therefore it is likely to suffer

Table 3. Examples of player types and behaviors commonly found in the game-related literature [25–27, 29, 30, 35]

	Player types		Performance		Who/what		Doing (*behavior*)	Who/what
The	Achiever	is	acting	on/ with	System	by	Tracking, Collecting, Gathering, Pursuing, Comparing, Bragging, Showing-off, Winning	Progress, point, medal, achievement, honor, currency, items, virtual goods, quests, status, leaderboard, prizes
	Explorer		interacting		System		Discovering, Exploring, Viewing, Investigating, Traveling, Searching, Looking for	Virtual world, Maps, remote places, secret places, Easter-eggs, hidden quests
	Killer		acting		Others		Harassing, Hacking, Killing, Disturbing Troublemaking, Defying, Cheating, Taunting, Teasing, Fighting	Players, characters, GMs (game masters) NPCs (non-player characters), guilds
	Socializer		interacting		Others		Helping, Greeting, Giving, Supporting, Sharing, Collaborating, Commenting	Players, characters, GMs (game masters) NPCs (non-player characters), information, forums, guilds
	Creator		interacting		System		Creating, Tweaking, Building, Customizing, Transforming, Adapting, Inventing, Crafting	Interface, maps, MODs (modification), avatar, weapons, armors, vehicles and mounts

from eventual drawbacks, such as overfitting or the missing of important interactions. Due to space constraints, in Table 4 we list only a subset of selected behaviors, one behavior for each player role.

Table 4. Example of player roles and potential behaviors

Player role	Behavior	Description	Source
Achiever	Tracking	To keep track of other learners progress and his/her own progress	[25, 27, 29, 35, 36]
Humanist	Empathizing	To have empathy for other learners	[25, 27, 29, 30]
Conqueror	Troublemaking	To unsettle the other learners by proposing solutions that are sometimes trustworthy but other times erroneous	[25, 27, 29, 30]
Explorer	Exploring	To unveil new things in the system as the learning process progresses (e.g., features, tasks, content)	[25, 26, 35, 36]
Creator	Tweaking	To tweak the system towards personalizing something (e.g. learning path, tasks)	[25, 26, 35, 36]

In Fig. 2, we present the basic structure of the conceptual framework. The first columns contain the planned ❶ Learner role and, for each learner role, all ❷ player roles we created. In the column ❸ Conditions, we describe the necessary conditions (*) and the desired conditions (−) that a learner should fulfill for each combination of the current learner role and respective player role. If a learner-player does not satisfy all necessary conditions, the student cannot play the role. The ❹ Expected effects column describes both learning and psychological outcomes, named (❹a) *pedagogical lenses* (PL) and (❹b) *motivational lenses* (ML). The last column, ❺ Source, summarizes the sources of the compiled information. The importance of this column is twofold, first, we believe it is important to keep track of such information because it will enable us to evolve and refine the framework. Second, it will be useful to support other designers, not only when checking the origin of the provided information, but also facilitating further corrections and/or enhancements.

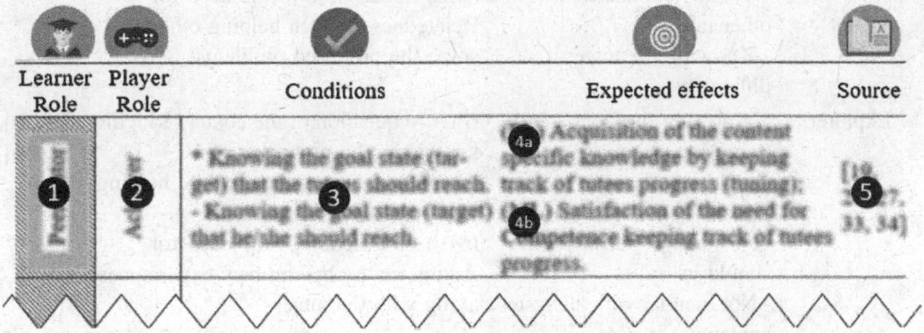

Fig. 2. Basic structure of the conceptual framework (adapted from [10, 35])

In the next subsection, we will demonstrate the viability of our framework using the Peer Tutoring theory. It is worth emphasizing that we have been working on other learning theories and instructional strategies, for instance: Anchored Instruction, Cognitive Apprenticeship, and Cognitive Flexibility. However, due to space constraints we will not present all schemes developed.

4.1 Conceptual Framework Using Peer Tutoring Theory

We filled out Tables 5 and 6 following our learner-player schema as illustrated in Fig. 2. We chose Peer learning as an example because it is a well-known theory [37], therefore minimizing our effort to explain both the learner roles and the player roles, as well as the interplay between the roles and the learning theory. Peer tutoring has being widely investigated and there are many useful techniques organized under such taxonomy [38], however it is not our intention to explore all these techniques. For simplicity's sake, we will consider Peer tutoring as a technique in which both tutor and tutee can gain benefits from their interactions.

Table 5. Peer tutor role, Player roles, Prerequisites, and Expected effects

Learner role	Player role	Conditions	Expected effects	Source
Peer Tutor	Achiever	* Knowing the goal state (target) that the tutees should reach - Knowing the goal state (target) that he/she should reach	(PL) Acquisition of the content specific knowledge by keeping track of tutees progress (tuning); (ML) Satisfaction of the need for Competence keeping track of tutees progress	[25, 27, 29, 35, 36]
	Conqueror	* Knowing the goal state (target) that the tutees should reach * Knowing the tutees' confidence level * Having the pedagogical expertise to maximize the impact of its interventions	(PL) Acquisition of the content specific knowledge by unsettling the tutees (tuning) (ML) Satisfaction of the need for Competence unsettling the tutees	[25, 29, 35, 36]
	Humanist	* Knowing the goal state (target) that the tutees should reach * Feeling connected with the other tutees - Knowing the tutees difficulties	(PL) Acquisition of the content specific knowledge by helping to solve the problems faced by the tutees (tuning); (ML) Satisfaction of the need for Relatedness though helping others to solve the proposed problems	[25, 30, 35, 36]
	Explorer	* Knowing the goal state (target) that the tutees should reach * Knowing how to discover new content that the tutees should learn - Not familiar with all system content	(PL) Acquisition of the content specific knowledge by progressively discovering new content while helping the tutees' (tuning); (ML) Satisfaction of the need for Autonomy by having new experiences along with the tutees	[25, 26, 35, 36]
	Creator	* Knowing the goal state (target) that the tutees should reach * Knowing how to choose which tasks the tutees should do - Knowing the tutees difficulties	(PL) Acquisition of the content specific knowledge by customizing the tutees' tasks (tuning); (ML) Satisfaction of the need for autonomy by having choices	[25, 26, 35, 36]

Essentially, the tutor is a more knowledgeable individual and the tutee is a less knowledgeable individual. However, tutor and tutee are learners who do not have an in-depth knowledge about the content. Therefore, by facing difficulties in teaching, the tutor needs to acquire more knowledge in order to teach and organize his thoughts in an understandable manner; and through the tutoring process, the tutee will acquire or construct his/her knowledge as well [36, 37, 39].

Any learner can play the role Peer Tutor, since he or she fits the specified conditions. In addition, since we are considering that learners have different game preferences, it is necessary to discover and map such preferences to be able to choose appropriate player roles for each learner. In our research, we carry this out by performing a cross-cultural adaptation of the original Motivations to Play Scale [25]. The scale was adapted to Brazilian Portuguese, so we can use it in real-world educational environments with Brazilian Portuguese native speaker students. In Table 6, we

Table 6. Peer tutee role, Player roles, Prerequisites, and Expected effects

Learner role	Player role	Conditions	Expected effects	Source
Peer Tutee	Achiever	* Knowing the goal state (target) that he/she should reach	(PL) Acquisition of the content specific knowledge progressively (accretion); (ML) Satisfaction of the need for Competence by keeping track of his/her progress	[27, 29, 35, 36]
	Conqueror	* Pushing the tutor by expressing his/her ideas in a convincing manner	(PL) Acquisition of the content specific knowledge by unsettling (flustering) the tutor (accretion) (ML) Satisfaction of the need for Competence by unsettling the tutor	[29, 35, 36, 40]
	Humanist	* Feeling connected with the tutor	(PL) Acquisition of the content specific knowledge by being assisted by the tutor (accretion); (ML) Satisfaction of the need for Relatedness through being helped to solve his/her problems	[30, 35, 36]
	Explorer	* Knowing how to discover new content - Not familiar with all system content	(PL) Acquisition of the content specific knowledge by progressively discovering new content (accretion); (ML) Satisfaction of the need for Autonomy by having new experiences	[25, 26, 35, 36]
	Creator	* Knowing how to choose tasks to do * Tweaking the system along with the tutor	(PL) Acquisition of the content specific knowledge by being able to choose the necessary tasks to reach the learning goal (accretion); (ML) Satisfaction of the need for Autonomy by having choices	[25, 26, 35, 36]

indicate examples of necessary and desired conditions defined in order to allow an instructor/designer choosing the appropriate game design elements that will help a peer tutor to reach the sought learner goals. Table 6 also lists examples of necessary and desired conditions defined in order to allow an instructor/designer to choose the appropriate game design elements that will help a peer tutee to reach the planned learner goals.

4.2   Case Study: Who Can Play the Peer-Tutoring Role, and Which Player Role is Appropriate?

We will demonstrate the viability of our framework using the Peer Tutoring theory [36]. Assume two students, one playing the Peer tutor role, while the other plays the Peer tutee role. Both learners take a test, and by the results of the Motivations to Play Scale, we set up their players' profiles. Assume the results indicate that the hypothetical learner, playing the tutor role, scored high as *achiever*, while the other hypothetical student, playing the tutee role, scored high as a *creator*. Checking information from Tables 5 and 6, we combine the pairs of learners as follows:

- Learner role: *Peer tutor* – Player role: *achiever* > ***Tutor-Achiever*** *role*
- Learner role: *Peer tutee* – Player role: *creator* > ***Tutee-Creator*** *role*

In Table 7, we present both roles extracted from Tables 5 and 6, respectively. We indicate the necessary and desired conditions in order to reach the learner goals planned for both learners. In Table 7, we suppressed the column "Source" due to space constraints. We filled out the column "Game" elements based on the information shown in Table 3. The game design elements presented are all related to each player role, consequently, all capable of influencing the psychological needs of each player role.

Table 7. Peer tutor-achiever, and peer tutee-creator roles

Learner role	Player role	Conditions	Expected effects	❻ Game elements
Peer Tutor	Achiever	* Knowing the goal state (target) that the tutees should reach * Knowing the goal state (target) that he/she should reach	(PL) Acquisition of the content specific knowledge by keeping track of tutees progress (tuning); (ML) Satisfaction of the need for Competence keeping track of tutees progress	*Progress bars, points, medals, achievements, honor system, currency, virtual goods, quests, leaderboard*
Peer tutee	Creator	* Knowing how to choose tasks to do * Tweaking the system along with the tutor	(PL) Acquisition of the content specific knowledge by being able to choose the necessary tasks to reach the learning goal (accretion); (ML) Satisfaction of the need for Autonomy by having choices	*Custom interface, progress map, knowledge map, avatars*

Based on information found in Table 7, designers/instructors can choose, more easily, ❻ game design elements that will support the necessary and desired conditions.

Setting up a gamified CL session:

1. Establish the desired learning groups;
2. Provide the ways to evaluate individual Motivations to play and Psychological needs for each learner. The results may have more than one scenario, which can help internalize the motivation and satisfy the psychological needs.
3. Set the Player roles for each learner based on the results from Step 3;
4. Check if each learner has the necessary and desired conditions to play the player roles for the CL scenarios defined in Step 1 (If the learner does not fulfill all conditions, our approach will not be useful).
5. Set the individual gameplay for each learner. This task is completed by the selection of proper game elements for each learner.
6. Set the group gameplay for each group. This task is carried out by selecting proper game elements for each group.

Explaining how to use/implement each game element is beyond the scope of this work. In Fig. 3, we present an example of a customized pop-up with instructions, tailored to fulfil psychological needs of both hypothetical peer learners described in our example working as a group. ❶ Each learner has a description of his or her task. The example is based on the Note-Taking technique [41]. We choose such technique to keep the example simple, while at same time still capable to illustrate our viewpoint. In ❷ we present two different kinds of rewards for fulfilling the proposed tasks. We choose which game element to emphasize checking the information provided by Table 7. In ❸ we illustrate the rewards of completing tasks using graphical elements more capable to appeal to each player role.

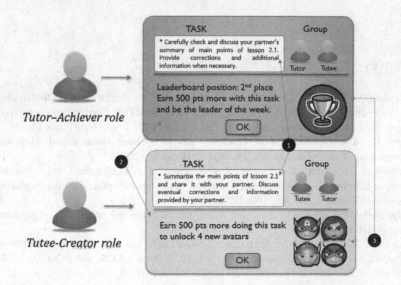

Fig. 3. Two versions of a gamified pop-up with personalized instructions

5 Concluding Remarks and Future Work

Currently, we have been gathering supportive theories from gamification and education. We outlined ways to relate player roles found in the game design and gamification literatures and possible ways to connect these player roles to CL learner roles in a systematic way. We posit that is possible to improve learners' experience by providing personalized gamified situations, thereby contributing to minimizing some potentially harmful aspects of gamification, such as being disruptive or unattractive to several users. By identifying learners' motivations to play, we can easily choose appropriate player roles for each learner in different gamified learning scenarios. Furthermore, instead of classifying learners in a static, brittle manner, we devised roles that can be played in order to satisfy not only temporal constraints related to the learning objectives but also constraints associated with the gamified CL environment. In this chapter, we presented one example of how our framework could be instantiated in a peer-tutoring scenario.

Although many studies have investigated the use of gamification in different education contexts, most studies do not explicitly provide a rationale to back up the pedagogical basis of such research efforts and these studies rely on ad hoc choices [15, 41]. The absence of some sort of rationale makes it difficult to reproduce or evolve these solutions [42]. A potential benefit of our approach is to provide replicable and scalable learner-player interactions. As future work, we plan to further investigate how gamification-related rewards can be linked to learner activities as well as design an adaptive reward system that takes into account intrinsic and extrinsic loadings. Currently, we are working on the implementation of a prototype that will provide the necessary computational support to evaluate the effectiveness of our proposal.

Acknowledgments. The authors would like to thank CNPq and CAPES for supporting this research.

References

1. Deterding, S., Dixon, D., Khaled, R., Nacke, L.: From game design elements to gamefulness. In: Proceedings of the 15th International Academic MindTrek Conference on Envisioning Future Media Environments - MindTrek 2011, p. 9. ACM Press, New York (2011)
2. Kapp, K.: The Gamification of Learning and Instruction: Game-Based Methods and Strategies for Training and Education. Wiley, Hoboken (2012)
3. Domínguez, A., Saenz-de-navarrete, J., Fernández-Sanz, L., Pagés, C., De-Marcos, L., Martínez-Herráiz, J.-J.: Gamifying learning experiences: practical implications and outcomes. Comput. Educ. **63**, 380–392 (2013)
4. Koivisto, J., Hamari, J.: Demographic differences in perceived benefits from gamification. Comput. Hum. Behav. **35**, 179–188 (2014)
5. Andrade, F.R.H., Mizoguchi, R., Isotani, S.: The bright and dark sides of gamification. In: Micarelli, A., Stamper, J., Panourgia, K. (eds.) ITS 2016. LNCS, vol. 9684, pp. 176–186. Springer, Heidelberg (2016). doi:10.1007/978-3-319-39583-8_17

6. Walz, S.P., Deterding, S.: The Gameful World: Approaches, Issues, Applications. The MIT Press, Cambridge (2014)
7. Chalco Challco, G., Andrade, F.R.H., Oliveira, T.M., Mizoguchi, R., Isotani, S.: An ontological model to apply gamification as persuasive technology in collaborative learning scenarios an ontological model to apply gamification as persuasive. In: Anais do XXVI Simpósio Brasileiro de Informática na Educação (SBIE 2015), pp. 499–508 (2015)
8. Dillenbourg, P., Järvelä, S., Fischer, F.: Technology-Enhanced Learning. Springer, Dordrecht (2009)
9. Schoor, C., Bannert, M.: Motivation in a computer-supported collaborative learning scenario and its impact on learning activities and knowledge acquisition. Learn. Instr. **21**, 560–573 (2011)
10. Isotani, S., Inaba, A., Ikeda, M., Mizoguchi, R.: An ontology engineering approach to the realization of theory-driven group formation. Int. J. Comput. Collab. Learn. **4**, 445–478 (2009)
11. Robinson, K.: The interrelationship of emotion and cognition when students undertake collaborative group work online: an interdisciplinary approach. Comput. Educ. **62**, 298–307 (2013)
12. Gomez, E.A., Wu, D., Passerini, K.: Computer-supported team-based learning: the impact of motivation, enjoyment and team contributions on learning outcomes. Comput. Educ. **55**, 378–390 (2010)
13. Ryan, R., Deci, E.: Self-determination theory and the facilitation of intrinsic motivation, social development, and well-being. Am. Psychol. **55**, 68–78 (2000)
14. Stone, D., Deci, E.L., Ryan, R.M.: Beyond talk: creating autonomous motivation through self-determination theory by. J. Gen. Manag. **1**, 75–91 (2009)
15. Borges, S.S., Durelli, V.H.S., Reis, H.M., Isotani, S.: A systematic mapping on gamification applied to education. In: Proceedings of the 29th Annual ACM Symposium on Applied Computing - SAC 2014, pp. 216–222. ACM Press, New York (2014)
16. Vassileva, J.: Motivating participation in social computing applications: a user modeling perspective. User Model. User-Adapt. Interact. **22**, 177–201 (2012)
17. Koch, F., Koster, A., Primo, T. (eds.): Social Computing in Digital Education. Springer International Publishing, Cham (2016)
18. Patall, E.A., Cooper, H., Robinson, J.C.: The effects of choice on intrinsic motivation and related outcomes: a meta-analysis of research findings. Psychol. Bull. **134**, 270–300 (2008)
19. Conole, G., Klobučar, T., Rensing, C., Konert, J., Lavoué, É. (eds.): EC-TEL 2015. LNCS, vol. 9307. Springer, Heidelberg (2015). doi:10.1007/978-3-319-24258-3
20. Wu, Y.: Designing gamification for collaborative learning in groupwork. Master thesis, Lappeenranta University of Technology, Lappeenranta, Finland (2015).http://urn.fi/URN:NBN:fi-fe2015120321938
21. Petersen, K., Feldt, R., Mujtaba, S., Mattsson, M.: Systematic mapping studies in software engineering. In: Proceedings of the 12th International Conference on Evaluation and Assessment in Software Engineering, pp. 68–77. British Computer Society, Swinton (2008)
22. Inaba, A., Supnithi, T., Ikeda, M., Mizoguchi, R., Toyoda, J.: How can we form effective collaborative learning groups? In: Gauthier, G., Frasson, C., VanLehn, K. (eds.) ITS 2000. LNCS, vol. 1839, pp. 282–291. Springer, Heidelberg (2000). doi:10.1007/3-540-45108-0_32
23. Inaba, A., Ohkubo, R., Ikeda, M., Mizoguchi, R.: Models and vocabulary to represent learner-to-learner interaction process in collaborative learning. In: Proceedings of the International Conference on Computers in Education, Hong Kong, pp. 1088–1096 (2003)
24. Isotani, S., Mizoguchi, R., Isotani, S., Capeli, Olimpio, M., Isotani, N., Albuquerque, Antonio, R.,P.,L.: An authoring tool to support the design and use of theory-based

collaborative learning activities. In: Aleven, V., Kay, J., Mostow, J. (eds.) ITS 2010. LNCS, vol. 6095, pp. 92–102. Springer, Heidelberg (2010). doi:10.1007/978-3-642-13437-1_10

25. Yee, N.: Motivations for play in online games. Cyberpsychol. Behav. **9**, 772–775 (2006)

26. Ferro, L.S., Walz, S.P., Greuter, S.: Towards personalised, gamified systems. In: Proceedings of the 9th Australasian Conference on Interactive Entertainment Matters of Life and Death - IE 2013, pp. 1–6. ACM Press, New York (2013)

27. Bateman, C., Bartle, R.A.: Step 4: understand the limits of theory. In: Beyond Game Design: Nine Steps Towards Creating Better Videogames, pp. 117–133 (2009)

28. Bartle, R.: Hearts, clubs, diamonds, spades: players who suit MUDs. J. MUD Res. **1**, 19 (1996)

29. Orji, R., Vassileva, J., Mandryk, R.L.: Modeling the efficacy of persuasive strategies for different gamer types in serious games for health. User Model. User-Adapt. Interact. **24**(5), 453–498 (2014)

30. Kim, A.J.: Beyond player types: Kim's social action matrix. Games, Apps & Services that Bring People Together. http://amyjokim.com/2014/02/28/beyond-player-types-kims-social-action-matrix/

31. Mizoguchi, R., Sunagawa, E., Kozaki, K., Kitamura, Y.: The model of roles within an ontology development tool: Hozo. Appl. Ontol. **2**, 159–179 (2007)

32. Heeter, C., Magerko, B., Medler, B., Fitzgerald, J.: Game design and the challenge-avoiding, self-validator player type. Int. J. Gaming Comput. Simul. **1**, 53–67 (2009)

33. Kuchera, B.: Blizzard silenced Hearthstone players, and it made the game amazing. http://www.polygon.com/2014/4/18/5625802/hearthstone-chat-Blizzard

34. Fullerton, T., Swain, C.: Chapter 3 - working with formal elements. In: Swain, T.F. (ed.) Game Design Workshop, 2nd edn, pp. 49–85. Morgan Kaufmann, Boston (2008)

35. Inaba, A., Mizoguchi, R.: Learners' roles and predictable educational benefits in collaborative learning. In: Lester, J.C., Vicari, R.M., Paraguaçu, F. (eds.) ITS 2004. LNCS, vol. 3220, pp. 285–294. Springer, Heidelberg (2004). doi:10.1007/978-3-540-30139-4_27

36. Endsley, W.: Peer Tutorial Instruction. Educational Technology Publications, Englewood Cliffs (1980)

37. Topping, K.J.: The effectiveness of peer tutoring in further and higher education: a typology and review of the literature. High. Educ. **32**, 321–345 (1996)

38. Falchikov, N., Blythman, M.: Learning Together: Peer Tutoring in Higher Education. Routledge/Falmer, Abingdon (2001)

39. Green, P.: Peer Assisted Learning: In and beyond the classroom. A Literature Review of Peer Assisted Learning (PAL) (2011)

40. Aïmeur, E.: Conflicting agents. In: Tessier, C., Chaudron, L., Müller, H.-J. (eds.) Conflicting Agents, pp. 223–250. Kluwer Academic Publishers, Boston (2002)

41. Barkley, E.F., Major, C.H., Cross, K.P.: Collaborative Learning Techniques: A Handbook for College Faculty. Wiley, Hoboken (2014)

42. Hamari, J., Koivisto, J., Sarsa, H.: Does gamification work? – A literature review of empirical studies on gamification. In: 2014 47th Hawaii International Conference on System Sciences, pp. 3025–3034. IEEE (2014)

Group Recommendation System
for E-Learning Communities:
A Multi-agent Approach

Mhd Irvan[✉] and Takao Terano

School of Computing, Department of Computer Science,
Tokyo Institute of Technology, Tokyo, Japan
irvan@trn.dis.titech.ac.jp, terano@dis.titech.ac.jp

Abstract. For many web services, recommendation system plays a very important role. In most situations, those recommendations are personalized to individual users. However in some services, like e-learning services, not all activities may be designed for personal usage, but rather to be conducted in a group. Group recommendation has been a very challenging problem to address due to the different preferences amongst members of a group. In this work, we propose a way to recommend courses to a group of e-learning students that considers the various preferences between students who happen to be online at the same time frame. We implement a multi-agent model to simulate the behaviors of those students and generate recommendations accordingly. By splitting the machine learning process across multiple intelligent agents, we found that our method managed to generate accurate recommendations.

Keywords: Multi-agent simulation · Recommender system · e-Learning

1 Introduction

Many web services now rely heavily on recommendation systems [1]. Music streaming services recommend what music to listen, video on-demand services suggest what movie to watch, or online shops recommend which products to buy. These services have become a part of many people's daily life. Web services grow and soon enough the number of items in the catalog becomes so large that users are overwhelmed by the massive list of choices [2]. In these cases, a recommendation system plays a vital role. Instead of letting people choose randomly in confusion, the system recommends things to do or to buy based on past activities or preferences.

Typically, recommendation systems are personalized for individual user [3]. However, situations exist where recommendations are necessary to be generated for several users as a group. Computer-supported collaborative learning (CSCL) environment [12] can be one of such situations. CSCL is a science branch concerns with how computers can help people learn together. Group recommendation can potentially play a vital role [4] in CSCL. In an e-learning environment, instead of to be taken individually, courses can be taken by a group of several students. The activities for these virtual courses may not be suitable for personal usage, but rather, for group

© Springer International Publishing AG 2016
F. Koch et al. (Eds.): CARE 2016/SocialEdu 2016, CCIS 677, pp. 35–46, 2016.
DOI: 10.1007/978-3-319-52039-1_3

consumption. Tasks and practice sessions may be offered as group works and interactive discussion between students may be necessary to reach understanding.

1.1 Literature Review

A literature by Stahl et al. [12] mentioned that the idea of CSCL is often associated with e-learning. However, collaborative learning in e-learning can be problematic. Simply posting slides or videos online is not a very attractive solution because it forces students to react in isolation to posted materials. The learning process can only be effective if the materials are compelling to students and the session is an interactive one, allowing students to interact with each other through questions, discussions, or debates.

Group recommendation is a very challenging task to solve [5, 11]. A literature by Mastoff [11], which discussed how to model users affective state to recommend to a group of users, found that some of the biggest challenge for making group recommendation is that a group can include users with different learning preferences and the users currently being online may be different from the previous group. Another research by Jameson [5], which proposed a preference aggregation mechanism to generate group recommendation, also concluded that finding an acceptable recommendation when a member of a group changes to a different person still remained an ongoing issue. A research paper by Irvan [9] about recommending TV shows also found that a good recommendation for an individual may not necessarily accurate for the same individual together with another person. For example, a fan of action movie may prefer watching family-oriented movie when watching together with a young child.

1.2 Research Goal

From the conclusions of other literatures mentioned at previous section, we found that for a group collaborative learning to be effective, it is important that the course is being attractive to the members of the group. In this research we present that finding an attractive course for a group can be done through recommender systems.

Our work is an effort to introduce a new approach to provide group recommendation in the field of social computing for education. We aim to build a system that can recognize a good course to recommend to a group and what other courses to recommend when part of the group members change.

1.3 Research Scope

It is commonly believed that students tend to learn better in a small group compared to a large one [12]. The more students participate in a group, the more likely that some of them turn to be passive learners. For this reason, as an initial step for our work, we limit our group recommendation for a group of three and four students.

To the best of our knowledge, there is no currently known public web service that is serving and recommending an interactive e-learning session to a group of users.

As such, there is no public data available to be used for our kind of research. Because of this limitation, we run our simulation in a virtually generated e-learning environment with students represented by artificial agents through a multi-agent simulation.

2 Proposed Method

In this research, we implement a Learning Classifier System (LCS) that adopts genetic algorithm operations and reinforcement learning's reward allocation method [8]. LCS has showed capabilities in providing good recommendations [9] and it has been implemented effectively in a multi-agent system [10].

This research aims to extend the multi-agent LCS model in [9], which implements an XCS model that emphasizes accuracy [13], to support group recommendations for multiple users, in addition to recommendation for individual users. We achieve this by adding an extra layer on top of the model that make the agents perform as a group, rather than simply exchange information of their past experience as individual agents.

2.1 Agents Role

Our research goal is to generate recommendations for a group. Before getting there, we start by training each agent to make accurate recommendation for an individual it represents. The multi-agent approach is necessary here because after training locally, the agents interact with each other and share their course preferences when they are grouped together. They negotiate which courses to recommend to the group they represent. Finally, the multi-agent system recommends a course that the agents agree on and see how the group reacts. The system repeats the training until it finds accurate recommendations.

2.2 Learning Classifier System (LCS)

LCS is a collection of condition-action classifiers that represent an agent's knowledge from previous experience. It receives input from an environment, informing agents about current situation such as the information about students currently being online. After gathering these inputs, agents perform a decision-making process and propose what actions to take (Fig. 1) in form recommendation. LCS allocates reward back to the classifiers that proposed the recommendation, essentially informing them the quality of their action and applies genetic algorithms to find and test new solutions.

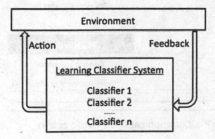

Fig. 1. Illustration of a learning classifier system

2.2.1   Classifier Representation

The condition part of a classifier is equivalent to the types of input string an agent receives from the environment. In our work, the classifier is represented as a string of profile of a user in form of:

| gender | age | location | favorite subject |

The action part of a classifier is the course that the classifier proposes to recommend. A simple example of a condition-action classifier would be:

| female | teenager | home | science | -> | course A |

The above classifier can be read as: *if a female teenager who likes science is accessing from home, recommend course A*. Additionally, each classifier maintains several properties attached to them:

- Prediction p reflects the reward that the classifier anticipate it will get when it execute then action when then condition is satisfied.
- Accuracy κ reflects the likelihood of the classifier actually getting the reward predicted by p when invoked.
- Prediction error ε reflects the absolute difference between the predicted reward and the actual reward received.
- Fitness f reflects the accuracy of the classifier relative to the other classifiers that also propose the same recommendation.

Each agent maintains knowledge in form of a population of classifiers. Classifiers inside the population reflect the situation that the agent has encountered in the past. The purpose of LCS is to keep a collection of classifiers with high accuracy inside the population.

2.2.2   Proposed Architecture

Agents collects knowledge by making recommendations, seeing the reward it receives, and interact with each other inside the environment (Fig. 2). They maintain several

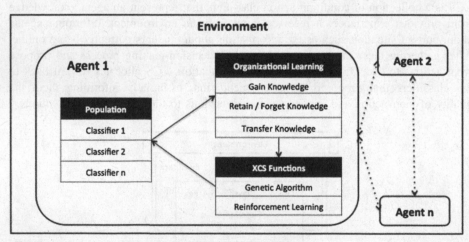

Note : <··············> Communication between agents

Fig. 2. Architecture of our proposed model

organizational learning functions [10] to separate rules to be kept from rules that may be "forgotten" or overwritten by new rules when the agent's memory is full. The memory is considered full when the capacity for the number of classifiers an agent can keep has reached its maximum. Communication happens between agents in a sense that they may exchange knowledge and perform as a group.

Our model used XCS functions [14] that concern about the accuracy of classifiers, an important factor in making recommendation. Thus, the genetic algorithms and reinforcement learning in our method are designed to lead LCS to evolve the rules into better accuracy. The aim is to collect as many accurate classifiers as possible allowed by each agent's memory into the knowledge population. Maintaining classifiers with high accuracy at the end of the learning process allows the agents to keep making good and reasonable recommendation afterwards.

2.2.3   Decision-Making Process

During the learning process (Fig. 3), an agent first receives an input from the environment. The input represents the current situation inside the environment, which essentially information about groups of students currently being online by extracting their profile (gender, age, and location) and their favorite topic.

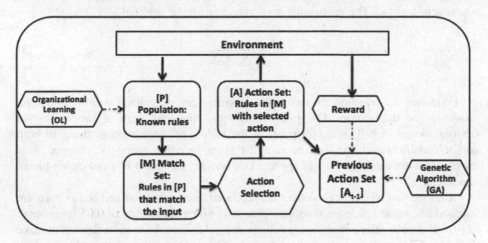

Fig. 3. The learning process of our proposed model

After it detects the environment, the agent checks to see whether it has encountered the same situation before by looking at its knowledge population [P]. If it found any condition-action classifiers C with the condition part matches the input from the environment, it stores those classifiers into a match set [M].

The agent continues to calculate the prediction array P(A) of the set [M] using the value of prediction (C.p) and fitness (C.f) of the classifiers within [M]:

$$P(A) = \frac{\sum_{C.a=a \wedge C \in [M]} C.p \times C.f}{\sum_{C.a=a \wedge C \in [M]} C.f} \tag{1}$$

The prediction array is used to choose the appropriate action. Recommendation proposed by the classifiers with the highest P(A) is selected and those classifiers proposing the same recommendation are stored in an action set [A].

A recommendation is put into action and action set [A] is moved into previous action set [A_{t-1}].

2.2.4   Genetic Algorithms

The agents' classifiers are evolved by genetic algorithm (GA) operations, including mutations and crossovers [6]. The classifiers act as GA's *genes* and GA is used to search and test the possible permutations for the classifiers by applying mutation and crossover operations upon them. GA is triggered (GA_TRIGGER) when the average time period for classifiers within the action set [A] since the last occurrence of genetic algorithm is greater than the frequency parameter θ:

$$GA\_TRIGGER([A]) \; if : \frac{\sum\limits_{C \in [A]} t - C.g}{[A].n} > \theta \tag{2}$$

GA selects two 'parent' classifiers from previous action set [A_{t-1}] using roulette wheel selection [6]. The probability p of classifier i to be selected is:

$$P_i = \frac{f}{\sum\limits_{C \in [A]} C.f} \tag{3}$$

Following the selection, two offspring classifiers are generated by either one-point crossover or duplication. One-point crossover, triggered with a probability of 0.8 (mentioned in [9]), selects a point in the middle of the condition string of both parent classifiers and the data behind that point in either string is swapped. If a crossover is not triggered, two offspring classifiers are generated by duplicating parent classifiers.

After the two offspring classifiers are produced, their condition and action parts are *mutated* (the value inside are randomly changed) with a probability of 0.05 (mentioned in [9]). If the classifier population is full, existing classifiers need to be deleted to make space for the new offspring classifiers. The classifier to be deleted is selected by roulette wheel algorithm using fitness f value as measurement. The lower the fitness value, the higher the probability that the classifier is being deleted.

2.2.5   Reinforcement Learning

Reacting to the actions taken by the agents', the LCS gives feedback in forms of reward allocation provided by reinforcement learning algorithms [7]. The reward varies based on the quality of the recommendations proposed by the agents.

Classifiers in previous action set [A_{t-1}] are credited reward r from the environment. Using this reward, the properties of each classifier is updated:

- Prediction error ε is updated by:

$$\varepsilon \leftarrow \varepsilon + \beta(|r - p| - \varepsilon) \tag{4}$$

- Prediction p is updated by:

$$p \leftarrow p + \beta(r - p) \tag{5}$$

- Accuracy κ is updated by:

$$\kappa = \begin{cases} 1 & \text{if } \varepsilon < \varepsilon_0 \\ \alpha\left(\frac{\varepsilon}{\varepsilon_0}\right)^{-\nu} & \text{otherwise} \end{cases} \tag{6}$$

- Fitness f is updated by:

$$f \leftarrow f + \beta(\kappa' - f) \tag{7}$$

The value for β and α are 0.2 and 0.1 respectively, as mentioned in [9], to control the learning rate. Payoff R is also allocated to the classifiers in the previous action set $[A_{t-1}]$, which derived from the maximum prediction value within the prediction array of the current iteration P(A), discounted by γ value:

$$Q = \max_A P(A) \tag{8}$$

$$R = r + \gamma Q \tag{9}$$

By applying reinforcement learning to classifiers generated by GA, LCS recognizes which offspring classifiers evolved into accurate classifiers. The evolution information gathered is used by organization learning algorithms.

2.2.6   Organizational Learning

The idea of organizational learning in LCS [10] is to give agents an idea which classifier is necessary to be tested further. GA sometimes too early deletes a classifier proven to grow accurate in the long run if it had stayed in the population and standard LCS (due its single agent approach) cannot distinguish which classifiers can potentially be useful other agents. If an agent encounters an input that another agent has encountered before, it can save time by making recommendation proven to be accurate that is proposed by the other agent's classifier.

Organizational learning is triggered when the last occurrence of its function is greater than frequency parameter φ. A timestamp parameter h is affixed to all classifier to act as the timestamp of the last occurrence:

$$OL\_TRIGGER([P]) \; if : \frac{\sum\limits_{C \in [P]} t - C.h}{[P].n} > \varphi \tag{10}$$

Organizational learning algorithms takes two extra parameters we refer as experience (*exp*) and immunity (*imm*). These parameters are included in every classifier inside the population. Experience parameter is a value that reflects how often a classifier was tested and selected into the action set. A classifier with high *exp* value is considered *experienced* enough to survive, and worth for further accuracy testing without the risk of being deleted.

Immunity parameter is a boolean flag that determines whether a classifier is immune against deletion. A classifier is immune to genetic algorithm's deletion algorithm if its experience is above threshold λ:

$$\forall C \in [P] : C.imm = \begin{cases} TRUE & if \ C.\exp > \lambda \\ FALSE & otherwise \end{cases} \qquad (11)$$

Furthermore, when organizational learning is triggered, an agent shares a classifier with other agents by copying the classifier with the highest *fitness* value to replace other agents' classifier with the lowest experience value. This operation reflects that agent who shared the classifier felt confidence that the classifier would be useful in case another agent encounters similar situation.

2.2.7 Making Group Recommendation

An agent initially learns to find a good recommendation for a user it represents and builds a population of accurate classifiers. When multiple agents are put together inside the same group, a combined population of classifiers from all participating agents is formed. For each course, our LCS model calculates how many classifiers are recommending that course, and what is the total fitness value. The system recommends the course that has the highest average fitness value (total fitness value divided by the number of the relevant classifiers).

Since each agent's population has evolved to contain accurate classifiers for an individual, our LCS model is tasked to recognize common preferred courses amongst the combined population and to find which common preferred course potentially leads to a good recommendation for the group.

3 Experiment

As mentioned in Sect. 1.3, currently there is no public e-learning service currently known to be providing group recommendation and there is no public data available to test our proposed method. For this reason, as initial step in our research, we tested our method against randomly generated data, reflecting what an actual data would seem to be if such e-learning is to be publicly available, where courses are intended to be taken by people of any age.

3.1 Data Generation

We generated 200 courses (categorized into science, social, or language studies) to be recommended to 1000 users through Gaussian distribution with standard deviation from 0.01 to 0.05 to fill their profiles in form of gender (male or female), age (kids, teens, or adults), location (at home or outside), and favorite subject (science, social, or language studies).

Staying inside the research scope mentioned in Sect. 1.3, each course is designed to be taken by a group of three users (experiment 1) and four users (experiment 2). Each user is set to "like" 50 of the courses and each group is set to "like" 25 of the courses. At each time frame during the simulation three or four agents are randomly selected to be "online". The system then try to recommend a course that suits the combination of these agents profiles.

3.2   Accuracy Measurement

Each agent can see 80% of "likes" of the user it represents. The agent is tasked to make course recommendation and a recommendation is considered to be good if the course exists inside the remaining 20% of "likes". Likewise, the group recommendation is considered to be good if it exist inside the group's "likes". We repeat the simulation 5 times by hiding different parts of the 20% of the "likes" at each simulation, essentially performing a 5-fold cross validation.

We measure the accuracy of the recommendation by using the precision value generated by the agents when performing group recommendation. We calculate the precision value as the occurrence of true positive (tp) divided by the sum of the true positive (tp) and false positive (fp).

3.3   Parameter Settings

Table 1 summarizes the parameter values we used for this experiment. These are standard values commonly chose by LCS researchers as an ideal setting [13, 14]. By using the same parameter settings in our initial research for group recommendation

Table 1. Parameter values for the experiment

Parameter	Value
Minimum reward R_{min}	0.0
Maximum reward R_{max}	1000.0
GA frequency θ	25
Crossover probability χ	0.8
Mutation probability μ	0.05
Wildcard '#' probability $p_{\#}$	0.3
Learning rate β	0.2
Discount factor Υ	0.7
Minimum error threshold α_0	0.01
Fall-off factor α	0.1
OL frequency Φ	3
Experience threshold λ	10

using LCS, other LCS researchers may easily compare their future research to our results. Additionally, each agent maintains a population of 1000 classifiers and we ran the simulation up until 10,000 simulation steps to see how the precision values progress over time.

3.4   Experiment Result

As mentioned in Sect. 3.2, we ran the simulation 5 times on different parts of the data to perform a 5-fold cross validation. Figures 4 and 5 show the average precision value at the same time steps after all 5 simulations have finished.

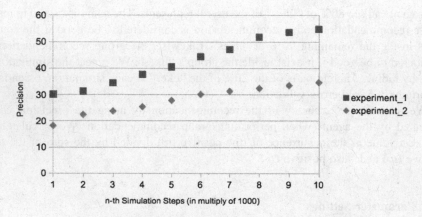

Fig. 4. Precision value of experiment 1 and experiment 2

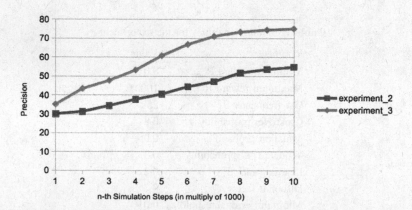

Fig. 5. Precision value of experiment 3 compared to experiment 2

Figure 4 illustrates the precision percentage of both experiment 1 and experiment 2 after every 1000th simulation steps. The figure shows that group recommendation for a group of four students took much longer time to produce the same range of precision than group recommendation for a group of three agents. This is expected as more agents means more permutation for the input to test and there is much deeper search space for the genetic algorithms to explore.

At some points during the experiment 1, we saw a sudden gap in precision increments. This happened because after a long run, more and more agents with similar profile showed up and the agents have built a large collection of classifiers that were already proven to be accurate. For similar reason, we saw the gap between precisions of both experiments was widening between both experiments during latter-half of the simulation because by the time experiment 1 had built a collection of accurate classifiers, experiment 2 still had more permutation to test and search.

Additionally, we also conducted a third experiment (experiment 3) which, like experiment 2, also had a group of four agents, but with one big difference: three of the agents came from experiment 1, carrying the classifiers learned from the previous experiment. Figure 5 illustrates the agents' performance for experiment 3 in comparison to the previous experiment 2.

We also detected that the precision does not increase very much beyond 8000th simulation steps in all three experiments. However, since it does slowly get better, we can conclude that from this step, the population has already reached a collection of classifiers mostly with similar fitness value, and even new offspring classifiers end up reaching that same range of fitness.

We saw that when a part of the group have been together before, agents tend to start better than a group of complete strangers, even if a new member is a later added to the group. Because the classifiers have been adjusted to match the recommendations for the first three agents, the system needed much less time to collect new accurate classifiers adjusted for the new agent. Toward the second half of experiment 3, we detected a smaller increment in precisions compared the first half. We found that most of the classifiers within the population already maintain a good fitness value by this time, the bigger classifier population size is necessary to include additional accurate classifiers to move beyond the 80% line. From this result, we can assume that a bigger group needs a bigger population size to keep the accuracy performance.

4   Conclusion and Future Works

We believe recommending ideal courses to be taken by a group of students can potentially leads to a fun learning experience. Our work presented a new approach to computationally generate group recommendation through learning classifier system. Our proposed method managed to achieve an acceptable precision in making recommendation to not an individual, but to several individuals as a group.

However, precision values almost stop increasing near the end of our simulations. We suspect the limit in population size and length of classifier are the cause. This issue is still under investigation and will be reported in our future publications.

We also found that bigger population size is necessary to keep up with larger group size and optimizing the algorithm to scale properly according to the population size remains a challenge. For easy comparison by other LCS researchers, we decided use a standard value for the parameter settings in this research, however different parameter settings may give varied results and we plan to investigate the impact of these settings for future work.

References

1. Bobadilla, J., et al.: Recommender systems survey. Knowl.-Based Syst. **46**, 109–132 (2013)
2. Bollen, D., et al.: Understanding choice overload in recommender systems. In: Proceedings of the Fourth ACM Conference on Recommender Systems, pp. 63–70 (2010)
3. Adomavicius, G.: Toward the next generation of recommender systems: a survey of the state-of-the-art and possible extensions. IEEE Trans. Knowl. Data Eng. **17**(6), 734–749 (2005)
4. Zhang, D., et al.: Can e-learning replace classroom learning? Commun. ACM **47**(5), 75–79 (2004)
5. Jameson, A.: More than the sum of its members: challenges for group recommender systems. In: Proceedings of the Working Conference on Advanced Visual Interfaces, pp. 48–54 (2004)
6. Goldberg, D.E., Holland, J.H.: Genetic algorithms and machine learning. Mach. Learn. **3**(2–3), 95–99 (1988)
7. Kaelbling, L.P., et al.: Reinforcement learning: a survey. J. Artif. Intell. Res. **4**, 237–285 (1996)
8. Holland, J.H., et al.: What is a learning classifier system? In: Lanzi, P.L., Stolzmann, W., Wilson, Stewart, W. (eds.) IWLCS 1999. LNCS (LNAI), vol. 1813, pp. 3–32. Springer, Heidelberg (2000). doi:10.1007/3-540-45027-0_1
9. Irvan, M., Chang, N., Terano, T.: Designing a situation-aware movie recommender system for smart devices. In: Proceeding of The Sixth International Conference on Information, Process, and Knowledge Management, pp. 24–27 (2014)
10. Irvan, M., Yamada, T., Terano, T.: Influence of organizational learning for multi-agent simulation based on an adaptive classifier system. IEEJ Trans. Electron. Inf. Syst. **133**(9), 1752–1761 (2013)
11. Mastoff, J.: Group recommender systems: combining individual models. In: Ricci, F., Rokach, L., Shapira, B., Kantor, P.B. (eds.) Recommender Systems Handbook, pp 677–702. Springer US, New York (2011)
12. Stahl, G., Koschmann, T., Suthers, D.: Computer-supported collaborative learning: an historical perspective. In: Cambridge Handbook of the Learning Sciences, pp. 409–426. Cambridge University Press (2006)
13. Wilson, S.W.: Classifier fitness based on accuracy. J. Evol. Comput. **3**(2), 149–175 (1995). MIT Press, Cambridge, USA
14. Wilson, S.W.: Get real! XCS with continuous-valued inputs. In: Lanzi, P.L., Stolzmann, W., Wilson, Stewart, W. (eds.) IWLCS 1999. LNCS (LNAI), vol. 1813, pp. 209–219. Springer, Heidelberg (2000). doi:10.1007/3-540-45027-0_11

The Impact of Social Similarities and Event Detection on Ranking Retrieved Resources in Collaborative E-Learning Systems

Samia Beldjoudi[1,2(✉)], Hassina Seridi[2], and Abdallah Bnzine[2]

[1] Preparatory School of Sciences and Technology, Annaba, Algeria
[2] Laboratory of Electronic Document Management LabGED,
Badji Mokhtar University, Annaba, Algeria
{beldjoudi, seridi}@labged.net,
abdoulahbenzine@gmail.com

Abstract. Recently, the social web has recognized a real attention by E-learning community. This collaborative space gave students new opportunities to share their contents and receive immediate feedback from other networkers. For instance, in folksonomies, learners are able to tag useful resources within a highly visible space, which allow sharing ideas that gives a basis for discussion, and thus other students can benefit from those resources. Actually, social environments offer a unique opportunity to personalize search spaces. The objective of this work is to achieve this opportunity and thus personalize tag-based search in E-learning folksonomy by extract implicitly the semantics of learners' tags. In this context, a social personalized ranking function is proposed; this function leverages the social aspect of folksonomy and events detection to estimate the relevance of given resources to a tag-based query issued by learners.

Keywords: Social tagging · Folksonomies · E-learning · Event detection · Ranking

1 Introduction

In social web, users produce, annotate and share what they find attractive on the web [5]. The appearance of relations between users creates the notion of social networking; which is an online community with a similar interest who use internet to communicate between them and share information. Folksonomies are one of these new social practices. These systems of classification result from the use of collaborative method to produce and organize tags to annotate content.

Recently, E-learning platforms focused on personalization to attain pedagogic scenarios or else unreachable by usual forms of learning. This work is oriented to personalize results proposed to each learner when he/she searches relevant resources by using tags.

Semantic web in turn plays an important role in developing the resources retrieval on the web. Ontologies that constitute the backbone of this tendency contribute

F. Koch et al. (Eds.): CARE 2016/SocialEdu 2016, CCIS 677, pp. 47–63, 2016.
DOI: 10.1007/978-3-319-52039-1_4

significantly in solving the semantics problems during the information retrieval. Although this, combining folksonomies and ontologies still a bothered task that suffers from some problems hinder the growth of these systems. Tags' ambiguity and the tags that are freely chosen in these systems are likely to contain spelling errors and therefore make the resources retrieval more doubtful than the metadata recovering from a lexicon examined by information professionals.

In another side, a big number of resources can match users' queries in folksonomies. Therefore, ranking these resources is required as a user cannot look through all the proposed results. The ranking task consists of defining a function that quantifies the similarities between results and queries. Thus, to define a valued ranking function in collaborative E-learning we focused on two features: social aspect and event detection. In the first feature, we based our approach on similarities calculation to overcome tags ambiguity problem. While in the second feature, we introduced a new dimension which is event detection to define the impact of resources popularity on ranking the retrieved resources.

Consequently, our main contributions in this work are: exploiting the power of social interactions between folksonomy learners in order to extract terms' meanings and thus overcome tags' ambiguity problem. In another hand, we aim at enhancing automatically the folksonomy by relevant facts in order to improve resources retrieval by reducing execution time. Also we want to benefit from the dependence between the presence of an event and the high number of similar queries transmitted in the same time period by different users to improve resources retrieval in collaborative E-learning applications. The next section presents a quick overview about the main contributions attached to our research field.

2 Related Work

Social web based approaches, like folksonomies, have achieved a high level of improvement even in E-learning practice. In this section, an overview about the main contribution attached to this field is proposed.

In [17], the authors proposed a method of assembling an on-demand curriculum from available learning objects specified by e-learning services suppliers. Fundamentally, the proposed approach is based on gathering all student relations representing them semantically, and using this information jointly with information of the student's. In the work of [15], the authors tried to propose a social semantic learning environment. The idea based on creating folksonomies from learners' tags and then helps to ontology maintenance.

Ranking the large number of resources in folksonomies is a key problem. In this contribution, to define a valued ranking function in collaborative E-learning, we focused on two features: the first one is social similarities to overcome tag ambiguity and the second is event detection.

Starting by the first feature, we will present an overview about the contributions oriented to overcome the lack of semantic links between tags: we start with [11] who has focused on social network analysis in order to extract lightweight ontologies, and therefore semantics between the terms used by the actors. According to [9], the problem of the lack of semantic links between terms in folksonomies can be easily resolved by representing folksonomies with ontologies. In [14], the authors in their turn have preferred reuse available ontologies on the semantic web in order to express correlations which can hold between tags. An attempt to automate this method has been done by [2]. In [8], the authors exploited the force of ontologies and semantic web standard languages in order to improve social tagging. According to the authors, with this approach, tagging remains easy and becomes both motivating and unambiguous. In the niceTag project of [10], the authors proposed methods to build lightweight ontologies which can be used to suggest terms semantically close during a tag-based search of documents. The work presented in [12] proposed to expand folksonomies in order to avoid bothering users with the rigidity of ontologies. During a keyword-based search of resources, the set of ambiguous used terms is concatenated with other tags so as to increase the precision of the search results. A new technique is presented in [4] for improving resources' search in folksonomies. In another contribution [6], the authors proposed new technique for improving the Social Semantic Web technologies in order to see how they overcome some semantics problems in folksonomies when representing these latter with ontologies.

In another side, event detection in social web has recognized a real success in the last years. In the contribution of [13], the authors considered the current interaction of events to suggest an algorithm for becoming aware of a target event. In the contribution of [3], the authors explored methods for examining the flow of messages in Twitter to differentiate between messages concerning real-world events and the ones related to non-event. The main contribution of [16] is to integrate social relations in event detection. In another contribution, [1] presented a framework to identify localized events from Twitter and also follow the progression of these events over time. To determine the most significant events, the authors introduced a score system for events.

To resume, we find that although the many contributions attached to folksonomies field, unfortunately resources retrieved in E-learning folksonomies still suffer from many problems. As a result we proposed a new approach for personalizing and improving resources retrieval in collaborative learning with tackling tags ambiguity and event detection impact on ranking retrieved resources.

3   Improving Tag Based Search in Collaborative E-Learning Environment

In e-learning applications, a folksonomy is a tuple $F = <L, T, R, A>$ where L, T and R represent respectively the set of learners, tags and resources, and A represents the relationship between the three preceding elements i.e. $A \subseteq L \times T \times R$. In our approach, we consider a folksonomy as being a tripartite model where we resources are associated with a learner (l) to a list of tags. Therefore we have extracted three social networks represented by three matrices LT (learner-tag), RT (resource-tag), RL (resource-learner).

3.1 Improving Resources Retrieval by Resolving Semantics Lack Problem in E-Learning Folksonomy

In social networks, especially in folksonomies users face some bothered problems like tags ambiguity, synonymy and lack of semantic links between the free used tags. These problems still the same when we speak about e-learning folksonomy. For example, a learner in computer-science department can want to obtain relevant resources about sun company, unfortunately the system will him propose not only the resources related to his preference but also those related to biological element (sun is an ambiguous tag) since such resources are used by learners of biology department.

Furthermore, in the case of resources tagged with the same tag, the system cannot access to the meaning of content in order to differentiate between them and thus personalized the retrieved results according to each learner interests. For instance, two learners in two different departments can study the same module "Algorithmic", but the module is different (in term of content and difficulty) from one specialty to another. For instance, a learner in computer-science department is interested by a high level of knowledge concerning the content of retrieved resources, contrary to a learner in economy department. It is clear that the two contents have not the same difficulty, and thus the first learner will not has the same feedback compared with the second one.

The proposed method to treat tag ambiguity problem is based on computing social similarities between learners. Thus, our approach takes benefits from the strength of community effect that characterizes web 2.0 technologies. The idea is analyzing the profile of each student, and then compares his preferences with other learners in order to extract those who are similar to him. In Table 1, we have four learners with the list of their tags:

Table 1. A set of learners with their tags

Learners	Tags
L1	Computer, mac, java, informatics (Learner interested with computer science)
L2	Sun, water, geography, nature (Learner interested with geography)
L10	Computer, sun, mac, informatics (Learner interested with computer science)
L12	Sun (No information about the interest of this learner)

Let us suppose that learner L_1 wants to retrieve resources relative to the tag *'sun'*. In the current folksonomies, the obtained result will contain all the resources tagged with *'sun'* i.e. those relative to biology and computer, even that it is clear for a human reading L_1's tags, that his preferences are relative to computer and not to biology.

In the next paragraph, we demonstrate that in the proposed approach if the learner L_1 searches resources tagged with 'sun'; our system will first propose him the resource corresponding to tag 'sun' which is used by the learner L_3 with a 'very strong' level of recommendation because the two learners L_1 and L_3 have similar preferences. On the contrary the resources corresponding to the tag 'sun' which is used by the learner L_2 will be given to L_1 with a percentage 'low' level of recommendation because L_1 and L_2

do not share the same interests. Now how should the system answer L_4 for whom it does not have much information about his interests?

For such cases, we propose to measure the similarity between the resources corresponding to the tag 'sun' which is used by L_4 and the resources already proposed to L_1 with a high percentage i.e. those of L_3. If the resources are similar, the system will propose them to L_1 with a 'very strong' level of recommendation, otherwise with a 'low' level of recommendation [5].

In order to facilitate the comprehension of the proposed approach, we suggest using an illustrative example in our description.

As we see in Fig. 1, the learner L1 want to obtain relevant resources (courses, video, etc.) related to 'sun'. It is clear that before seeing the profile of this learner, we cannot know his preferences because the used tag is ambiguous. For a human reading L_1's tags, we can conclude that L1's preferences are relative to computer and not to biology.

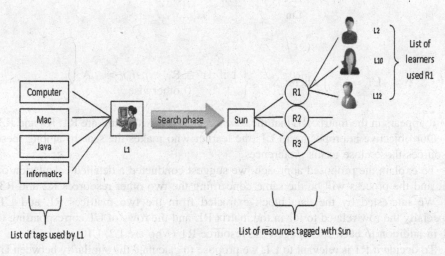

Fig. 1. An illustrative example (A real case study)

To let the machine understand this, we propose the following steps:

First, construct the matrix RL for the tag 'sun', in which we find the resources tagged with sun and by whom (Table 2).

Table 2. The matrix RL related to the tag sun

	L1	L2	...	L10	L11	L12	Lm
R1	0	1	0	1	0	1	0
R2	1	1	...	...	...	...	...
R3	...	...	...	...	...	...	...

$$RL = [Z_{ij}] \text{ where: } Z_{ij} = \left\{ \begin{array}{c} 1 \text{ if } \exists \text{ sun} \in T, <li, sun, rj> \in A \\ 0 \text{ otherwise} \end{array} \right\}$$

Second, construct the matrix LT that constitute the profile of each learner in the matrix RL as follow (Table 3):

Table 3. The matrix LT with the learners presented in RL

	T1	T2	T3	...	...	Tn
L1	1	0	1	1	0	0
L2	...	...	...	...	...	...
...	...	...	...	0	...	...
L10	...	...	...	...	...	...
L11	...	1	...	...	...	...
L12	...	...	...	0	...	...
Lm	...	...	...	...	...	...

$$LT = [X_{ij}] \text{ where: } X_{ij} = \left\{ \begin{array}{c} 1 \text{ if } \exists r \in R, <lj, ti, r> \in A \\ 0 \text{ otherwise} \end{array} \right\}$$

It appears in the matrix RL that the resources tagged with 'sun' are R1, R2 and R3.

Our objective is proposing to L1 (the learner who makes the search) among these resources those close to his preferences.

To explain the proposed approach, we suggest conducted a detailed calculation on R1, and the process will be the same concerning the two other resources R2 and R3.

We interested by the data block extracted from the two matrices RL and LT, especially the row related to R1 in the matrix RL and the rows of LT corresponding to L1 in addition to each user tagged the resource R1 (who are L2, L10 and L12).

To decide if R1 is relevant to L1, we propose to calculate the similarity between L1 and these users. At this stage, we was interested by three sub-blocks because we have 3 users (L2, L10 and L12), in each sub-block we have sub-matrices constructed from two rows of LT one of L1 and the other one from user among those used R1. We need also the transposed matrix (TL) of this later in order to calculate the matrix LL = LT*TL.

Thus, to calculate the similarity between two learners, for example L_1 and L_2, we calculate the cosines of the angle between their associated vectors v_1 and v_2 (designates a series of numbers defined the set of learners' tags).

After similarity calculation of the users who tagged R1, we calculated the average value of the above similarities to obtain the final value that will be compared with a defined threshold S.

If the average similarity is greater or equal than S, then the resource R1 is relevant to L1.

Otherwise, to avoid the cold start problem which generally results from a lack of data required by the system in order to make a good recommendation, when the learner of the system is not yet similar to other students, we also measure the similarity between the resources which would be recommended by the system and those which are already used by the learner.

To measure the similarity between two resources r_1 and r_2, we represent each of them by the vector of numbers representing all its tags (extracted from matrix RT) and we calculate the cosines of the angle between the two vectors.

The same, we suggest detailing the applied calculation on R1, and the process will be the same concerning the two other resources R2 and R3.

We used the data block extracted from the two matrices LR (the transposed matrix of RL) and RT that is constructed as follow:

$$RT = [Y_{ij}] \text{ where: } Y_{ij} = \left\{ \begin{matrix} 1 \text{ if } \exists 1 \in L, <l, ti, rj> \in A \\ 0 \text{ otherwise} \end{matrix} \right\}$$

Especially the row related to L1 in the matrix LR and the rows of RT corresponding to R1, R2 and R3 (the resources that we will be studied) in addition to each resource tagged with the learner L1.

For example, to decide if R1 is relevant to L1, we propose to calculate the similarity between the resources which would be recommended by the system and those which are already used by the learner. At this stage, we used two sub-blocks because we have 2 resources (R6 and R9).

In each sub-block we have a sub matrices constructed from two rows of RT one of R1 and the other of the resource used by L1. We need also the transposed matrix (TR) of this later in order to calculate the matrix RR = RT*TR.

Thus, to calculate the similarity between two resources, for example R_1 and R_6, we calculate the cosines of the angle between their associated vectors v_1 and v_6 (designates a series of numbers defined the set of learners' tags).

After the similarity calculation, we calculated the average value of these similarities to obtain the final value that will be compared with a defined threshold Z.

If the average similarity is greater or equal than Z, then R1 is relevant to L1, otherwise the resource will not be recommended to this learner.

3.2 Personalized Ranking Function in E-Learning Folksonomy

In folksonomies, a large number of resources can match users' queries. Therefore, ranking these web resources is necessary. In this section, a personalized social ranking function is proposed to rank the retrieved resources according to their importance to the users.

Within the context of E-learning folksonomies, we can formalize the ranking problem as follows: Let's consider an E-learning folksonomy F (L, T, and R) from which a learner $l \in$ L submits a query t to a search engine. We would like to rank the set of resources that match t, such that relevant resources for l are highlighted and pressed to the top for maximizing his satisfaction and personalizing the search results (Fig. 2).

Folksonomies allow users to distribute and receive significant resources about real-world events. The objective of this approach is improving resources retrieval by

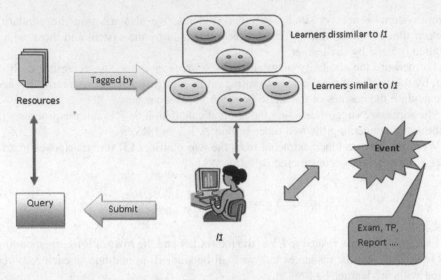

Fig. 2. Overall of tag-based search in collaborative learning

exploiting the dependence between event detection and the high number of similar queries transmitted in the same time period.

It is clear that with the presence of a particular event, the number of similar queries in search engines increases considerably. The presence of an event *e* involves increasing the number of searches performed on this event. Real time event (RTE) [7] is a formula that can detect the presence of an event related to a given query since the increase of similar queries in a particular time period.

The RTE score is defined by the following equation:

$$RTE = \sqrt[3]{\frac{A+B}{B}} - 1 \tag{1}$$

where A is the number of related queries in n time units, B is the number of queries m units during earlier times, such as $n \geq 2$ and $m = n/2$.

For example, taking a week as a time unit, if n = 2, the RTE score will determine the increase of the number of queries submitted about a given topic in two weeks.

To achieve a good ranking, we must sort the retrieved resources according to some criterion so that the most relevant results appear early in the retrieved list displayed to the learner. Two cases can be observed:

(1) There is not an event detected during the search phase (i.e. the RTE score is lower than a defined threshold z): in this case the retrieved resources will be ranked only according to social similarities values.
(2) Otherwise, when the value of RTE is greater or equal than z, the proposed ranking function incorporated two features to be effective: the social aspect and the number of visit of each resource during the same time period of event detection.

Thus the proposed function $Rank(r, t, l)$ is computed by merging the average similarities values $\frac{\sum_{i=k}^{j} sim(l1, li)}{j}$ and $Nbr\_visit(r)$. This merge is computed as follows:

$$Rank(r, t, l) = \alpha \times \frac{\sum_{i=k}^{j} sim(l1, \ li)}{j} + (1 - \alpha) \times \frac{Nbr\_visit(r)}{total} \qquad (2)$$

where, the parameter α denotes the weight that satisfies $0 \leq \alpha \leq 1$ and represents the importance one wants to give to the two types of features, i.e. social similarities or most popular resource in n time unites.

Depending on the context, one may want to give a higher importance to learners' similarities. Another user may want to give more importance to special events that can be occurring, and so prefers the most popular resources.

Note that, the first side of the formula (2) represents the average value of similarities between l and (j) other learners who tagged a given resource (r) with the tag (t). It is clear that if two users are dissimilar, then similarity between resources replace that between those two users.

The introduction of last feature in the definition of the ranking function is crucial, because the presence of an event can have a real influence on the popularity of resources and thus influenced the meaning of tags in the query even if those later are ambiguous.

Examples of events that can affect the learners search are: Exams, TPs, Reports, BAC, etc. where learners can submit similar queries in these times periods.

In order to estimate the utility of taking into account event detection in the definition of ranking function, let us consider the following example where we have four learners' profiles described with their tag list as follow:

L1 (TP, Java, Apple)
L2 (Eclipse 3.4, TP, Java)
L3 (Apple, Java, Programming, Eclipse)
L4 (Eclipse 3.5, Java, TP)

If the learner L1 wants to search relevant resources related to the tag 'Eclipse', all the resources tagged with the tags (Eclipse 3.4, Eclipse, Eclipse 3.5) will be proposed to our learner. But the question in which order those resources should be retrieved?

We distinguish between two different cases:

Case 1: if there is not an event presented during this period, our approach was focused only on social similarities (by taking the value of α equal to 1) in order to rank the retrieved resources.

Case 2: suppose that we have the following event: there is a new version of Eclipse in the net. Thus, if L1 wants to obtain resources about the tag 'Eclipse', it appears relevant to him propose firstly the resources tagged with *eclipse 3.5* before those tagged with *eclipse 3.4* and even with *eclipse*.

We conclude that event detection can play a crucial role in ranking retrieved resources within E-learning folksonomies.

3.3   Folksonomy's Enrichment

In order to reduce repeated calculation and thus economize execution time, we propose to enrich the E-learning folksonomy with a significant fact as follows:

Enrich the database by facts extracted from the above similarities' calculations as follow: *resource X is similar to resource Y*. In the form: is-similar-to (X, Y).

The choice of this kind of facts was based on resources and not on users because we must be aware that the profiles of users can be changed at any time by adding or removing new tags or new resources and therefore we can't say that "two users have always the same interests".

On the contrary if a large number of learners have already agreed that two resources are similar, this information becomes an assertion even if the profiles of those users can be changed in the future. And so we conclude that: Two resources are similar if they are already judged as similar by a large group of users.

For example, if we found that a resource R1 is similar to another resource R2 then we add this information in our database, i.e. we add the following fact: is-similar-to (R1, R2).

In Fig. 3, an activity diagram is introduced in order to illustrate the complete search's procedure followed by our approach.

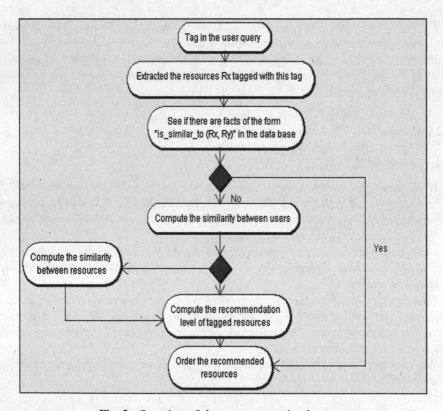

Fig. 3. Overview of the resources retrieval process

The complete code of the proposed algorithm is:

Algorithm
Input: Tag in the form of user query.
Output: A set of ordered personalized resources.
Method
1.Extract the resources tagged with the tag founded in the user query;
2. **For** each resource Rx related to this tag **do**
If there are resources similar to this one in the database **then** propose them to current user;
End For
3. Calculate the similarity between this user and the others whom used this tag;
3.1- **If** *users are not similar* **then** calculate the similarity between resources;
3.2- Ranking the retrieved resources;
End.

In step (1), the system must extract the resources tagged with the tag used in the user's query. This can be done by a simple select command. In step (2), for each resource R_x retrieved in the first step, the system will detect if this latter is similar to other resources already recommended to this user. This can be done by seeking facts of the form is-similar-to (R_x, R_y): if it is the case, then recommend the resource R_x to our user.

In the step (3), our system must calculate the similarity between the user who wants obtaining a set of relevant resources and the other users who have used resources tagged with the tag employed in the query but they wasn't similar yet to any other resources: if the users are not similar (3.1), then the system must calculate the similarity between resources. Finally (step 3.2), the ranking function should be calculated in order to rank all the retrieved resources.

4 Experiments and Evaluation

In this section, experiment over a popular dataset is described and results are analyzed and discussed. The dataset exploited in our test is del.icio.us: a web-based social bookmarking tool which let a user manage a personal set of web resources and annotate them with tags.

In this experiment we were interested with data sample constructed from users who tagged resources about education. Thus our data base comprises 20432 tag assignments involving 7898 users, 15439 tags some of which are ambiguous, 10527 resources each having possibly several tags and several users. Note that, the used dataset include also the date of each tagging operation, this can help us in event detection.

4.1 Experimental Results

In order to evaluate the quality of the proposed approach, we used the following three metrics: recall, precision and F1 metric. In order to evaluate our work, the three metrics listed above are calculated for each user, and then the average of each metric in the system is calculated. The results are shown in the Table 4:

Table 4. The average value of the three metrics

	Precision	Recall	F1
Ambiguous tags	85%	80%	83%
Not ambiguous tags	93%	85%	89%

From the analysis of the Table 4 we can conclude that, the values of Precision, Recall and the metric F1 are very promising both in the case of ambiguous tag-based queries and also not ambiguous tag-based queries. This result indicates that social similarities and event detection performed by our approach are really able to help learners when they query a folksonomy.

The experiment has showed that the resources associated to no ambiguous tags are highly recommended. It has also showed that, in the case of ambiguous tags, our system proposes to the learner the resources which are close to his interests with a high level of recommendation and, on the contrary, those which are far from his interests with a low level of recommendation.

Also, we have found when a user want obtain relevant resources related to a specific tag, the majority of pertinent resources related to tags which are spelling variations of the entered one; are given to this user with respecting his preferences.

The results presented in the Table 4 show a rate of precision and recall very optimistic seeing the data set tested in this experience. Indeed our approach is succeeded in distinguishing between ambiguous tags.

4.2 Analyze the Approach Accuracy in Resources Retrieved

In order to analyze the accuracy of our approach, we compared our results against the null hypothesis where every resource tagged with an ambiguous tag is returned. We consider a naive folksonomy without any method to overcome the semantics problems between tags. The average rates of precision, recall, and metric F1 obtained are presented in Table 5.

Table 5. The average values of the three metrics concerning the problem of tags' ambiguity and spelling variations without following our proposed approach

Problem	Database	Precision	Recall	F1
Tags ambiguity	Del.icio.us	10%	100%	18%
Spelling variations		30%	15%	20%

Tags Ambiguity: When omitting the steps proposed in our approach, the rates of precision become very low, which confirms that the folksonomy suffers from the precision of results and so the ambiguity problem in the step of resources retrieval, and no respect of users' preferences in the resources retrieval process. Also the metric F1 rate decreases according to the diminution of precision. On the contrary the rates of recall are very high (100%), this can be explained by the ability of our system to retrieve all the existing resources by a simple selection query.

Spelling Variations: When omitting the steps proposed in our approach the rates of precision becomes very low, which confirms that the folksonomy suffers from the precision of results in resources retrieval. The rates of recall are also much lower than with our approach. This can be explained by the inability of the system to retrieve all the relevant resources tagged with tags related to the one found in the learner's query. The rate of the metric F1 also decreases.

To conclude, the values of precision and recall achieved with our approach are very promising. Especially when we consider the F1 metric, we can observe that our approach achieves the best values. This implies that it is the most adequate when the user wants to obtain a trade-off between precision and recall. The use of social similarities really enable to satisfy the user's need when retrieving him a set of resources.

Tables 6 and 7 present the deviation value of precision, recall and the F1 metric in del.icio.us datasets for tags ambiguity and spelling variations problems respectively.

Table 6. The standard deviation value of the three metrics concerning tags ambiguity problem

	Precision	Recall	F1
Del.icio.us dataset	6%	8%	7%

Table 7. The standard deviation value of the three metrics concerning spelling variations problem

	Precision	Recall	F1
Del.icio.us dataset	10%	7%	8%

In both cases, these values are very small which indicates that the value of these measures for each user tend to be very close to the average. Since the averages values are very promising for the community in general, the small values of standard deviations indicate that the metrics are also promising for each user individually. An analysis of the impact of α value setting will be presented in the next subsection.

4.3   The Impact of α Value in the Ranking Function

In this experiment, we detected the presence of 19 events by using the formula (1). To evaluate the impact of these events on ranking the retrieved resources, we proceeded as follow:

In the same time periods where we have detected the presence of an event, two experimental scenarios related to choosing the value of parameter α were proposed:

(a) The α value is between 0 and 0.4 ($0 \leq \alpha \leq 0.4$)

In this case, we remarked that when the value of α is between 0 and 0.4 the ranking function is focused much more on the second feature of the formula (2), which is the popularity of resources when event detection.

Experiments demonstrated that in the case of ambiguous tag, when two different events are detected, precision value is bended down because we have neglected the social similarities between users that can personalized the retrieved results. Thus focusing only on event detection can decrease the pertinence of ranking function.

For example, suppose that a learner want to obtain relevant resources related to the software (eclipse). In the same time period when this learner searches these resources, two different events were detected: the first one there is a new version of eclipse software and the second one there is the natural event (eclipse).

In this case, when we neglect the social similarities between users, resources that are related to natural event (eclipse) can be proposed to this learner, which decrease the precision of results.

(b) The α value is between 0.5 and 1 ($0.5 \leq \alpha < 1$)

It is clear that in this second case; the ranking function is focused on the social aspect more than the influence of new event on resource popularity.

This can degrade the result precision because even with the fact that users are similar, there are some resources became not relevant to an active learner because they are very ancient and thus their popularity decreased comparing with new resources that are presented recently with the new event detection.

Figure 4 demonstrates that the most appropriate value of α that produces the highest value of precision, recall and F1 metric is 0.6. This implies that it is the most sufficient when the user wants to gain a trade-off between social similarities and new events detection.

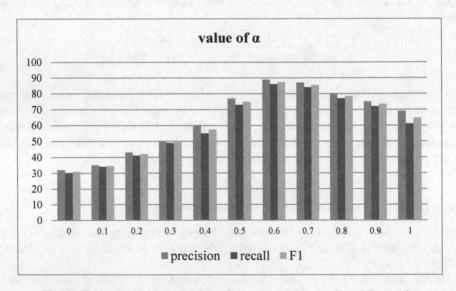

Fig. 4. Evaluation the impact of α values on precision, recall and F1 metrics

4.4 Scalability Evaluation

As information retrieval systems are designed to help users to navigate in huge collections of resources, one of our goals is to scale up to big datasets. So, it is significant to determine how fast our approach provides results.

In this subsection we analyze the impact of increasing the number of learners on the execution time.

In order to demonstrate the scalability of our approach, we measured the execution time necessary to make appropriate ranking in del.icio.us database, with a number of learners increasing from 2000 to 7898.

Figure 5 shows that the execution time of our approach linearly increases as the database size increase, meaning that our approach have relatively good scale-up behavior since the increase of the number of learners in the database will lead to approximately the linear increase of the processing time, which is wanted in the processing of big databases.

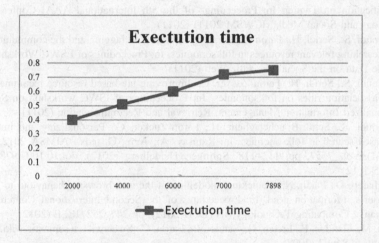

Fig. 5. Evaluation performance of our approach when the database size increases

5 Conclusion and Future Work

Information Retrieval is still a growing research area in computer science. In this context, the presented work investigated the social information retrieval in order to enhance and improve the classic information retrieval process within social technologies in E-learning area.

Our investigations in the field of E-learning folksonomies have allowed us to make a contribution in which we are interested to personalize resources retrieval according to learners' levels and specialties. The proposed approach was based on social interactions between learners where the objective was the combination between social similarities and event detection to rank retrieved resources. We used a formula that can detect the presence of an event related to a given query since the increase of similar queries in a particular period.

We have tested the approach on a baseline dataset. In order to continue and improve our work, we aim to test our approach on other big datasets, compare it with other ranking functions and also used the map-reduce framework in order to let our approach scale with very large databases.

References

1. Abdelhaq, H., Sengstock, C., Gertz, M.,: Eventweet: online localized event detection from twitter. In: Proceedings of the 39th International Conference on Very Large Data Bases (VLDB 2013), vol. 6, No. 12 (2013)
2. Angeletou, S., Sabou, M., Specia, L. Motta, E.: Bridging the gap between folksonomies and the semantic web: an experience report. In: Proceedings of ESWC Workshop on Bridging the Gap Between Semantic Web and Web (2007)
3. Becker, H., Naaman, M., Gravano, L.: Beyond trending topics: real-world event identification on Twitter. In: Proceedings of the 5th International AAAI Conference on Weblogs and Social Media (ICWSM 2011) (2011)
4. Beldjoudi, S., Seridi, H., Faron-Zucker, C.: Ambiguity in tagging and the community effect in researching relevant resources in folksonomies. In: Proceedings of ESWC Workshop User Profile Data on the Social Semantic Web (2011)
5. Beldjoudi, S., Seridi, H., Faron-Zucker, C.: Improving tag-based resource recommendation with association rules on folksonomies. In: Proceedings of ISWC workshop on Semantic Personalized Information Management: Retrieval and Recommendation (2011)
6. Beldjoudi, S., Seridi-Bouchelaghem, H., Faron-Zucker, C.: Personalizing and improving tag-based search in folksonomies. In: Ramsay, A., Agre, G. (eds.) AIMSA 2012. LNCS (LNAI), vol. 7557, pp. 112–118. Springer, Heidelberg (2012). doi:10.1007/978-3-642-33185-5_12
7. Boughareb, D., Farah, N.: Contextual modelling of the user browsing behaviour to identify the user's information need. In: Proceedings of the Second International Conference on Innovative Computing Technology (INTECH 2012), pp 247–252. IEEE (2012)
8. Buffa, M., Gandon, F., Ereteo, G., Sander, P., Faron, C.: Sweetwiki: a semantic wiki. J. Web Semant. 6, 84–97 (2008)
9. Gruber, T.: TagOntology - a way to agree on the semantics of tagging data (2005). http://tomgruber.org/writing/tagontology.htm
10. Limpens, F., Gandon, F. Buffa, M.: Collaborative semantic structuring of folksonomies. In: Proceedings of IEEE/WIC/ACM International Conference on Web Intelligence (WI 2009) (2009)
11. Mika, P.: Ontologies are us: a unified model of social networks and semantics. In: Gil, Y., Motta, E., Benjamins, V.R., Musen, M.A. (eds.) ISWC 2005. LNCS, vol. 3729, pp. 522–536. Springer, Heidelberg (2005). doi:10.1007/11574620_38
12. Pan, J.Z., Taylor, S., Thomas, E.: Reducing ambiguity in tagging systems with folksonomy search expansion. In: Aroyo, L., et al. (eds.) ESWC 2009. LNCS, vol. 5554, pp. 669–683. Springer, Heidelberg (2009). doi:10.1007/978-3-642-02121-3_49
13. Sakaki, T., Okazaki, M., Matsuo, Y.: Tweet analysis for real-time event detection and earthquake reporting system development. IEEE Trans. Knowl. Data Eng. 25(4), 919–931 (2010)

14. Specia, L., Motta, E.: Integrating folksonomies with the semantic web. In: Franconi, E., Kifer, M., May, W. (eds.) ESWC 2007. LNCS, vol. 4519, pp. 624–639. Springer, Heidelberg (2007). doi:10.1007/978-3-540-72667-8_44
15. Torniai, C., Jovanović, J., Gašević, D., Bateman, S., Hatala, M.: E-learning meets the social semantic web. In: Proceedings of Eighth IEEE International Conference on Advanced Learning Technologies (2008)
16. Wang, Y., Sundaram, H., Xie, L.: Social event detection with interaction graph modeling. In: Proceedings of ACM International Conference on Multimedia, Association for Computing Machinery Inc., pp. 1–4. ACM, Nara (2012)
17. Westerski, A., Kruk, S.R., Samp, K., Woroniecki, T., Czaja, F. O'Nuallain, C.: E-learning based on the social semantic information sources. In: Proceedings of LACLO (2006)

Using Semantic Web Technologies to Describe an Educational Domain

Tiago Thompsen Primo[1(✉)], André Behr[2], and Rosa Viccari[2]

[1] SRBR - Samsung Research Institute Brazil, Campinas, SP, Brazil
tiago.t@samsung.com
[2] Instituto de Informática, Avenida Bento Gonalves,
Porto Alegre, RS 9500, Brazil

Abstract. This research presents a method to describe Learning Objects as Semantic Web compatible Ontologies. The proposed method divides the Ontologies among three layers. The first is composed by the knowledge domain, the second by the LOs and their relations, and the third is responsible for knowledge inference and reasoning. As study case, it is presented the Ontologies of LOM and OBAA metadata standards as part of the Layer One. The layer two is composed by the description of sample Learning Objects based on the properties and restrictions defines by the layer one ontologies. The layer three describes the knowledge inference axioms, which we defined as Application Profiles. Our current results can be resumed as a contribution to Ontology Engineering for Semantic Web applied to Digital Education.

1 Introduction

Nowadays the availability of alternatives to access information is extensive. Television, Internet, and mobile devices are platforms that ease the access of various types of information in different situations. What if we could use the Internet as a source of personalized information for learning systems?

Explore such technologies can benefit Educators and Students. Educators can reuse part of a documentary from Youtube in a class. Students can use their own social networks to share with colleagues educational materials. Both of them can share educational contents between them.

To materialize this scenario and allow the interoperability of distinct applications, we must exceed the layers of protocol communication. It is important to build an interoperable knowledge representation.

The idea of standard Knowledge Representations is not a novelty. The Learning Object communities, and other research groups are proposing standards since the early days of the Web to cope with such scenarios. What changed so far is the amount of content; the where and how to find it; and how the content can be made available. Thus, the focus of this research is to integrate the standard technologies provided by the Semantic Web with Knowledge Representation and Reasoning methods to use the Semantic Web as a source of Educational Materials to support Personalized Learning.

F. Koch et al. (Eds.): CARE 2016/SocialEdu 2016, CCIS 677, pp. 64–80, 2016.
DOI: 10.1007/978-3-319-52039-1_5

In [15], the authors argue that educational content discovery should be personalized based on contextual factors such as prior knowledge, learning goals and learning pace. Our approach makes use of Linked Data [6] methods and technologies to represent the knowledge domain. This approach allows an expressive representation of user requirements and context.

With this representation, it is possible to focus on recommendations to support the students pedagogical necessities. To accomplish this, we propose an alternative to model Learning Objects using ontologies.

The variables related to the learning process of a student can be perceived from numerous perspectives (e.g. Pedagogy, Philosophy, Psychology, Human Computer Interaction) [9]. It is necessary to use a flexible and extensible approach to model the student, the interactions with a system and their LOs. Therefore, we propose the utilization of the standard languages from the Semantic Web together with reasoning techniques of the Descriptive Logic.

In this work, we will present our ontological proposal to describe Learning Objects, Students Profiles and their relationships allowing a two-fold contribution: (I) An ontological knowledge representation to describe Learning Objects, Students Profiles and (II) a practice to describe axiom with description logic to perform basic inferences and to support Intelligent Agents.

This representation and reasoning scheme allow the user model to have multiple facets, such as context, a level of instruction, and cognitive learning style. Those facets can be also modeled as an Agent.

The core idea is that the user agent is composed of a set of annotations that are defined and maintained by specific ontologies. Besides modeling the user, it is possible to adopt the same approach to representing the Learning Objects. In this work, we restrict the content to Learning Objects [8], allowing us to open space for Agents to deal with incomplete metadata information and different metadata standards.

Related to the objective the contributions are: 1 - A method to describe Learning Objects as Ontology individuals compatible with the Semantic Web; 2 - A method to describe the relationships among Learning Objects; and 3 - An ontology engineering approach to describe ontologies and axioms to reason over specific domain information (Application Profiles).

2   Related Work

The research of [5], presents a comparative study between solutions to support educational applications using ontologies and Semantic Web. [5] also classifies the educational systems in three generations: The First generation is characterized by the Learning Management Systems (LMS), whose example is Moodle; The second generation is characterized by the use of AI techniques to support the learning process, for instance, the Intelligent Tutoring Systems; and the third is characterized by the use of ontologies and the Semantic Web, an example is this current proposal that intends to cope with educational systems in a decentralized manner. Although they relate the importance of utilizing Semantic Web and ontologies, they do not provide a general methodology to engineer those ontologies, their relationships, and a real case usage scenario. As stated by [5] the state-of-the-art educational applications are between the first and second generation. This fact motivates the appearance of initiatives that stimulates the transition to the third generation, such as this work.

Following this third generation of educational systems, as proposed by the work of Dicheva, [1] presents two approaches using ontologies and Semantic Web techniques to support instructional design activities, in other words, allowing personalization alternatives to the pedagogical engineering process. Along with this, they present the concept of anytime-anywhere learning based on Semantic Web techniques. Their relation with the present work resides in the use of Semantic Web and ontologies for reasoning. Although their proposal is majorly based on Semantic Web techniques, they do not provide alternatives to fulfill the communication gap between this alternative and the current learning systems.

The work of [10] reinforce the necessity for broad solutions to cope with large-scale personalized education. It means that the current learning systems and technologies should not be discontinued immediately and they need alternatives to migrated to a semantic environment.

In the work of [14], they are concerned with the data that is generated by the use of educational applications. In their proposal, they mention that this data should be available by other applications and users. The alternative would be the use of Semantic Web technologies, especially to describe and share information among educational applications. The underlying idea is that currently we already have several educational applications and we have to recommend the suitable application according to a student need. Albeit they acknowledge that Semantic Web can be used along with legacy learning systems, they have not proposed any alternative to describe and share the students data.

This approach is also based on the research of [13], where one of the areas that need to be explored by educational systems, is the ability to have intelligent software that can help learners to filter information for quality and importance. The Semantic Web is a rich source to accomplish this [3], along with current interoperability issues that must be considered to deal with this challenge.

Over the next sections, we will describe our approach to represent educational content and user profiles using domain ontologies.

3   Building the Knowledge Representation

Users in the educational domain can be perceived accordingly to several perspectives (e.g. pedagogy, psychology, cognitive sciences, and social behavior). In addition, a user profile is dynamic, instead of being previously determined, and is dynamic during the learning process.

Therefore, we choose to represent the user model as ontologies based on descriptive logic. This representation allows to cope with incomplete information and also to manage consistency-check of the students profile during information updates.

For the purpose of this work, we will focus on the use of the OWL due to its compatibility with the Semantic Web, its ability to provide decidable reasoning mechanisms and its status as a W3C recommendation.

The proposed ontologies are divided into three layers. The Layer One is composed by ontologies that describe metadata schemas, for instance, the LOM Ontology; the Layer Two ontologies, describes a User Profile, Learning Objects or their relationships with properties from a Layer One Ontology; and the Layer Three Ontologies comprehend the description of Applications Profiles that will provide reasoning over the Layer One and Layer Two.

To describe the method we use several key terms of OWL ontologies: **Class:** Describe concepts of a domain, a structure that can encompass a set of Data Properties or Object Properties and individuals; **Properties:** Is a binary relation on individuals; **Object Properties:** Relations between individuals; **Data Properties:** Relationships among individuals and an XML Schema Datatype value or a literal; **Axiom:** A premise or a point to begin the reasoning process; **Range:** Links a property to either a class description or a data range; **Domain:** It is used to link a property to a class description; **Cardinality:** It is a restriction, defines the maximum or minimum number of individuals to link with a property; **Individuals:** represent the objects in the domain that we are interested in.

3.1 Describing Layer One Ontologies

The Layer One ontologies are used to describe classes and properties that are used to represent individuals in the Layer Two ontologies. This layer stores ontologies with the semantics of a metadata schema, considering: cardinality; data ranges; association properties; and the necessary axioms to describe the application domain.

The first thing to consider is the application domain: A Standard for User Profile representation; an educational metadata standard; a relationship standard; among other possible top layer descriptions.

For example, in this work the Layer One ontologies comprehend the LOM Metadata Standard[1], the OBAA metadata standard[2], the FOAF metadata standard[3].

To design Layer One ontologies, we propose the following set of practices: Metadata became Class and Subclass; Properties became Data Properties and Object Properties according to their semantic; The semantic of a metadata is described as restriction axioms.

---

[1] The Learning Object Metadata Standard [8] has an element set used to describe Learning Objects, it is considered a reference for such activity.

[2] [17] was build mainly to extend LOM with platform interoperability aspects. It is a Brazilian Standard.

[3] The Friend Of A Friend vocabulary is used to describe the relationships among Agents for the Semantic Web.

3.2 Describing Layer Two Ontologies

The Layer Two ontologies describes the User Profiles, Learning Objects and their relationships. Those ontologies import the properties of the n Layer One ontologies allowing the standardized description of individuals.

This method, allows the application of reasoning mechanisms to verify the consistency of an individual trough some Layer One ontology. For instance, if we describe a Learning Object as an individual of the OBAA Standard layer one ontology, we can verify if the cardinality, range, and value space were properly used. Also, if some description is incorrect we can apply an *explanation* algorithm to understand what was described wrong.

Considering storage purposes, those ontologies can be stored in some formal repository, e.g. a Triple-Store, or even simply defining a URI for its access. This alternative gives flexibility to content designers that can simply build and publish their contents on the Web.

Layer Two ontologies are appropriated to describe: User Profiles; Learning Objects; application contexts; and relationships. Each one of them can be described in one or several ontologies. There is a payoff to consider when dealing with granularity matters. Higher granularities allows by on side to delimit the processing unities and reduce computer processing, but, by the other side, the human cost to brake the information in several ontologies are elevated. Take this in consideration when describing your application domain with this method.

3.3 Describing Layer Three Ontologies

Layer Three ontologies are mainly developed to represent Application Profiles. [11] defined an Application Profile as compositions of metadata elements from one or more metadata schemas. They are used to describe an application domain.

This work add to the application profiles computations means to reason knowledge and verify the consistency of Layer Two individuals. This process can be used to derive, for example, the users that have specific pedagogical characteristics, which Learning Objects can be used in a specific domain. Those inferences are done exploring the deduction rules of OWL ontologies.

Basically, an Application Profile ontology will be composed, at least, by a class with an axiom that will infer the individuals that match the axiom description. For example, it can be created a class *UsersWithSpecialNeeds* with an axiom that describes that individual with the property *hasVisual* are inferred as an instance of the class *UsersWithSpecialNeeds*. To create Layer Three ontologies we can use as many classes with domain axioms as necessary.

4 Example Application

In this section we describe a Learning Object based in the three ontology layers method described in Sect. 3. For that, we will present the Educational Metadata Standard for the Layer One ontology, the Learning Objects ontology in the Layer Two, and the Application Profile ontology in the Layer Three.

This study case was built with the intend to bridge the gap between the theoretical definitions presented in Sect. 3 and real works Learning Objects.

4.1   The Layer One Ontology

Building Layer One Ontologies regards the definition of the properties that are necessary to describe the Layer Two individuals and the Layer Three ontologies Application Profiles.

To design the Layer One Ontology, we will use as case study the LOM Metadata Standard for three reasons: LOM is considered an international *de Facto* standard to describe Learning Objects [4]; It is common for researcher of educational technology, and, there is an opportunity to describe a standardized LOM OWL ontology.

There are a few steps to follow in order to describe this ontology:

- Study and understand the whole standard;
- define the set of Classes and Properties exactly as the standard incorporating their Ranges and Cardinalities;
- choose a Reasoner to test the ontology;
- provide an URI to publish the ontology.

LOM is an extensive educational standard, because of this, we will describe some classes and properties. The chosen LOM group (LifeCycle) is complex enough (cardinality restrictions, domain and range restriction) to demonstrate our method.[4]

We choose to present the study case using the LOM LifeCycle group because of its characteristics. It is relatively small but preserves the semantic complexity of the larger groups, such as General or Educational. Following we present the Classes and Properties described according to our ontology engineering approach.

The LifeCycle group presents the LOM metadata Standard group 2 and its contents are presented in Table 1. The column **Nr** enumerates the internal metadata identification according the standard; the column **Name** has the metadata

Table 1. Group 2 of the LOM metadata standard

Nr	Name	Cardinality	Value space	Datatype
2	Life Cycle	1		
2.1	Version	1		LangString max 50
2.2	Status	1	Draft, final, revised	
2.3	Contribute	30		
2.3.1	Role	1	Author, publisher	
2.3.2	Entity	40	Delimited vocabulary	CharString max 1000
2.3.3	Date	1	DateTime	2001-08-23

---

[4] The LOM ontology is available to reuse through the following URI[5].

names; the column **Cardinality** has the metadata restriction in terms of usage quantity; the column **Value Space** contains the values to be used in the metadata, and the column **Datatype** the computational data-type restriction.

Classes. Each metadata from LifeCycle group became a class and a subclass with cardinality restrictions according to the chosen standards. For instance, Contribute is a subclass of Life Cycle and has a cardinality *max* 30.

Properties. Properties can be classified as Data Properties or Object Properties. Data Properties are the data itself (e.g. *has_name* String "james"). Object Properties describe the relationships between classes and individuals (e.g. *has_classes*). Object Properties are also associated with the metadata cardinality (e.g. Max 10 *has_classes*).

The cardinality restrictions can be used with Object Properties. They can be used to group individuals with specific characteristics. As an illustrative example of those relationships, refer to Fig. 1.

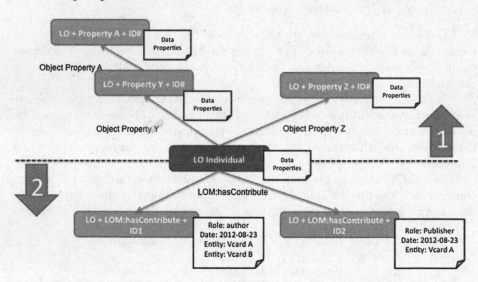

Fig. 1. Sample learning objects with Life Cycle information

In Fig. 1, at its center, it is illustrated a sample **Learning Objects Individual** that is divided into two parts. The number one (1), illustrates a generic Learning Objects representation model; The number two (2) illustrates the usage of the Object Properties Contribute, in this case, named LOM:hasContribute. As can be seen, there are three individuals represented. The higher Layer **Learning Objects Individual** and two other individuals linked by the Object Properties LOM:hasContribute and each one of them, with specific Data Properties.

This kind of relationship allows, for instance, the reuse of the individuals **LO + LOM:hasContribute + ID1** and/or **LO + LOM:hasContribute + ID1** in different versions of an Learning Objects.

This example was prepared to exemplify the description of a Learning Objects with such ontology engineering method, the next section will present the characteristics of the Layer Two Ontologies.

4.2 The Layer Two Ontology

The Layer Two Ontologies to provide the representation of Learning Objects, User Profiles, Educational Applications and their relationships.

For example, the description of a Learning Object as instance of the LOM ontology is performed within the following steps: convert or create a Learning Object; create an OWL file to represent the information of the Learning Objects; import the LOM OWL ontology; describe the individuals to represent information of the Learning Objects; create Object Properties and Data Properties relationships as necessary.

To illustrate this scenario, we present the *Ramis* Learning Object. *Ramis* uses two metadata standards, IEEE-LOM and OBAA. The underlying purpose for its creation was to simulate the description of an interoperable Learning Object compatible with three hardware platforms: Internet, Digital Television, and Mobile Devices.

Ramis has a set of metadata as presented in Table 2. We started our conversion by analyzing that meta-information and illustrate its complexity with Fig. 2.

Table 2 is divided into four columns to present the whole set of metadata utilized to describe it. The Column **Metadata Index and Name** is the identification according to the metadata standard; the Learning Objects standard by the column **Standard**; the associated value of a metadata by the column **Value**, also this column describes the metadata cardinality, when applicable. And the column **Type** can be a Class, if it is a container and has cardinality one (1), can be a DP when it was used a data property or an Object Properties if it was used an object property to represent it.

As can be seen in Table 2, there are several Data Properties and some Object Properties. If we take for example the metadata **Requirement**, the index 4.4, it has the cardinality of forty individuals. To exemplify the *Ramis* Learning Objects OWL ontology, we present the Fig. 2 that illustrates the individuals that were built to describe the Learning Objects *Ramis*[6].

Figure 2, has the indication **1** that emphasizes the higher layer individual; the indication **2** the Object Properties *hasRequirement*; the indication **3** the Object Properties *hasPlatformSpecificFeatures*; the indication **4** emphasizes the Object Properties hasSpecificRequirement; The indication **5** the Object Properties hasSpecificOrComposite and finally the indication **6** the Object Properties hasOrComposite. Each individual has its own set of Data Properties.

---

[6] The full OWL file can be accessed here: http://gia.inf.ufrgs.br/ontologies/OAS/ Ramis/Ramis.owl.

Table 2. The metadata for the Learning Object *Ramis*

Metadata index and name	Standard	Value.	Type
1 - General	LOM	Cardinality one (1)	Class
1.3 - Language	LOM	pt-br	DP
1.4 - Description	LOM	Apresenta ideias para melhorar o estilo de vida	DP
1.5 - Keywords	LOM	hábitos alimentares, IMC, Atividade Física	DP
4 - Technical	LOM	Cardinality one (1)	Class
4.1 - Format	LOM	Texto XHTML, CSS, Imagens JPEG, Vídeos H.264	DP
4.2 - Size	LOM	14	DP
4.3 - Location	LOM	http://...oaramisindex.jsf	DP
4.4 - Requirement	LOM	Cardinality forty (40)	OP
4.4.1 - OrComposite	LOM	Cardinality forty (40)	OP
4.4.1.1 - Type	LOM	Web Browser, Operating System	DP
4.4.1.2 - Name	LOM	IE, Firefox, Win Mobile, IE Mobile, Symbian, S60	DP
4.4.1.3 - Version	LOM	7.0, 3.0, 6.1	DP
4.7 - Duration	LOM	PT00H17M00S	DP
4.8 - SupportedPlatforms	OBAA	Web, Mobile, Digital TV	DP
4.9 - PlatformSpecificFeatures	OBAA	Unlimited	OP
4.9.1 - SpecificPlatform	OBAA	TV Digital	DP
4.9.2 - SpecificFormat	OBAA	ZIP	DP
4.9.3 - SpecificSize	OBAA	1.8	DP
4.9.4 - SpecificLocation	OBAA	http://...oaramisramis_tvd.zip	DP
4.9.5 - SpecificRequirements	OBAA	Unlimited	OP
4.9.5.1 - SpecificOrComposite	OBAA	Unlimited	OP
4.9.5.1.1 - SpecificType	OBAA	Middleware	DP
4.9.5.1.2 - SpecificName	OBAA	Ginga NCL Live CD	DP
4.9.5.1.3 - SpecificVersion	OBAA	1.0	DP
4.9.6 - SpecificInstallationRemarks	OBAA	Descompactar e Transferir	DP

4.3   The Layer Three Ontology

The Layer Three ontology is in charge of the reasoning over the Layer Two ontologies. To this proposal, this type of ontology is classified as Application Profile. Application Profile is an ontology composed of a class or a set of classes that describes specific domain knowledge and has at least one axiom for reasoning.

The reasoning is useful to verify if a Learning Objects is properly described according to some standard; to provide inferences according to specific domain characteristics; infer new relationships between Learning Objects; to support some statistical process; among others.

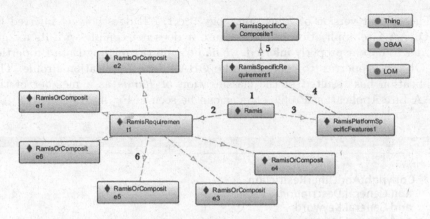

Fig. 2. The representation of individuals for the *Ramis* OWL file

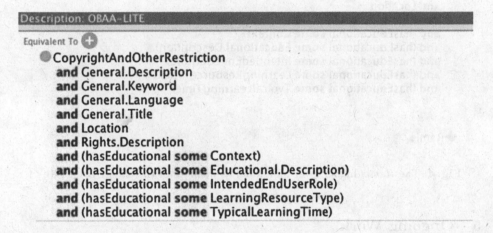

Fig. 3. OBAA Lite ontology axiom

To describe the Application Profile OWL ontology we must consider: What is the knowledge to be derived from the Layer Two ontologies? Is it possible to retrieved by a SPARQL query? Reasoners are not extremely powerful, one axiom is enough? How many class are necessary?

As an example, we shall describe an Application Profile that will infer Learning Objects, only if this Learning Object has a specific set of metadata. Considering this, we present the OBAA Lite Application Profile. This Application Profile was developed by [16]. The presented research used OBAA and LOM standards to define the minimum set of metadata information that is necessary to describe domain specific Learning Objects. Figure 3 presents the class and the axiom built to infer which Learning Objects are compliant with the OBAA Lite Application Profile.

The current version of *Ramis* ontology (Sect. 4.2) does not get inferred by the OBAA Lite application profile because it does not comply with its axiom. In order to have it properly inferred, we had to add the missing Data Properties and Object Properties to cope with the OBAA Lite Application Profile. The modification has resulted in the classification of *Ramis* as a member of the OBAA Lite Application Profile class as can be seen in Fig. 4.

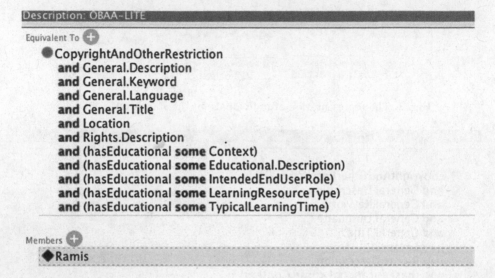

Fig. 4. The *Ramis* higher layer individual as member of the class OBAA Lite

5   Ongoing Work

Alternatively, Application Profiles can be expressed as a set of triples or a set of rules, to be used in SPARQL and SQWRL queries, respectively. These query languages are commonly used within OWL ontologies, dealing with different levels of expressivity.

Our ongoing work is being performed in order to measure the computational time and complexity of the inference model based on the use of logical reasoners such as Hermitt vs the use of Semantic Web Query Languages.

5.1   SPARQL

SPARQL is a W3C recommendation[7] of a query language for RDF sources. It is able to retrieve and manipulate data over semantic repositories (known as Triple-Stores). In this kind of database, in fully compatible with OWL ontologies and stored structures of "Subject - Predicate - Object" triples.

---

[7] https://www.w3.org/TR/rdf-sparql-query/.

Figure 5 shows how to retrieve learning objects over the OBAA Lite represented as a set of triples. As the triple query returned the same individual more than one time, we used the *DISTINCT* operator to just return one. The query acted directly over the Data Properties and Object Properties of the triples.

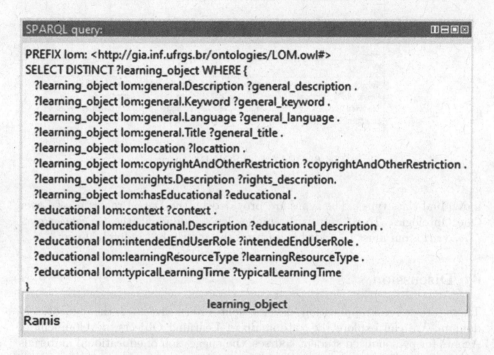

Fig. 5. OBAA Lite SPARQL query

5.2   SQWRL

The Semantic Query-enhanced Web Rule Language (SQWRL) is a query language based on the Semantic Web Rule Language (SWRL). This query language is a proposal that can be used to query over OWL ontologies.

SWRL [7] is an extended proposal of OWL axioms to include rules similar to the Horn clauses. These rules are in form of implication by antecedent and consequent. Both consist of zero or more atoms.

The information extraction in OWL ontologies is an underlying requirement. SQWRL furnishes basic operators to search in OWL, such as *select, count, orderBy*, that gives the resulting query without modifying the OWL ontology. Besides that, the language does not violate the open world assumption. The use of set elements provides a closure world mechanism. In this way, operators to build and manage sets are proposed as language features [12].

Figure 6 depicts how the OBAA Lite Application Profile could be transposed to a set of rules. The query (**S1**) is composed of antecedents that capture the

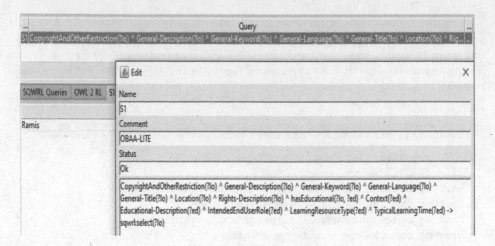

Fig. 6. OBAA Lite SQWRL query

individual class types. The types are provided by the Data Properties of Layer One Ontologies. To **S1** return the higher level individual, the *hasEducational (?lo, ?ed)* atom must be added to capture the interlinked individual types.

6   Discussion

There are several application development alternatives for the educational domain. We can explore the authorship of Learning Objects, development of Agents for personalized student courses, the suggestion of educational materials among others. The present work had presented an alternative to represent User Profiles and Learning Objects by ontologies to allow a reasoning alternative for educational applications based on Semantic Web.

The work of [2] divides the Semantic Web educational applications into three columns. This work was able to contribute with the two first columns. To cope with the first column, an alternative to reduce computational costs related to exploring SPARQL queries for simple application profiles. E.g., search Learning Objects with a specific property value. To cope with the second column our major challenge will be to reuse the educational ontologies that are already available and are not compliant with Semantic Web, also, privacy is a delicate matter, especially in this case when dealing with private and personal information.

The described ontologies were built according to the three layer proposal ontology engineering proposal. During this task, it is important to mention that the LOM ontology is considered complex due to its specifications and restrictions. This fact, in some cases, caused the reasoner to be overwhelmed with ontologies of the Layer Two that were composed by many individuals. An alternative could be separate each group of the LOM metadata in a single ontology. In the best case scenario, the reasoner would only have to cope with a limited set of properties.

The *Ramis* ontology used properties from the LOM and OBAA ontologies. This Layer Two ontology had complex sets of Data Properties and Object Properties to be described. Although it can be considered a complex ontology, in an automatic process we could obtain several interesting benefits such as: Easy update, for instance, an individual that is updated can be linked through an Object Properties; the reuse of some individuals by other Learning Objects, for instance, a technical individual that is common to several other Learning Objects; the described individuals can be validated according to a Layer one ontology; the storage can be made by a URI; it is possible to build relationships between Learning Objects ontologies by properties and it is compatible with the current Semantic Web stack.

The method to build a Layer Two ontology can be used to describe the user profile ontologies, educational domain ontologies, relationship ontologies, or any other that might describe an educational activity. Such amount of relationships can lead to performance issues, especially by the reasoner.

The use of query languages, such as SPARQL and SQWRL, to classify Layer Two Ontologies seems to be more efficient than using Description Logic because they act over the close world assumption, despite the open world assumption by the OWL ontologies. However, does it worth for Intelligent Agents? According to [12], the serialization of OWL ontologies to RDF/XML can lead to slightly different results in applications because it does not have the native meaning of OWL. In this way, SPARQL queries can produce distinct results for the same OWL ontologies in some cases.

Beyond that, the use of SPARQL does not unify with the proposed Knowledge Representation, because it is not represented by the OWL ontology. Otherwise, SQWRL copes with the proposed Knowledge Representation adding the rules in the OWL ontology, precisely in *DLSafeRule* tag.

A related research opportunity is to conserve and securely transpose the information of Learning Objects and User Profiles among those generations. Such effort may lead to a better user profiling and the singularity of educational technologies.

The usage of service-oriented architectures emerges as an alternative for the transition among "generations, their major characteristic is to focus on the definition of a standard communication format between the applications on the Web. Using such approach leads the communication between different applications in distinct programming languages and/or architectures.

Beyond communicating among educational applications, understand what is stored is crucial to provide personalization alternatives. Provide computational structures that can manipulate the information and derive knowledge, autonomously, became fundamental. The tendency to achieve such interoperability is explored by the use of ontologies. The presented approach provides a method to describe and store information allowing extensions, the connection between information, and compatibility across multiple domains.

To cope with this tendency, it had opened space for the creative development of service-based applications mainly supported by AI techniques. Those applications can derive knowledge, provide inferences, retrieve content from different servers, build flexible networks to support educational applications, stimulate the relationships between students and teachers that are geographically distributed, and mostly to provide the possibility that the users being immersed in a permanent learning environment.

7 Conclusion

There can be several application development alternatives for the educational domain. We can explore the authorship of Learning Objects, development of Agents for personalized student courses, the suggestion of educational materials among others. The present work had presented an alternative to represent User Profiles and Learning Objects by ontologies to allow a reasoning alternative for educational applications.

The presented ontologies made use of the three layer proposal to describe the knowledge domain. In each one, we described and presented an example of them. The LOM ontology is considered complex due to its specifications and characteristics. This fact, in some cases, caused the reasoner to be overwhelmed with ontologies of the Layer Two that were composed by many individuals. An alternative could be separate each group of the LOM metadata in a single ontology. In the best case scenario, the reasoner would only have to cope with a limited set of properties.

The *Ramis* ontology made use of properties from the LOM and OBAA ontologies. This Layer Two ontology had to deal with a complex set of Data Properties and Object Properties to be described. Although it can be considered a complex ontology, in an automatic process we could obtain several interesting benefits such as: Easy update, for instance, an individual that is updated can be linked through an Object Properties; the reuse of some individuals by other Learning Objects, for instance, a technical individual that is common to several other Learning Objects; the described individuals can be validated according to a Layer one ontology; the storage can be made by a URI; it is possible to build relationships between Learning Objects ontologies by properties and it is compatible with the current Semantic Web stack.

The method to build a Layer Two ontology can be used to describe the user profile ontologies, educational domain ontologies, relationship ontologies, or any other that might describe an educational activity. Such amount of relationships can lead to performance issues, especially by the reasoner.

There is a lot of work that yet need to be done, especially when considering students privacy matters, content usage rights, security policies over such information and, not most important, public policies that stimulate and popularize the principals of open knowledge. This can lead to a large-scale evaluation that can measure the effective of this approach for the current learning system.

As future work, we will explore a Triple-Store alternative to index and store Layer Two Ontologies such as LOs, User Profiles and Relationships between them, a Service Oriented alternative to integrating this proposal with some current educational application and describe new APs, to evaluate if the use of OWL-DL is the adequate solution to represent such kind of knowledge and explore the automatic conversion of Legacy Learning Objects repositories according to this proposal.

As stated by [5] the state-of-the-art educational applications are between the first and second generation. This fact motivates the appearance of initiatives that stimulates the transition to the third generation, such as this work.

The work of [2] divides the Semantic Web educational applications into three columns. This work was able to contribute with the two first columns. To cope with the first column, an alternative to reduce computational costs related to exploring SPARQL queries for simple application profiles. E.g., search Learning Objects with a specific property value. To cope with the second column our major challenge will be to reuse the educational ontologies that are already available and are not compliant with Semantic Web, also, privacy is a delicate matter, especially in this case when dealing with private and personal information.

Measure the efficiency of Query languages over Reasoning approaches.

More importantly, the grounding on descriptive logic provides inference services to automatically discover implicit information using classification (subsumption).

References

1. Adorni, G., Battigelli, S.: CADDIE and IWT: two different ontology-based approaches to anytime, anywhere and anybody learning. J. e-Learn. (2010)
2. Anderson, T., Whitelock, D.: The educational semantic web: visioning and practicing the future of education (2004)
3. d'Aquin, M.: Linked data for open and distance learning. Commonwealth of Learning report (2012)
4. Devedzic, V., Jovanovic, J., Gasevic, D.: The pragmatics of current e-learning standards. Internet Comput. IEEE **11**(3), 19–27 (2007)
5. Dicheva, D.: Ontologies and semantic web for e-learning. In: Adelsberger, H.H., Kinshuk, Pawlowski, J.M., Sampson, D.G. (eds.) Handbook on Information Technologies for Education and Training, pp. 47–65. Springer, Heidelberg (2008)
6. Dietze, S.: Interlinking educational resources and the web of data: a survey of challenges and approaches. Progr.: Electron. Libr. Inf. Syst. **47**(1), 60–91 (2013)
7. Horrocks, I., Patel-Schneider, P.F., Boley, H., Tabet, S., Grosof, B., Dean, M., et al.: SWRL: a semantic web rule language combining OWL and RuleML. W3C Memb. Submiss. **21**, 79 (2004)
8. IEEE. IEEE LOM final standard metadata (2002)
9. Kantor, P., Ricci, F., Rokach, L., Shapira, B.: Recommender Systems Handbook. Springer, Heidelberg (2011)
10. Klašnja-Milićević, A., Vesin, B., Ivanovic, M., Budimac, Z.: E-learning personalization based on hybrid recommendation strategy and learning style identification. Comput. Educ. **56**(3), 885–899 (2011)
11. Manouselis, N., Kastrantas, K.: An IEEE LOM application profile to describe training resources for agricultural & rural SMEs. In: Proceedings of Metadata and Semantics Research Conference (2007)

12. O'Connor, M., Das, A.: SQWRL: a query language for OWL. In: Proceedings of the 6th International Conference on OWL: Experiences and Directions, vol. 529, pp. 208–215. CEUR-WS.org (2009)

13. Plesch, C., Kaendler, C., Rummel, N., Wiedmann, M., Spada, H.: Identifying Areas of Tension in the field of technology-enhanced learning: results of an international Delphi study. Comput. Educ. **65**(c), 92–105 (2013)

14. Ruiz-Calleja, A., Vega-Gorgojo, G., Asensio-Pérez, J.I., Bote-Lorenzo, M.L., Gómez-Sánchez, E., Alario-Hoyos, C.: A linked data approach for the discovery of educational ICT tools in the web of data. Comput. Educ. **59**(3), 952–962 (2012)

15. Santos, O.C., Boticario, J.G.: Requirements for semantic educational recommender systems in formal e-learning scenarios. Algorithms **4**(2), 131–154 (2011)

16. Silva, J.M.C.D.: Análise técnica e pedagógica de metadados para objetos de aprendizagem (2011)

17. Vicari, R.M., Ribeiro, A., Silva, J.M.C., Santos, E.R., Primo, T., Bez, M.: Brazilian proposal for agent-based learning objects metadata standard - OBAA. In: Sánchez-Alonso, S., Athanasiadis, I.N. (eds.) MTSR 2010. CCIS, vol. 108, pp. 300–311. Springer, Heidelberg (2010). doi:10.1007/978-3-642-16552-8_27

Forming Tests from Questions with Different Theoretical and Practical Degree

Doru Popescu Anastasiu[1(✉)] and Nicolae Bold[2]

[1] Faculty of Mathematics and Computer Science,
University of Pitesti, Pitești, Romania
dopopan@gmail.com
[2] Faculty of Management, Economic Engineering in Agriculture and Rural ·
Development, University of Agronomic Sciences and Veterinary Medicine
Bucharest, Slatina Branch, Bucharest, Romania
bold_nicolae@yahoo.com

Abstract. The assessment process must meet certain requirements in order to be correct and real-based. Through this process, the assessor discovers the degree of knowledge of the taught notions. Various degrees of difficulty help the student to diversify the learning and to meet all certain types of exercises and problems. In the context of the development of technology, models of assessment diversified or were updated using technology means. This work shows a type of model of generating tests using questions with different degrees of difficulty, given a desired interval of difficulty. This model is based on an algorithm which uses genetic notions. This model has several domains of applicability, one of the main being assessment within education. Also, it consists in a structure of a future web application which will use technology-based means for the assessment of students and which will be described in detail in the work.

Keywords: Test · Genetic algorithm · Difficulty · Assessment

1 Introduction

Generating assessment tests with the characteristics of equitability and efficiency for both the assessor and the assessed persons can be a challenging task. Equitability is referred to fair build tests and efficiency relates to the best covering of the taught concepts and the exact finding of the right difficulty. Moreover, the high number of questions which consist in the question database for a test is a serious time-related obstacle for the selection of the most adequate questions for a specific situation. Some presentations of this issue and some solutions to the general process of education based on the needs of the learner, using e-learning platforms, can be found in papers [6, 18].

Assessment is an important part within the educational process. A list of subjects that were studied or can be studied in case of educational process is shown in Fig. 1. Also, we can see the context of assessment within the other processes of education and the situation of the proposed theme within the assessment process. Problematic items that appear frequently within the general context of assessment can be considered:

© Springer International Publishing AG 2016
F. Koch et al. (Eds.): CARE 2016/SocialEdu 2016, CCIS 677, pp. 81–96, 2016.
DOI: 10.1007/978-3-319-52039-1_6

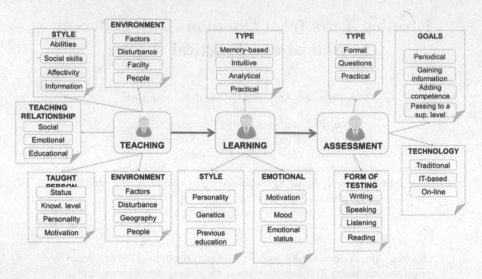

Fig. 1. The learning process and the context of the proposed theme

- the creation of an equitable assessment for a group of students which have been taught as a group. Equitability refers to a correct distribution of balanced assessment items for each student within a group. A preventive solution would be the setting of straight rules for the assessment process, that can be accomplished by each student. Another proactive approach of this issue is the generation of tests/items with equal levels of difficulty for each student;
- the human errors that appear. Due to tiredness or external factors, in the process of verification of certain items, some errors can appear. Thus, a double IT-based check can always be a good solution;
- the covering of a large area of subjects learned before. Within the evaluation, the generated items must cover a larger specific area of the subjects learned before. These subjects must be tested in order for the learner to check if these have been understood;
- the mix between practical and theoretical character of assessment. A larger proportion of one of the two types of assessment can lead to a sub-development of the other type. Moreover, some situations require a larger proportion of theoretical assessment, while other situations need a practical assessment. A solution of this issue is presented in this work.

Each one of the issues can find a solution in the system described in this work or in previous papers of the authors which are linked to this topic.

These reasons have led to the creation of a model called The Dynamic Model of Assessment and Interpretation of Results (DMAIR) which would encapsulate all this requests in a single web or offline application. This model has several components which will be presented in Sect. 2.

Diverse models for generating specific tests were presented in literature. These models use questions with different characteristics. The methods presented in these papers are different, using evolution-based algorithms (such as in papers [7, 20]), including genetic algorithms and memetic ones, combined with divide-and-conquer elements, such as in [11] or just plain generation, such as in [8]. Other cases are studied in the literature, such as generation of tests taking into account the notion of concept-effect model [13]. All of these papers study some traditional models of technology-assisted assessment and have good results in terms of runtime and general results.

Besides these traditional approaches in the field, this work introduces concepts such as theoretic difficulty degree (TDD) or practical difficulty degree (PDD). Based on these coefficients, a degree of difficulty (DD) of a question is calculated using a formula which will be presented in Sect. 3. In this way, the user has the possibility to generate items with a larger proportion of theoretical or practical character. The degree of difficulty of the test will be the sum of all the difficulty degrees of the questions that form the test. Moreover, the user can generate items that fit within an interval [A, B] or which have a practical or theoretical degree between certain limits. The questions within the test are ordered ascendingly by their DD, the difficulty increasing once the test is processed.

This work presents both the DMAIR model (in Sect. 2) and a specific case of condition (in Sect. 3). This condition consists in determining a difficulty degree for a question based on the TDD and PDD, which are given by the user.

2 Description of the Dynamic Model for Assessment and Interpretation of Results (DMAIR)

As seen in Fig. 1, the assessment is a delimited component within the educational process, among the three main important components that succeed, each one having its own characteristics. Thus, the IT-based assessment is a type of evaluation that finds many connections with other characteristics of assessment.

This model of assessment is part of a larger system which reunites database-related elements, graphic user interfaces, generation models and mechanisms of data interpretation and analysis. This system is intended to be used with the scope of the assessment of the students. The general scheme of this model is presented in Fig. 2.

The general form of the model states that the two main actors of the model are the assessor (usually, a teacher) and the assessed person (or persons, usually students). Using a different login form, the assessor has extended rights within the model. The main actions that can be made are: the insertion of questions in the database, the generation of tests with given conditions (keywords, difficulty etc.), test check and analysis of responses. Using a GUI, the assessor generates a dynamic web page for each student which contains the generated test. Using a Student Login Form, the student logins in this dynamic page and solves the test. After a checking mechanism is applied, the interpretation of the results is made and sent to both the assessor and the assessed person, through the GUI. Also, using the interpretations, some adjustments to the generation and conditions can be made. The questions can have various types, from multiple-choice to discursive or problem solving (where answers are numbers).

The most changeable elements within this model are the conditions, which can vary depending on the needs of the assessor. In previous papers, we made implementation of

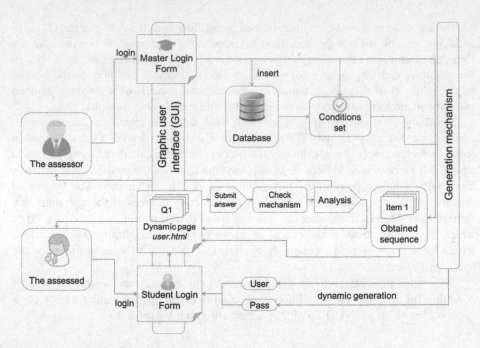

Fig. 2. The DMAIR assessment model proposed by the authors

algorithms that treat various conditions. For example, paper [12] presents an implementation based on trees, where tests are related depending on a difficulty degree. Papers [14, 15] show implementations and results for genetic algorithms where tests/questions are isolated and are/are not characterized by keywords. Paper [5] shows a model of generating different versions of tests by generating permutations of the same questions and variants.

In the next section, we will present a method that treats the case of generating question based on TDD and PDD.

3   Description of the Method Based on a Genetic Algorithm

Before starting the description of the method, we must define some notions that we will use in the work. The first definition is based on a traditional method of calculating the degree of difficulty of a question.

Definition 1. Given a question q_i, whose number of given answers is k and number of correct answers is k', the degree of difficulty is considered the ratio between k' and k. The degree of difficulty can also be approximated by the teacher.

$$DI = \frac{k'}{k} \tag{1}$$

At a simpler structure of answers (e.g., the answer is a number), the number of correct answers (k') can be easily determined. However, in case of more complex answers (e.g., words or simple statements), k' can have a confusing determination. Thus, we can use the editing distance (also called Levenshtein distance) between the given answer and the correct one in order to determine exactly whether an answer is correct or not. Usage of the editing distance can be studied in [2].

Definition 2. Given a question q_i, the theoretical difficulty degree (TDD) of q_i is considered as being the degree in which q_i is considered difficult from a theoretical point of view. Theoretical character means that the question can be solved using methods such as memorization or by presentation of short classifications.

Definition 3. Given a question q_i, the practical difficulty degree (PDD) of q_i is considered as being the degree in which q_i is considered difficult from a practical point of view. Practical character is given by the nature of the question, which demands thinking, analysis, data interpretations, deductions and connections with other notions.

Definition 4. For a specific question q_i, the degree of difficulty (DD) based on TDD and PDD is calculated using the formula:

$$DD = \frac{(TDD \times \alpha) + (PDD \times \beta)}{\alpha + \beta} \tag{2}$$

where $0 \leq \alpha \leq 1, 0 \leq \beta \leq 1$ are proportions given by the user and symbolize:

- α is the theoretical proportion given by the user, which determines the proportion in which the theoretical questions will be found in the test;
- β is the practical proportion, also given by the user, determines the proportion of practical questions in the test.

The sum of these two coefficients can be 1 or less than 1, depending on the needs of the user.

Intuitively, the larger the theoretical coefficient (α) will be, the larger the proportion of the theory-based will be. This coefficient is bigger when the assessor wants to test notions at first sight, in order to find out the level where he would like to start the learning process with his assessed persons, or to test theoretical concepts.

Analogous, a higher value of the practical coefficient (β) will determine the generation of more practical problems (generally, the problems with numbers). This value is higher in case the assessor wants to apply the theoretical notions in practical problems, related to human activity in the domain.

Based on these notions, we will present a method for the generation mechanism of the DMAIR. The method we will use for generating test is based on genetic algorithms.

Genetic algorithms are a specific part within a set of heuristic algorithms (as shown in [1]. Genetic algorithms are a strong alternative to classical methods of data analysis. Their heuristic character gives them some key characteristics that make them preferable to more exact, but slower algorithms. Practically, as their name suggests, the genetic algorithm use nature-inspired phenomena and structures and mime their behavior, in order to obtain a close-to-optimal solution to a specific problem. Usually, the genetic algorithms are used in case of problems that cannot be solved using exact algorithms, such as the NP-complete problems.

GA are also used in issues related to domains such as mathematics, statistics, physics, engineering, transportation, chemistry [3], fashion issues [9], web programming [16], agriculture [17], and pollution cases [19]. Their importance within the educational process is given by their usage in assessment issues, as shown in papers [7, 20], where there are presented studies regarding the generation of assessment tests using genetic-based and related algorithms.

Genetic algorithms use genes and chromosomes as representations of data and several methods (such as selection, mutation, crossover etc.) in order to modify these chromosomes and to choose the most optimal ones. A genetic algorithm has to deal with some issues and the most important of them are the codification of the problem and the fitness value, which defines the optimality of a chromosome [4, 10].

Basically, the algorithm contains specific steps that use genetic-based elements, such as genes and chromosomes and operations such as mutation or crossover with one point. The questions will be codified with numbers from 1 to the total number of questions. The genetic algorithms were used because of their lower runtime in case of large sets of data.

In the case of our problem, the genes will be considered the questions and the chromosomes will be the tests. The optimality of a chromosome will be given by its general degree of difficulty. This means that the fitness value of a chromosome will be considered as the sum of the general degrees of difficulty of all genes within that chromosome. We have used several variations of mutation and crossover, until this configuration was chosen as the one with the best results.

We will use some variables and structures within the algorithm. These are:

- N – the number of questions found in the database;
- M – the number of questions wanted to be found in a test;
- $Q[N]$ – a structure that contains several characteristics for each question. For a question $Q[i]$, $i \in \{1, ..., N\}$ these characteristics are:
  - nr_ord – the order number of $Q[i]$; nr_ord $\in \{1, 2, ..., N\}$;
  - state – the statement of $Q[i]$; state is a string of characters;
  - c_answ – the correct answer of $Q[i]$; the type can vary;
  - deg1 – the TDD of $Q[i]$; deg1 $\in \{0.0, ..., 1.0\}$;
  - deg2 – the PDD of $Q[i]$; deg2 $\in \{0.0, ..., 1.0\}$;
  - deg – the DD of $Q[i]$; deg $\in \{0.0, ..., 1.0\}$.
- A – the lower limit wanted by the user for deg;
- B – the upper limit wanted by the user for deg;
- $A1$ – the lower limit wanted by the user for deg1;
- $B1$ – the upper limit wanted by the user for deg1;
- $A2$ – the lower limit wanted by the user for deg2;
- $B2$ – the upper limit wanted by the user for deg2;
- NG – the number of generations; the higher NG is, the finer the results will be;
- NrPop – the number of chromosomes in the population;
- sol[NrPop][M] – the array that contains the solutions.

We want to generate M distinct questions Q_1, ..., Q_M, each Q_i with deg $\in$ [A, B], deg1 $\in$ [A1, B1] and deg2 $\in$ [A2, B2], i = 1, M. Within the algorithm, the gene of a chromosome is considered a question and the chromosome is considered a test. The degree of difficulty of a test is the sum of all the DDs of the questions that form a test. The formula is shown in (3).

$$DD_{test} = \sum_{i=1}^{M} deg \ of \ Q_{sol_i} \qquad (3)$$

The steps of the algorithms and the pseudocode are presented next.

Step 1. Input data is read. Input data consists of N, M, Q[N] and NG. Depending on the programming language, the type of Q[N] may vary. For example, we can use *struct* type for storing this variable in C++ and Java.

Step 2. The initial population is generated, using random generation. At this step, the conditions are verified. We calculate for each chromosome the degree of difficulty. The next steps will be repeated for NG times (Fig. 3).

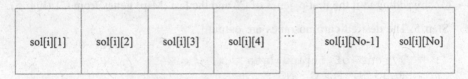

Fig. 3. General form of a chromosome

Step 3. The mutation operation is applied. That is, we generate a random number m, a position p and a chromosome n. The gene in the position p in the chromosome n is swapped with the random number m (Fig. 4).

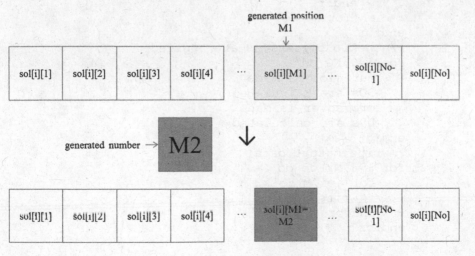

Fig. 4. Operation of mutation for a chromosome (M1 $\leq$ No, M2 $\leq$ N)

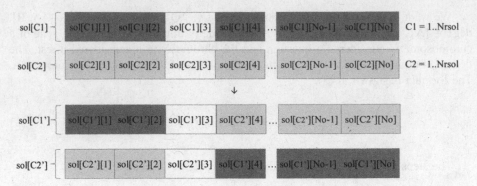

Fig. 5. Operation of crossover for a chromosome

Step 4. The crossover in one point is applied. That is, we randomly choose two chromosomes (C1 and C2) and a position p. From the two chromosomes we obtain two distinct chromosomes:

- C1' by adding to it the first p genes of C1 and the last (M-p) genes from C2;
- C2' by adding to it the first p genes of C2 and the last (M-p) genes from C1 (Fig. 5).

Step 5. The desired chromosomes are output.

```
//read of input data
Read N, M, Q, NG
//generation is made
for i=1,NrPop do
    for j=1,M do
        if (requirements are respected) then
                sol[i][j] ← random value
                DD[sol[i][j]] is calculated
        endif
    endfor
endfor
//genetic operations are applied
for i=1,NG do
    mutation is made
    DDs are calculated
    crossover is made
    DDs are calculated
endfor
//write output data
for i=1,NrPop do
    for j=1,M do
        write sol[i][j]
    endfor
endfor
```

Following these steps, the algorithm will output the desired tests that respect the restrictions given by the user.

4 Implementation and Results

For showing the veracity of this method, we will focus on two main aspects of this method: the runtime of the algorithm and the viability of the method for situations from reality. As for the environment, the generations were made on a system, using Windows 8 environment, on an i3-3217U CPU microprocessor, 1.80 GHz, with 4 GB of RAM.

Taking into account the viability, we took a generated test using the algorithm and we gave it to a number of 20 students to solve it. Because of the low development of the GUI, we used Google Forms for the answer to the questions. In order to show the closeness to real situations, we will show the distribution of scores and a comparison between the degrees of difficulty found by the algorithm and the degrees of difficulty calculated with the traditional method (in this case, the DD is called Difficulty Index).

The number of questions in the database was set to 400 (N = 400) and the test had 20 questions (M = 20). The assessor wanted to test some theoretical issues, so α = 0.9 and β = 0.1. A and B were set to 11.0, respectively 14.5. A1 and A2 were set to 0.0, B1 and B2 were set to 20.0. At a number of 1000 generations (NG = 1000), we obtained some sequences. A random sequence was chosen, that is the test contained the questions with order numbers (97 145 126 32 325 319 44 337 300 61 95 70 361 183 208 264 42 240 98 283). The degree of difficulty of this test (the sum of DDs of all questions within the sequence) was 13.99 (Table 1).

Table 1. Degrees of difficulty for the sequence taken as example

Q 1–10	97	145	126	32	325	319	44	337	300	61
DD	0.26	0.34	0.66	0.66	0.74	0.74	0.74	0.74	0.74	0.74
Q 11–20	95	70	361	183	208	264	42	240	98	283
DD	0.74	0.74	0.74	0.82	0.82	0.82	0.82	0.82	0.82	0.82

The test was indeed 90% with theoretical issues. Only the first 2 questions requested solving some practical problems. Figure 6 shows some data analysis after the tests were solved by the students. The data consist in:

- the number of question solved correctly by each student, which helps at showing the normal distribution of the answers and which proves that the built test using the genetic algorithm is balanced and have a good structure;
- the number of correct answers per question, which helps at establishing the DI;

Regarding the calculus of the degree of difficulty using the editing distance (EDDD), we calculated this value for every question. The answers were considered the variants in front of answers (e.g., 'a', 'b', 'bc' or 'abc'). We obtained the values shown in Table 2.

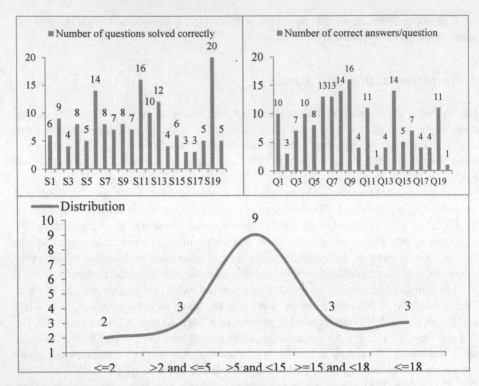

Fig. 6. Answers and distribution of answers

Table 2. Editing distance for the 20 questions and the 20 students

	Q1	Q2	Q3	Q4	Q5	Q6	Q7	Q8	Q9	Q10	Q11	Q12	Q13	Q14	Q15	Q16	Q17	Q18	Q19	Q20
S1	1	1	1	2	2	0	1	0	0	1	0	1	2	0	1	1	1	1	0	1
S2	0	1	1	0	1	0	0	0	0	1	0	1	2	0	1	1	1	1	0	1
S3	0	1	1	0	1	2	1	0	0	1	1	1	2	1	0	2	1	1	1	2
S4	1	1	1	1	2	0	0	0	0	1	0	1	1	0	1	1	1	2	1	1
S5	0	2	1	1	1	0	1	1	0	1	1	2	2	1	1	0	2	1	0	1
S6	1	0	0	0	1	0	0	0	0	1	0	1	1	0	0	0	0	0	0	1
S7	1	2	1	0	2	0	1	0	0	1	0	2	2	0	1	1	0	1	0	1
S8	0	2	0	0	1	2	0	0	1	1	0	2	2	0	1	0	1	1	1	2
S9	1	1	0	2	2	2	0	0	0	1	0	1	2	0	1	0	1	2	0	1
S10	0	1	1	0	1	0	0	0	0	1	1	2	2	1	1	1	2	2	0	2
S11	1	1	0	0	1	0	0	0	0	1	0	1	1	0	0	0	1	0	0	1
S12	1	2	0	1	2	0	0	0	0	1	0	1	2	0	1	1	1	1	0	1
S13	1	1	0	0	2	0	0	0	0	1	1	1	1	0	1	2	0	0	0	2
S14	0	1	1	2	2	0	1	0	0	2	1	1	2	0	1	1	1	2	1	1
S15	0	2	1	1	2	0	1	0	2	0	0	2	2	0	1	0	1	1	1	1
S16	1	1	1	0	2	0	0	1	1	1	1	1	2	1	1	1	2	1	1	2
S17	1	1	1	1	2	0	0	0	0	1	1	1	2	1	1	1	1	1	1	2
S18	1	1	1	2	2	2	1	0	0	1	1	1	2	0	0	1	1	1	1	2
S19	1	1	0	0	1	0	0	0	0	0	0	1	0	0	0	0	0	0	0	0
S20	1	1	1	1	2	0	0	0	0	0	1	2	2	1	0	1	1	1	1	2
#0	7	1	7	10	0	16	13	18	17	3	11	0	1	14	6	7	4	4	11	1
#1	13	14	13	6	8	0	7	2	2	16	9	14	4	6	14	11	13	12	9	11
#2	0	5	0	4	12	4	0	0	1	1	0	6	15	0	0	2	3	4	0	8
	0.38	0.71	0.38	0.41	0.94	0.24	0.21	0.06	0.12	0.53	0.26	0.76	1.00	0.18	0.41	0.44	0.56	0.59	0.26	0.79

The last column in Table 2 shows us the degree of difficulty based on the editing distance (EDDD). The formula used to calculate it is based on the mean of the editing distances which is reported to the maximum value of all means. The equation is shown in (4).

$$EDDD = \frac{\frac{\sum_{i=1}^{N} d(aQi,ac)}{N}}{\max\left(\frac{\sum_{i=1}^{N} d(aQi,ac)}{N}\right)} \tag{4}$$

where:

- N is the total number of questions
- aQi is the number of correct answers of the question Qi
- ac is the total number of answers of the question Qi
- d(aQi, ac) is the editing distance between an answer of a student and the correct answer

The lower the EDDD will be, the harder the question will be considered. Figure 7 shows a graphical representation of the responses regarding the editing distance between the given answers and the correct answer. The line shows the values obtained after Eq. (4) is applied to all answers. As we can see, the DI calculated after the determination of correct answers using the editing distance is the same after the traditional determination of DI.

Given the degree of difficulty obtained by using the algorithm (DD), the comparison with the Difficulty Index (DI) is made in Fig. 8. Remember, the less the value of the Difficulty Index, the greater the difficulty of the question. Thus, the DI axis must have a decreasing slope. We can mention that DD is somehow approximate, because it is calculated before the results are found, while the Difficulty Index is calculated after the results are shown. This comparison is made with the purpose of showing that the DD is respecting the acknowledged metrics in terms of difficulty, but also to see the differences between the traditional approach and our approach, based on slightly different requirements (i.e., differentiation of theoretical by practical).

We can observe in Fig. 9 the comparison between the calculated DD and the degree of difficulty based on the editing distance. As we said, the greater the EDDD, the harder the question will be. We make this comparison to show the closeness to reality to the proposed method based on the theoretical and practical character of a question. We can observe that the degrees of difficulty regarding the general character, regardless the theoretical and practical character, shows the average degree of difficulty. In the same time, it is shown the practical, theoretical and the general degree of difficulty.

Figure 10 shows the comparison bewteen all the studied degrees of difficulty. The DD and the EDDD are inversely proportional, showing the average general degree of difficulty. This general degree supports the study of the theoretical and practical degrees of difficulty, showing the fact that the practical and theoretical difficulties are shown in a relative increasing, well-assigned within the test.

The behavior of the two axes is somehow normal. DD must have an increasing slope, because the greater the DD, the harder the question. Here, we must differentiate

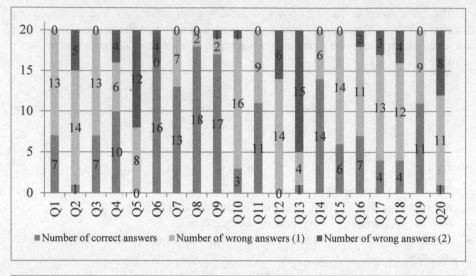

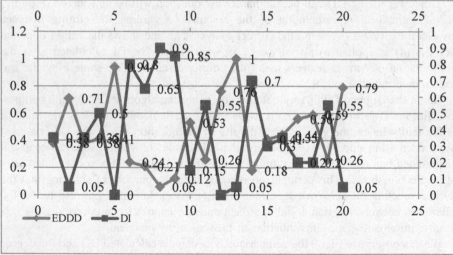

Fig. 7. Correct and incorrect answers found after the determination of the editing distance between the given and correct answers

between practical and theoretical questions. For example, if α is greater, than a practical question can be seen as an "easy" question, even if its DD can be bigger (the question is "hard") when β is bigger. Also, there may be some differences between DI and DD, because their modalities of calculations are different and they must be taken both as trend lines.

We observe that there exist a local minimum for the DI at Q2. This happens because in the calculus of the DI, there is not taken into account the differentiation between theoretical and practical character. Thus, Q2 is seen as a "difficult" question in

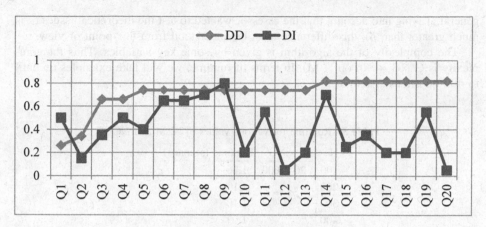

Fig. 8. DD compared with DI

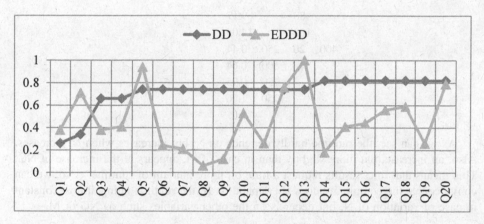

Fig. 9. Comparison between the DD and the EDDD

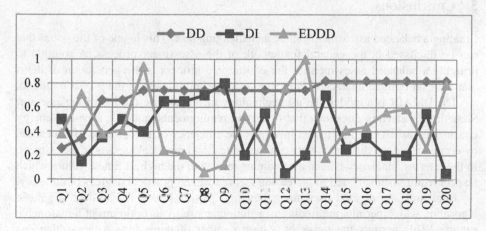

Fig. 10. Comparison between DI, DD and EDDD

general. Taking into account that the assessor wanted to test the theoretical issues (α is much greater than β), this difference must be understood from this point of view.

The complexity of the algorithm is given by some key variables. Thus the complexity is O(NG $\times$ NrPop $\times$ M). In terms of runtime, we will take examples up until to 400 questions (Table 3).

Table 3. Runtime for various values of N, M and NG

N	M	NG	Runtime (seconds)
100	20	1000	1.16
200			1.19
300			1.10
400			1.03
400	40	1000	2.87
	60		5.53
	80		9.17
	100		14.05
400	20	250	0.44
		500	0.64
		750	0.95
		1250	1.76

As we can see, the runtime hardly depends on N, but increases when M increases. Also, an increase, but more slightly than in case of M, appears at the increase of NG. This means that finer results request a little bit more amount of runtime. Also, we can convince that the complexity does not depend on N, the runtime being almost constant in case of variation of N, but depends on the other variables such as NG or M.

5 Conclusions

Creating a balanced assessment can be a challenging task. This is one of the issues that can be discussed in the general framework of the assessment process. A solution to bringing a balanced assessment to the educational process is the generation of items that have an optimal character. Thus, the local optimum leads to the global optimum.

The DMAIR is a model that use technology means to ease the job of the assessor. Sometimes, selecting questions that fit certain requirements can be a time-and-energy consuming task. Thus, this model increases the efficiency of this process of education, by emphasizing the difference between theoretical and practical aspects of assessment. In these terms, efficiency is seen as obtaining tests with the highest fitness values which respect requirements related to increasing theoretical and practical degrees of difficulty.

Regarding the method used for generating questions, this is based on a genetic algorithm, which permits the finding of solutions close to an optimum at a reasonable runtime. This permits the usage of a high number of items in a database that can represent a data pool for the algorithm. This can be effectively integrated into the DMAIR model as a generator mechanism.

As future work, we would like to implement the model using past research that can be found in papers [5, 12, 14, 15], giving some improvements to other mechanisms within the model. Thus, a DMAIR element that has not been studied in detail is the modality of checking the correctness of the answers and their interpretation, a thing that will be made in future papers, as well as the implementation of the DMAIR model in a web or offline application.

References

1. Back, T., Fogel, D.B., Michalewicz, Z.: Handbook of Evolutionary Computation. Oxford University Press, Institute of Physics, New York, Oxford (1997)
2. Cormen, T.H., Leiserson, C.E., Rivest, R.L., Stein, C.: Introduction to Algorithms, 3rd edn. MIT Press, Cambridge (2009)
3. Darby, S., Mortimer-Jones, Th.V., Johnston Roy, L., Roberts, C.: Theoretical study of Cu–Au nanoalloy clusters using a genetic algorithm. J. Chem. Phys. **116**, 1536 (2002). J. Chem. Phys. **116**(4) (2002)
4. Davis, L.: Handbook of Genetic Algorithms. Van Nostrand Rainhold, New York (1991)
5. Domşa, O., Bold, N.: Generator of variants of tests using the same questions. In: The 12th International Scientific Conference eLearning and Software for Education, Bucharest, 21–22 April 2016 (2016)
6. Holotescu, C.: A conceptual model for open learning environments. In: International Conference on Virtual Learning – ICVL, pp. 54–61 (2015)
7. Hwang, G.-J., Bertrand, M.T.L., Tseng, H.-H., Lin, T.-L.: On the development of a computer-assisted testing system with genetic test-sheet generating approach. IEEE Trans. Syst. Man Cybern. **35**(4), 590–594 (2005)
8. Hwang, G.-J.: A test-sheet-generating algorithm for multiple assessment requirements. IEEE Trans. Educ. **46**(3), 329–337 (2003)
9. Kim, H.-S., Cho, S.-B.: Application of interactive genetic algorithm to fashion design. Eng. Appl. Artif. Intell. **13**(6), 635–644 (2000)
10. Koza, J.R.: Genetic Programming. MIT Press, Cambridge (1992)
11. Minh, L.N., Siu, C.H., Alvis, C.M.F.: Divide and conquer memetic algorithm for online multi-objective test paper generation. Regul. Res. Pap. Memetic Comput. **4**(1), 33–47 (2012)
12. Nijloveanu, D., Bold, N., Bold, A.-C.: A hierarchical model of test generation within a battery of tests. In: International Conference on Virtual Learning, Timişoara, pp. 147–153 (2015)
13. Panjaburee, P., Hwang, G.-J., Triampo, W., Shih, B.-Y.: A multi-expert approach for developing testing and diagnostic systems based on the concept-effect model. Comput. Educ. **55**, 527–540 (2010)
14. Popescu, D.A., Bold, N., Nijloveanu D.: A method based on genetic algorithms for generating assessment tests used for learning. In: 17th International Conference on Intelligent Text Processing and Computational Linguistics, 3–9 April 2016 (2016)
15. Popescu, D.A., Bold, N., Domşa, O.: Generating assessment tests with restrictions using genetic algorithms. In: 12th IEEE International Conference on Control and Automation, Kathmandu, Nepal, 1–3 June 2016 (2016)

16. Popescu, D.A., Radulescu, D.: Approximately similarity measurement of web sites. In: Arik, S., Huang, T., Lai, W.K., Liu, Q. (eds.) ICONIP 2015. LNCS, vol. 9492, pp. 624–630. Springer, Heidelberg (2015). doi:10.1007/978-3-319-26561-2_73
17. Popescu, D. A., Radulescu, D.: Monitoring of irrigation systems using genetic algorithms. In: IMCSA (2015)
18. Popescu, E.: Adaptation provisioning with respect to learning styles in a web-based educational system: an experimental study. J. Comput. Assist. Learn. **26**(4), 243–257 (2010). Wiley
19. Rahmani, S., Mousavi, S.M., Kamali, M.J.: Modeling of road-traffic noise with the use of genetic algorithm. Appl. Soft Comput. **11**(1), 1008–1013 (2011)
20. Wang, F.-R., Wang, W.-H., Yang, H.-Q., Pan Q.-K.: A novel discrete differential evolution algorithm for computer-aided test-sheet composition problems. In: Information Engineering and Computer Science, ICIECS 2009, Wuhan, 19–20 December 2009, pp. 1–4 (2009)

Collaborative Assessments
in On-Line Classrooms

Nardine Osman[1]($\boxtimes$), Ewa Andrejczuk[1,2], Juan A. Rodriguez-Aguilar[1],
and Carles Sierra[1]

[1] Artificial Intelligence Research Institute (IIIA-CSIC), Barcelona, Spain
{nardine,ewa,jar,sierra}@iiia.csic.es
[2] Change Management Tool S.L., Barcelona, Spain

Abstract. With massive open on-line courses (MOOCs) gaining momentum, it is now common for thousands of students to enrol in a course, making manual assessments by teachers simply unfeasible. Peer assessments is one way to go when auto-scoring approaches are not possible. Current on-line courses usually use a simple aggregation of peer assessments, but these suffer from two main pitfalls. First, simple aggregation does not take into consideration the reliability of a peer assessment. Second, simple aggregation calculates what the students think of an assignment as opposed to what the teacher thinks of it (the far more important opinion). This work proposes two different models to address these two different pitfalls. These models lay the foundation for future work, where we intend to combine both models into a single one that addresses both pitfalls at once. The aim is to build an automated assessment system that results from the collaboration of both students and teachers.

1 Introduction

Self and peer assessment have clear pedagogical advantages. Students increase their responsibility and autonomy, get a deeper understanding of the subject, become more active and reflect on their role in group learning, and improve their judgement skills. However, in this work, we are interested in relying on peer assessments for reducing the marking load of teachers. This is specially critical when teachers face the challenge of marking large quantities of students as needed in the increasingly popular Massive Open Online Courses (MOOC). Existing platforms for on-line courses, like Coursera (coursera.org), apply a simple assessment aggregation method. This work proposes two different models to address two different pitfalls of the simple aggregation method. The first pitfall is that a simple aggregation does not take into consideration how good is each peer assessment.[1] The academic publishing field has attempted to address the pitfall of the simple aggregation method when aggregating reviews by asking each reviewer to specify their confidence level. This confidence level is then used to weigh the review. This work proposes the Collaborative Judgements (CJ) model, our first proposed model, where we go even further by stating that the

---

[1] Some MOOCS are using the mean or median of the students peer assessments.

© Springer International Publishing AG 2016
F. Koch et al. (Eds.): CARE 2016/SocialEdu 2016, CCIS 677, pp. 97–116, 2016.
DOI: 10.1007/978-3-319-52039-1_7

confidence level provided by a reviewer is not sufficient as it completely relies on how much objective is that reviewer in assessing himself. As such, our CJ model proposes that peers judge each others assessments (or reviews). As such, the weight used when aggregating assessments is then based on the judgements that this assessment has received. In other words, instead of relying on one's self-confidence, we rely on how other peers judge each other's assessments.

The second pitfall of the simple aggregation method of on-line courses is that they solely aggregate student assessments, that is they aggregate what students think of their peers assignment results. In classrooms, we believe the teacher's assessment of an assignment is far more important (and credible) than the student assessments. As such, we propose the personalised automated assessment service (PAAS), which modifies peer assessments to approximate the unknown teacher assessments. PAAS basically predicts how the teacher will assess an assignment, given how the fellow peers have assessed it. In other words, the aggregation is tuned to the point of view of the teacher.

While each of the models addresses a different problem of the simple aggregation method used by current on-line courses, these models lay the foundation for future work, where we intend to combine both models into a single one that addresses both pitfalls at once. The aim is to build an automated assessment system that results from the collaboration of both students and teachers.

2 Background

Peer assessments in education have been gaining momentum [8,14,15]. Previous works have proposed several methods to generate student assessments based on peer-student assessments. Table 1 categorises the related work, including our CJ and PAAS models, with respect to whether the model aggregates peer opinions by tuning them to the teacher's view or not (where T2T stands for 'Tuned to Teacher'), and whether they weigh assessments by their reliability (where WbR stand for 'Weighed by Reliability'). We briefly present these models next.

CrowdGrader [1] is a framework which defines a crowdsourcing algorithm for peer assessments. The authors claim that, when performing assessments, relying on a single person is often impractical and can be perceived as unfair. Their method aggregates the assessments of an assignment made by several students into an overall assessment for the assignment, relying on a reputation system. The reputation of each student (or their *accuracy degree* as they call

Table 1. Categorisation of related work

	WbR	¬ WbR
T2T	Future work	**PAAS**, LocPat [5], Collaborative Filtering [12]
¬ T2T	**CJ**, CrowdGrader [1], PeerRank [16], Piech et al. [10]	Simple aggregation (mean or median)

it) is measured by comparing the student's assessments with the assessments of their fellow students for the same assignments. In other words, the reputation of a student describes how far are her assessments from those of her fellow students. The overall assessment (consensus grade) is calculated by aggregating all student assessments weighted by the reputation of the students providing them. The algorithm executes a fixed number of iterations using the consensus grade to estimate the reputation (or accuracy degree) of students, and then uses the updated student's reputation to compute more precise suggested assessments.

PeerRank [16] is based on the idea that the grade of an agent is constructed from the grades it receives from other agents, and the grade an agent gives to another agent is weighted by the grading agent's own grade. Thus, the grade of each agent α is calculated as a weighted average of the grades of the agents evaluating α, and thus the grades of α's evaluators are themselves weighted averages of the grades of other agents evaluating them, and so on. The final grades are defined as a fixed point of an equation, similar to PageRank, where web-pages are ranked according to the ranks of the web-pages that link to them.

Piech et al. [10] propose a method to estimate student reliability and to correct student biases in an online learning scenario, presenting results over two Coursera courses. They assume the existence of a true score for every assignment, which is unobserved and to be estimated. Every grader is associated with a bias, which reflects the grader's tendency to inflate or deflate her assessments with respect to the true score. Also, graders are associated with a reliability which reflects how close the grader's assessments tend to land near the corresponding true score, after having them corrected for bias. Authors infer the values of these unobserved variables using known approximated inference methods such as Gibbs sampling. The model proposed is therefore probabilistic and is compared to the grade estimation algorithm used on Coursera's platform (mean of assessments), which does not take into account individual biases and reliability.

Next, we present relevant recommender systems, as recommender systems tune their results to the point of view of a specific person (as in PAAS). One relevant system is LocPat [5], a generalised framework for personalised recommendations in agent networks. LocPat builds trust measures based on mining the graph of an agent network. For instance, trustworthy relationships are discovered by studying the link structure (e.g., the number of common neighbours). Then, it suggests to a specific requester (who requests a recommendation in the agent network) a list of trustworthy agents for the requester to interact with.

Collaborative Filtering [12] is a classical social information filtering algorithm that recommends content to users based on their previous ratings, exploiting similarities between the tastes of different users. In summary:

1. The system maintains a user profile, which is a record of the user ratings over specific items.
2. Then, the system computes a similarity measure among users' profiles.
3. Finally, the system recommends items to users with a rating that is a weighted average of the ratings on that item given by other users. The weights are the similarity measures between the profiles of users rating the item and the profile of the user receiving the recommendation.

3   CJ: Collaborative Judgements Model

Recall that the collaborative judgements model (CJ) aggregates peer assessments by weighing each assessment with respect to its reliability, where reliability in this model is referred to as the peer's reputation, and it is based on the judgements that this peer has received. In this section we detail our CJ algorithm, but first, we introduce the notation, which we will use in the rest of this section.

3.1   Notation

We say an *appraisal* is a tuple $\langle P, R, E, o, v \rangle$, where $P = \{p_i\}_{i \in \mathcal{P}}$ is a set of works (that is students' solutions for the assignment); $R = \{r_j\}_{j \in \mathcal{R}}$ is a set of peers (or students) evaluating someone' works; $E = \{e_i\}_{i \in \mathcal{E}} \cup \{\bot\}$ is a totally ordered evaluation space, where $e_i \in \mathbb{N}$ and $e_i < e_j$ iff $i < j$ and $\bot$ stands for the absence of evaluation; $o : R \times P \to E$ is a function giving the opinions of peers on someone's work; and $v : R \times R \times P \to E$ is a function giving the judgements of peers over opinions on someone' works.

In general we might have different dimensions of evaluation, that is a number of E spaces over which to express opinions and judgements. For instance, originality, soundness, etc. Nonetheless, here for simplicity reasons we will assume that the evaluation of a work is made over a single dimension. Actually, the 'overall' opinion is what is aggregated in many real systems.

3.2   The CJ Algorithm

The steps of the CJ algorithm applied over an appraisal $\langle P, R, E, o, v \rangle$ are:

Step 1. Compute the *agreement level* between each pair of peers r_i and r_j as a function $a : R \times R \to [0, 1] \cup \{\bot\}$. This computation involves the set of works jointly assessed by peers r_i and r_j, which we will formally define as $P_{ij} = \{p_k \in P | o(r_i, p_k) \neq \bot, o(r_j, p_k) \neq \bot\}$. If two peers jointly reviewed works, then their agreement level is based on the similarities of their opinions on common works as well as on their judgements. Formally, we say:

$$a(r_i, r_j) = \begin{cases} \frac{\sum_{p_k \in P_{ij}} s(r_i, r_j, p_k)}{|P_{ij}| \cdot d} & \text{if } P_{ij} \neq \emptyset \\ \bot & \text{otherwise} \end{cases} \quad (1)$$

where d is the maximum distance in the evaluation space and:

$$s(r_i, r_j, p_k) = \begin{cases} v(r_i, r_j, p_k) & \text{if } P_{ij} \neq \emptyset \text{ and } v(r_i, r_j, p_k) \neq \bot \\ Sim(o(r_i, p_k), o(r_j, p_k)) & \text{if } P_{ij} \neq \emptyset \text{ and } v(r_i, r_j, p_k) = \bot \\ \bot & \text{otherwise} \end{cases} \quad (2)$$

Sim stands for an appropriate similarity measure. When no explicit judgements are given, we use the similarity between opinions as a heuristic. This is based on the following assumption: the more similar an opinion is to my opinion, the better I am bound to judge that opinion.

Step 2. Compute a complete *Trust Graph* as an adjacency function matrix $C = \{c_{ij}\}_{i,j \in R}$ such that:

$$c(r_i, r_j) = \begin{cases} a(r_i, r_j) & \text{if } a(r_i, r_j) \neq \bot \\ \max_{h \in chains(r_i, r_j)} \prod_{(k,k') \in h} a(r_k, r_{k'}) & \text{otherwise} \end{cases} \quad (3)$$

where $chains(r_i, r_j)$ is the set of sequences of peer indexes connecting i and j. Formally, a chain h between peers i and j is a sequence $\langle l_1, \ldots, l_{n_h} \rangle$ such that $l_1 = i$, $l_{n_h} = j$, and $a(r_k, r_{k+1}) \neq \bot$ for each pair $(k, k+1)$ of consecutive values in the sequence. To compute this step we use a version of Dijkstra's algorithm that instead of looking for the shortest path (using + and min as mathematical operations), it looks for the path with the largest edge product (using $\cdot$ and max as mathematical operators).

Step 3. Compute a *reputation* for each peer in R, $\{t_i\}_{i \in R}$. We follow the notion of transitive trust: If a peer i trusts any peer j, it would also trust the peers trusted by j. Since this principle is employed by the Eigentrust algorithm [7], we use it to compute peer reputations. The use of Eigentrust allows us to obtain a global trust value for each peer by the repeated and iterative multiplication and aggregation of reputation values until the trust grades for all peers converge to stable values. Note that the trust graph generated in step 2 is aperiodic and strongly connected as required by the Eigentrust algorithm. Furthermore, we normalise the powers of the matrix C at each step to ensure its convergence. In vectorial notation, the trust vector is assessed as $\bar{t} = \lim_{k \to \infty} \bar{t}^{k+1}$ with $\bar{t}^{k+1} = C^T \bar{t}^k$ and $\bar{t}^0 = \bar{e}$ being $\bar{e}_i = 1/|\bar{e}|$.

Step 4. Compute the *collective opinion* on each work as a weighted average of the opinions of those that expressed an opinion on the work. In other words, given a work p_j, we only consider the opinions of those peers that reviewed p_j, which we formally define as $R_j \subseteq R, R_j = \{r \in R | o(r, p_j) \neq \bot\}$. We can then compute the collective opinion on a work p_j as a weighted average of the opinions of the peers in R_j using as weights the peers' reputations. Finally, the collective opinion computed by our collaborative judgements algorithm for a work p_j, noted as $o_{CJ}(p_j)$, is:

$$o_{CJ}(p_j) = \frac{\sum_{r \in R_j} \bar{t}_r \cdot o(r, p_j)}{\sum_{r \in R_j} \bar{t}_r} \quad (4)$$

where $\bar{t}_r$ stands for the reputation value of peer r as computed in Step 3.

Step 5. Generate a partial ranking based on the set of collective opinions $O_{CJ}(P)$. CJ sorts works in descending order by the collective opinion values. Thus, the work with the highest value of collective opinion gets the first ranking position. Works with equal collective opinion receive the same ranking number, and the work(s) on the next position receive the immediately following ranking number (i.e. bucket index). The procedure continues until CJ assigns bucket indexes to all works.

3.3   Comparing CJ to Related Literature

As illustrated by Table 1, several approaches have been proposed to aggregate peer assessments by weighing each with respect to its reliability. The main difference between these approaches and CJ is the usage of judgement information over such assessments. Here, we focus on comparing CJ to those models.

The reliability of a student in the Crowd Grader model is measured by comparing the student's assessments with the assessments of their fellow students for the same assignments. In other words, when one student's assessments are similar to his friends, then he is considered reliable, and vice versa. We believe our proposed CJ model is more accurate than the Crowd Grader model as one's assessment need not be similar to others, but needs to be highly viewed by others. For instance, think of the clever student who always makes excellent observations that have gone unnoticed by others.

PeerRank is another model that takes into consideration the reliability of an assessment as the reliability of the student providing that assessment. And the reliability of a student is calculated following an approach similar to Google's PageRank, where the assessment of each student is calculated as a weighted average of the assessments of the students evaluating the student in question. In other words, PeerRank assumes that if you are assessed highly by reliable friends, then your own assessments will be more reliable. CJ, on the other hand, differentiates between one performing well in an assignment and one who provides good assessments. For instance, one might fail at solving a difficult problem, but might still be exceedingly capable of spotting out the mistakes of others. Unlike PeerRank, CJ allows for that, because one's assessments are judged by his peers independently of his own performance in an assignment.

The model by Piech et al. [10] also uses reliability of assessments, where reliability is defined as the distance between one's score and the assignment's true score. They assume true scores exist for assignments, and they use Gibbs sampling to infer these values. CJ on the other hand does not assume true scores exist and reliability simply depends on how others judge one's assessment.

4   The PAAS Model

After presenting our CJ model that introduces judgements as a way for calculating the reliability of an assessment, we now present our PAAS model that tunes assessments to the point of view of the teacher.

4.1   Notation and Problem Definition

Let ϵ represent the teacher who needs to assess a large set of students' works $\mathcal{I}$, and let $\mathcal{P}$ be a set of peers able to assess works in $\mathcal{I}$. We define a peer assessment e_{μ}^{α} (also referred to as evaluation or opinion) as an element from a numerically ordered evaluation space $\mathcal{E}$, where $\alpha \in \mathcal{I}$ is the work being evaluated and $\mu \in \{\epsilon\} \cup \mathcal{P}$ is the evaluating peer. We define an automated assessment e^{α} for student work α as a metric (which could be the mean, the median, the maximum, etc.) built from a probability distribution $\mathbb{P}$ over the evaluation space $\mathcal{E}$. We say $\mathbb{P} = \{x_1 \mapsto v_1, \ldots, x_n \mapsto v_n\}$, where $\{x_1, \ldots, x_n\} = \mathcal{E}$ and $v_i \in [0, 1]$ represents the value assigned to each element $x_i \in \mathcal{E}$, with the condition that $\sum_{0 < i \leq |\mathcal{E}|} v_i = 1$.

For example, one can define the evaluation space of the quality of an English classroom homework as $\mathcal{E} = \{1, 2, 3, 4\}$. The distribution $\{1 \mapsto 0, 2 \mapsto 0, 3 \mapsto 0, 4 \mapsto 1\}$ would represent the best possible assessment, whereas the distribution $\{1 \mapsto 0, 2 \mapsto 1/2, 3 \mapsto 1/2, 4 \mapsto 0\}$ would represent that the quality of the homework is most probably average, and so on.

Finally, we define $\mathcal{H}$ as the history of all assessments performed, and $\mathcal{O}^\alpha \subset \mathcal{H}$ as the set of past peer assessments over the work α.

4.2   The PAAS Algorithm

The ultimate goal of our model is to compute the probability distribution of ϵ's assessment over a certain work α, given the assessments of several peers over that same work α. In other words, what is the probability that ϵ's assessment of α is x given the set of peers' assessments $\mathcal{O}^\alpha$?

We base the computation on the notion of *trust* between peers built from previous experiences, where trust is understood as the similarity between the assessments made by those peers for the same works. In other words, our intuition is that we expect ϵ will tend to agree with μ's assessment on a work if her trust on μ is high. Otherwise, ϵ's assessment will probably be different. To build a trust measure between ϵ and μ we perform a sort of analogical reasoning: if in the past μ gave opinions that were similar to ϵ's opinions to a certain degree (trust), then ϵ is likely to coincide with μ's opinion again now to the same degree. The steps needed for calculating the teacher's assessment are presented next.

Step 1. How much should I trust a peer? ϵ needs to decide how much can she trust the assessment of a peer μ. We base this trust measure on two intuitions. First, if ϵ and μ have both assessed the same work in the past, then the similarity of their assessments for that work can give a hint on how close their judgements/thinking are. When there are no works evaluated by both ϵ and μ, ϵ would not know how much to trust μ's assessments. Second, and to cover this latter situation, we approximate the unknown trust between ϵ and μ by transitivity over the path with direct trust links between ϵ and μ. In the following, we make these two intuitions concrete through two different types of trust relations: *direct trust* and *indirect trust*.

Direct Trust. Direct trust is the trust relation that emerges between two people or two agents that have already assessed the same works in the past.

We will define the direct trust between two peers i and j as a probability distribution $\mathbb{T}_{i,j}$ over assessment differences built from the historical data of previous evaluations performed by i and j. First, we define the *evaluation difference* between two assessments performed by i and j as:

$$diff(e_i^\alpha, e_j^\alpha) = e_i^\alpha - e_j^\alpha \tag{5}$$

We use the euclidean distance between assessments as the measure of dissimilarity, as it is the most used distance in the literature on similarity in metric spaces. If $diff(e_i^\alpha, e_j^\alpha) = 0$, it means that i and j provide the same assessment for α. If $diff(e_i^\alpha, e_j^\alpha) > 0$, it means that i *over rates* α with respect to j, if $diff(e_i^\alpha, e_j^\alpha) < 0$, it means that i *under rates* α with respect to j. Note that $diff(e_i^\alpha, e_j^\alpha) \neq diff(e_j^\alpha, e_i^\alpha)$.

When defining $\mathbb{T}_{i,j}$, we are interested in maintaining information about whether a peer under rates or over rates with respect to another peer. As such, the *support* of the distribution representing i's direct trust on j (i.e. the x-axis of $\mathbb{T}_{i,j}$) consists of the possible evaluation difference values between i and j. Trust distribution $\mathbb{T}_{i,j}(x)$ then describes the probability that i and j would assess a work with an evaluation difference x. Therefore, the distribution $\mathbb{T}_{i,j}(0) = 1$ represents a trust distribution where i *fully* trusts on j's opinion, since the probability that their assessments are the same is 1.

Definition 1. *Given a numeric evaluation space $\mathcal{E} = [0, b]$, a Trust Distribution is any probability distribution over the differences in $\mathcal{E}$, that is the interval $[-b, b]$.*

We now explain how we build direct trust distributions computationally, based on previous experiences. We use an information theory approach where the behaviour of the studied phenomenon is modelled by probability distributions which are updated with every new observation. This approach is inspired by [2].

Initially, the direct trust distribution between any two peers i and j is the distribution describing ignorance (i.e. the uniform distribution). Then, whenever j evaluates a work α that was already evaluated by i we update $\mathbb{T}_{i,j}$ as follows:

1. We find the element x in $\mathbb{T}_{i,j}$'s support whose probability needs to be adjusted: $x = diff(e_i^\alpha, e_j^\alpha)$.
2. We increase the probability of x in $\mathbb{T}_{i,j}$ $(p(X = x))$ as follows:

$$p(X = x) = p(X = x) + \gamma \cdot (1 - p(X = x)) \tag{6}$$

The update is based on increasing the current probability $p(X = x)$ by a fraction $\gamma \in [0, 1]$ of the total potential increase $(1 - p(X = x))$. For instance, if the probability of x is 0.6 and γ is 0.1, then the new probability of x becomes $0.6 + 0.1 \cdot (1 - 0.6) = 0.64$. We note that the ideal value of γ should be closer to 0 than to 1 so that one single experience does not result in considerable changes in the distribution. In other words, a *single* assessment cannot result in a *significant* change in the probability distribution.

3. We normalize $\mathbb{T}_{i,j}$ by following the entropy based approach of [13]. The entropy-based approach updates $\mathbb{T}_{i,j}$ such that: (1) the value $p(X = x)$ is maintained and (2) the resulting distribution has a minimal relative entropy with respect to the previous one. In other words, we look for a distribution that contains the updated probability value $p(X = x)$ and that is at a minimal distance from the previous $\mathbb{T}_{i,j}$:

$$\mathbb{T}_{i,j}(X) = \arg\min_{\mathbb{P}'(X)} \sum_{x'} p(X = x') \log \frac{p(X = x')}{p'(X = x')} \tag{7}$$
$$\text{such that} \quad \{p(X = x) = p'(X = x)\}$$

where $p(X = x')$ is a probability value in the original distribution, $p'(X = x')$ is a probability value in the potential new distribution $\mathbb{P}'$, and $\{p(X = x) = p'(X = x)\}$ is the constraint that needs to be satisfied by the new distribution.

Indirect Trust. Indirect trust is the trust relation that is deduced between peers when they have not assessed any works in common and thus a direct trust relation cannot be computed. The notion of indirect trust is inspired in the Eigentrust algorithm for reputation management [7]. In Eigentrust the transitivity in trust is based on products and additions of positive real numbers. For example, for a difference in opinion x between peers β and α and a difference in opinion y between β and the teacher, the overall difference between the teacher and α is $z = x + y$, when we are in an ordinal space. However, in our case we need to define operators to compute the transitive trust distribution from two *distributions*. When we move to probabilities, we then say that $\mathbb{P}(z) = \mathbb{P}(x) * \mathbb{P}(y)$, as we assume independence between opinions. Following this intuition, we define the combined distance distribution between two peers as follows.

Definition 2. *Given Trust Distributions* $\mathbb{P}$ *and* $\mathbb{Q}$ *over the numeric interval* $[-b, b]$ *we define their* Combined Distance Distribution, *noted* $\mathbb{R} = \mathbb{P} \otimes \mathbb{Q}$, *as:*

$$
r(X = x) = \begin{cases} \sum_{x_1 + x_2 = x} p(X = x_1) * q(X = x_2) & \text{if } x \in (-b, b) \\ \sum_{x_1 + x_2 \leq -b} p(X = x_1) * q(X = x_2) & \text{if } x = -b \\ \sum_{x_1 + x_2 \geq b} p(X = x_1) * q(X = x_2) & \text{if } x = b \end{cases} \tag{8}
$$

This operation can be nicely applied to our case of evaluation differences as the transitive trust is nothing else than the aggregation (addition) of the combined probability (product) of given evaluation differences happening.

The $\leq$ and $\geq$ (in cases $x = b$ and $x = -b$) are used to maintain the range of the evaluation distance within the $[-b, b]$ limits. For example, assume $\mathbb{P} = \{0, 0, 1\}$ and $\mathbb{Q} = \{1, 0, 0\}$, over the support (x-axis) [-1,1]. Now assume we need to calculate $\mathbb{R}(-1)$. We say $\mathbb{R}(-1)$ should aggregate the product of the probabilities of $\mathbb{P}(-1)$ and $\mathbb{Q}(0)$ (since $(-1) + 0 = -1$), the product of the probabilities of $\mathbb{P}(0)$ and $\mathbb{Q}(-1)$ (since $0 + (-1) = -1$), as well as the product of the probabilities of $\mathbb{P}(-1)$ and $\mathbb{Q}(-1)$ (since $(-1) + (-1) = -2$, and -2 is outside the limits of the numeric interval of the evaluation distance).

Note that the $\otimes$ operator is commutative. The neutral element of $\otimes$ is the distribution $\mathbb{O}$ (the ideal, or optimal, distribution), which describes the probability of the evaluation difference between two peers being 0 is 1, that is $p(X = 0) = 1$.

The next problem to tackle is how to aggregate combined distances calculated from different sources (different peers). In this case, from several distance distributions, we select the one that is closer to $\mathbb{O}$, that is, the one that makes the teacher and student closer in their judgements. In the Eigentrust algorithm, this would be equivalent to selecting the maximum combination (modelled as the product of the values in the links) instead of the used weighted sum of all the combinations. We note that other operators could be used here, such as selecting the distribution with minimum entropy. In the following we define this operator.

Definition 3. *Given probability distributions* $\mathbb{P}$ *and* $\mathbb{Q}$ *over the numeric interval* $[a, b]$ *we define* $\mathbb{P} \oplus \mathbb{Q}$, *as:*

$$\mathbb{P} \oplus \mathbb{Q} = \arg \min_{\mathbb{T} \in \{\mathbb{P}, \mathbb{Q}\}} (emd(\mathbb{T}, \mathbb{O})) \tag{9}$$

with emd standing for the earth mover's distance [11].

Note that this operator, $\oplus$, is commutative and associative so the order in which we combine the trust distributions is irrelevant.

Next, we show how we use these operators following a similar approach to Eigentrust. First, we store the direct trust distributions between ϵ's peers in a matrix C^T, where at the position (i, j) we store the current probability distribution between peers i and j: $\mathbb{T}_{i,j}$. We store the indirect trust distributions between the teacher ϵ and each community member in a vector t_ϵ, where at each position i we have $\mathbb{T}_{\epsilon,i}$. Initially, t_ϵ contains the probability distributions describing ignorance (i.e. the uniform distribution) in all rows. Let us call this initial vector t_ϵ^0. In Eigentrust, the t_ϵ vector is updated as follows:

$$t_\epsilon^{k+1} = C^T i_\epsilon^k \tag{10}$$

until $\|t_\epsilon^{k+1} - t_\epsilon^k\| < \eta$, where η is a specified threshold to determine that we have reached a fix point. The trust vector t_ϵ then converges after a certain amount of iterations. In this way, the trust that ϵ has on i is built aggregating the direct trust distributions between community members and peer i weighted by the trust (initially ignorance) that ϵ has on each community member. In our model, however, the product between matrix C^T and t_ϵ^k is defined using the previous definitions of $\otimes$ and $\oplus$, resulting in:

$$t_{\epsilon,j}^{k+1} = \bigoplus_{0 < i \leq n} \mathbb{T}_{i,j} \otimes \mathbb{T}_{\epsilon,i}^k \tag{11}$$

Finally, if a direct trust distribution is already built between ϵ and j, $\mathbb{T}_{i,j}$, then after each step of the algorithm, $t_{\epsilon,j}^{k+1}$ is overwritten with $\mathbb{T}_{i,j}$, since we prefer to preserve direct trust distributions.

Information Decay. An important notion in PAAS is the *decay* of information. We say the integrity of information decreases with time. So information provided by a trust probability distribution should lose its value over time by decaying towards a default value, which we refer to as the *decay limit distribution* $\mathbb{D}$. For instance, $\mathbb{D}$ may represent ignorance (e.g. uniform distribution), implying that information learned from past experiences tends to ignorance over time. Information in a probability distribution $\mathbb{T}$ decays from t to t' as follows:

$$\mathbb{T}^{t \rightsquigarrow t'} = \Lambda(\mathbb{D}, \mathbb{T}^t) \tag{12}$$

where $t' > t$, and Λ is the *decay function* satisfying the property: $\lim_{t' \to \infty} \mathbb{T}^{t \rightsquigarrow t'} = \mathbb{D}$. In our implementation, we adopt the decay function of [9].

Naturally, to implement such a decay mechanism in our model, we will need to add a timestamp t to every assessment $(e_\mu^{\alpha^t})$ and every trust distribution, direct or indirect, $(\mathbb{T}_{i,j}^t)$. Note that while the timestamp of an assessment is fixed, the timestamp of a trust distribution should refer to the timestamp of the latest assessment that modified this distribution.

Step 2: What to believe when a peer gives an opinion? Given a peer assessment e_μ^α, the question now is how to compute the probability distribution of ϵ's assessment. That is, what is the probability that ϵ's assessment of α is x given that μ evaluated α with e_μ^α. This is expressed as the conditional probability:

$$\mathbb{P}(X^\alpha = x \mid e_\mu^\alpha)$$

To calculate this conditional probability, the intuition is that ϵ would tend to agree with μ's assessment if his trust on μ is high (that is, the expected assessment difference between their assessments is close to 0). Otherwise, ϵ's assessment would probably be different. We perform then a sort of analogical reasoning: if in the past μ gave assessments with a certain evaluation difference with respect to ϵ, then this will probably happen again now.

We thus calculate the above conditional probability simply as:

$$p(X^\alpha = x \mid e_\mu^\alpha) = \begin{cases} \displaystyle\sum_{y \leq \mathit{diff}(x, e_\mu^\alpha)} \mathbb{T}_{\epsilon,\mu}(y) & \text{if } x = 0 \\ \displaystyle\sum_{y \geq \mathit{diff}(x, e_\mu^\alpha)} \mathbb{T}_{\epsilon,\mu}(y) & \text{if } x = b \\ \mathbb{T}_{\epsilon,\mu}(\mathit{diff}(x, e_\mu^\alpha)) & \text{otherwise} \end{cases} \tag{13}$$

Observe that in the first two cases, the probabilities are computed as the summation of the probability mass of $\mathbb{T}_{\epsilon,\mu}$ for points below or over the difference between the new opinion and the point x being considered. This is done to cope with the fact that we cannot under rate or over rate further as we are already at the extremes. For example, assume μ's assessment is 2 when the maximum mark is 3, we are calculating the probability of ϵ's assessment, and ϵ usually over rates μ by 2 marks. The probability of ϵ's assessment being 2 will essentially be $\mathbb{T}(0)$ (since the difference $2 - 2 = 0$). However, the probability of ϵ's assessment being 3 cannot simply be $\mathbb{T}(1)$ (since the difference $3 - 2 = 1$), because it is the maximum value of the evaluation space and so it needs to consider all over rating possibilities described by $\mathbb{T}(2)$ and $\mathbb{T}(3)$ as well. As such, the probability of ϵ's assessment being 3 aggregates $\mathbb{T}(1)$, $\mathbb{T}(2)$, and $\mathbb{T}(3)$.

Step 3: What to believe when many give opinions? In the previous section we computed $\mathbb{P}(X^\alpha \mid e_\mu^\alpha)$. That is, the probability distribution of ϵ's assessment on α given the assessment of a peer μ on α. But what does ϵ do when there is more than one peer assessing α?

Given the set of opinions $\mathcal{O}^\alpha = \{e^\alpha_{\mu_1}, e^\alpha_{\mu_2}, \ldots, e^\alpha_{\mu_n}\}$ of a group of peers over the work α, we define the probability of ϵ's assessment being x as follows:

$$p(X^\alpha = x \mid \mathcal{O}^\alpha) = \begin{cases} \bigvee_{i=1}^n (\mathbb{I}(\mathbb{T}_{\epsilon,\mu_i}) \cdot p(X^\alpha = x \mid e^\alpha_{\mu_i})) & \sum_{i=1}^n \mathbb{I}(\mathbb{T}_{\epsilon,\mu_i}) > \delta \\ 1/n & \text{otherwise} \end{cases} \tag{14}$$

where $\vee$ is an operator that combines probabilities assuming the sources are independent:[2] $a \vee b = a + b - a * b$, and $\mathbb{I}(\mathbb{T}_{\epsilon,\mu})$ measures the information content of the probability distribution $\mathbb{T}_{\epsilon,\mu}$ as the earth mover's distance to the ignorance distribution (the uniform distribution $\mathbb{F}$). In other words, the probability of ϵ's assessment being x given the set of opinions $\mathcal{O}^\alpha$ is a disjunction of the probabilities of ϵ's assessment being x given each assessment $e^\alpha_{\mu_i} \in \mathcal{O}^\alpha$ and diminished by the information content of the assessment distributions $\mathbb{I}(\mathbb{T}_{\epsilon,\mu_i})$. We diminish the probability derived from a particular opinion when that opinion is actually not very informative and thus very close to ignorance. In the case that most opinions are close to ignorance, $\sum_{i=1}^n \mathbb{I}(\mathbb{T}_{\epsilon,\mu_i}) \leq \delta$, the result of such combination might be too close to zero (for a small δ) and thus we prefer to assume ignorance, $1/n$, for the probability value.

Finally, for several purposes (give a mark to a student, rank objects to purchase, ...) it is practical to 'summarise' distributions $\mathbb{P}(X^\alpha \mid \mathcal{O}^\alpha)$ into a number. From the several methods that can be used (centre of gravity, mean, median, ...) in the experiments we use the mode value of the distribution.

Step 4: What should be evaluated next? The previous steps compute assessments of students' works that have not been assessed by ϵ, based on peers opinions. The level of uncertainty of the assessments generated by our method can be calculated as the uncertainty of the probability distribution $\mathbb{P}(X^\alpha \mid \mathcal{O}^\alpha)$. A classical method to measure this uncertainty is the the distribution's entropy:

$$\mathbb{H}(\mathbb{P}(X^\alpha \mid \mathcal{O}^\alpha)) = \sum_{x \in X^\alpha} p(X^\alpha = x \mid \mathcal{O}^\alpha) \cdot \ln p(X^\alpha = x \mid \mathcal{O}^\alpha) \tag{15}$$

We will explore in the experiments a heuristic that aims at reducing the number of assessments made by the teacher. In other words, what work should be assessed next by ϵ in order to maximally decrease the overall uncertainty? For example, what students' works and in which order should a tutor evaluate so that the uncertainty of the computed assessments, i.e. the uncertainty on the students' marks, becomes *acceptable*. The heuristic is simple: we suggest that ϵ evaluates works by decreasing value of the entropy of their assessment distribution, that is the next work α that the teacher should assess is:

$$\alpha = arg \max_\alpha \mathbb{H}(\mathbb{P}(X^\alpha \mid \mathcal{O}^\alpha)$$

---

[2] This assumption is not very restrictive for the scenarios we are considering: peer assessments in online education or e-commerce as opinions are expressed by people that do not know each other.

4.3   Comparing PAAS to Related Literature

What is fundamentally different between our PAAS model and the related work presented earlier is that the computation of our automated assessments is tuned to the perspective of a specific community member, a teacher. We clarify that our target is to accurately estimate those unknown assessments *from the teacher's point of view*. PAAS aggregates peer assessments giving more weight to those peers that are trusted by the teacher. Such trust metrics are built, as we will see shortly, using probability distributions based on the history of past assessments between the teacher and his/her peers, rather than using aggregations.

Unlike LocPat, PAAS bases trust measures on the similarity of assessments. If the student's assessments are similar to the teacher, then the student will be considered trustworthy by the teacher. LocPat, on the other hand, bases trustworthiness on characteristics of the social graph, which we believe are not as important as the similarity of assessments in the specific domain of automatic assessment calculation for online courses.

In the experimental evaluation of our system, we compare PAAS to Collaborative Filtering (CF), since CF (like PAAS) biases the final computation towards the opinion of a particular member of the community. Furthermore, CF has been widely adopted by the industry. Typical recommendation services, as the ones provided by Amazon, Youtube or Last.fm, are based on the CF algorithm.

5   The English Classroom Experiment

5.1   Experimental Setting

In this section, we present experiments performed over real data coming from two English language classrooms (30 14-years old students) at the Secondary School 'Torras i Bages' in L'Hospitalet de Llobregat, near Barcelona. Two different tasks were given to the classroom: an English composition task and a song vocabulary task. A total of 71 assignments were submitted by the students and marked by the teacher. Students assessed their fellow students during a 1 h period. A total of 168 student assessments were completed by the students (each student assessed on average 2.4 assignments). Marks vary from 1 (very bad) to 4 (very good). Students evaluated different criteria from the assignments: *focus, coherence, grammar* in the composition task and *in-time submission, requirements, lyrics* in the song vocabulary task.

We calculate the error of the generated assessments, noted as e_-^α, as the average difference between them and the tutor assessments, that is:

$$error = \frac{\sum_{\alpha \in \mathcal{I}} \|e_-^\alpha - e_\epsilon^\alpha\|}{|\mathcal{I}|}$$

Additionally, we are also interested in plotting the number of computed assessments. Note that when there is no peer or tutor assessment for a particular assignment, an automated mark for that assignments can not be generated.

In this experiment, we compare PAAS with the well known Collaborative Filtering (CF) algorithm [12]. (Please note that the CJ model is evaluated in the following section.) As discussed in Sect. 2, CF is a social information filtering algorithm that recommends content to users based on their previous preferences. CF biases the final computation towards a particular member: the person being recommended, as our algorithm does.

In this experiment, we randomly select a subset of 6 teacher assessments to use in both PAAS and CF (this subset represents 8.4% of the total number of teacher assessments, the rest are used to calculate the error). Then, several iterations are performed, one for each student assessment. At each iteration: (1) one student assessment is selected randomly and added to PAAS and CF; and (2) automated assessments are generated by PAAS and CF and the error is calculated. To calculate the error, our groundtruth is the set of all tutor assessments. Results are averaged over 50 executions. When an assessment could not be deduced, a default mark (ignorance) 2 is given, since this value is situated more or less in the middle of the evaluation space. Default marks are used in both PAAS and CF error calculations.

5.2   Results

Figure 1 shows the results of comparing PAAS to CF. As the assignments are different with different evaluation criteria we choose a criterion per group, necessarily different, so that we can have a larger number of assignments in the experiments. Figure 1 presents the results of one such pairing of criteria ("focus" and "in-time submission"), although the results of other pairings (not presented here) are very similar. The results highlight the remarkable improvement of PAAS over CF, considering the number of final marks generated (see the right column of graphics in the figure). PAAS has an added capability with respect to CF in using indirect trust measures to generate assessments. In CF the opinion of someone without any similarity in her profile with the teacher (in our case, without any common assignment being assessed) cannot be used to suggest a recommendation (an assessement). Thus, PAAS is capable of generating many more assessments, specially once the graph of indirect trust relationships becomes more and more connected. This highlights PAAS's first point of strength: *PAAS increases the number of assessments that can be calculated.* On the left, we show the improvement of PAAS over CF in terms of the error with respect to the ground truth that we know (the actual teacher assessments). The error is calculated over the entire set of assignments, including assignments that receive the default mark. This highlights PAAS's second point of strength in outperforming CF: *PAAS decreases the error of the assessments calculated.* We note that when the number of peer assessments increases PAAS and CF's error get closer because the effect of indirect trust diminishes. However, we are much better than CF for a small effort per peer (for instance, think of 5 or 6 assessments per peer instead of hundreds).

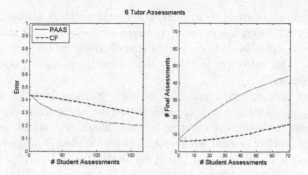

Fig. 1. Results of the English classroom experiment

6 The Simulation-Based Experiment

Students failed to provide sufficient judgements to allow us to properly evaluate our CJ model. As such, the data obtained from the real experiment of Sect. 5 was used to evaluate PAAS, whereas we simulated data for evaluating CJ. This section presents our simulation.

6.1 Experimental Setting

We assume a set $P = \{p_1, \ldots, p_n\}$ of students' works (assignments) and a function for their true quality in a range $[0, 1]$,[3] $q : P \to [0, 1]$. We use the following evaluation space $E = \{0.1, 0.2, 0.3, 0.4, 0.5, 0.6, 0.7, 0.8, 0.9, 1\}$.

We use beta distributions to model students' opinions and judgements as it is an appropriate distribution to simulate a behaviour that is subject to random variation and is limited on both extremes, i.e. represents processes with natural lower and upper boundaries [6].

We model two types of student assessors: good and bad, accordingly:

- *Good student assessor.* She provides fair opinions and fair judgements. Her opinion on any work p_k is always close to its true quality $q(p_k)$. We assume that the absolute value of the difference between the opinion of a student assessor and the true quality of a work (as a percent) follows a beta distribution, $Beta(\alpha, \beta)$, very positively skewed, for instance with $\alpha = 1$ and $\beta = 30$. For each work p_k reviewed by a good student assessor, we sample the assessor's associated beta distribution for a percentage difference, apply it to the work quality $q(p_k)$ (up or down randomly) and round the result to fit an element in E. Her judgements on someone's opinion are close to 0 if that opinion is far from the true quality of the work, and close to 1 otherwise. We implement this as the following function:

$$v(r_i, r_j, p_k) = 1 - |o(r_j, p_k) - q(p_k)|$$

---

[3] Assessing the true quality of an object may be difficult and it is certainly a domain dependent issue.

and self-judgements from $Beta(5,2)$, slightly negatively skewed.

We assume that when a good student assessor judges a bad student assessor she samples a value in E from a beta distribution rather positively skewed: $Beta(2,40)$. The intuition is that good student assessor poorly mark bad student assessor.

– *Bad student assessor.* She provides unfair opinions, because she is incompetent, but provides reasonable judgements as she can interpret the opinions of others as being informative or not. Thus, we sample opinions from $Beta(20,12)$ (rather central with a slight positive skew), judgements for good assessments (or opinions) and self-judgements from $Beta(5,2)$ as for good student assessors (negatively skewed), and judgements on bad reviews from $Beta(2,5)$ (slightly positively skewed). The overall idea is that bad student assessors stay mostly in the central area of the evaluation space.

We use $Sim(x,y) = (|E| - 1 - |\tau(x) - \tau(y)|)/(|E| - 1)$ as a simple linear similarity function where τ is a function that gives the position of an element in the ordered set E.

6.2 Simulation Results

Analysing the Accuracy of Opinions. Here, we consider the accuracy of a collective opinion on a work as the difference between that opinion and the true quality of that work. We compare CJ to the algorithm that weighs opinions with the assessors' self-assessments. This is because the models presented in Sect. 2 that consider the reliability of an assessment have not been adopted yet, and as such, we compare to one that is commonly used in academia (specifically in online conference management systems, such as Confmaster or Easychair). There, each reviewer states his self-confidence when it comes to the assessment he has given, and the aggregation of assessments uses this measure as a weight describing the reliability of assessments. We will call this simple algorithm the *Self-Assessment Weighted Algorithm* (SAWA).

We compare the accuracy of the opinions computed by CJ and SAWA as the percentage of good student assessors increases. We compute the accuracy of both CJ and SAWA as the mean absolute error of their opinions with respect to the true qualities using the following expressions:

$$MAE_{CJ} = \frac{\sum_{p \in P} |o_{CJ}(p) - q(p)|}{|P|} \qquad MAE_{SAWA} = \frac{\sum_{p \in P} |o_{SAWA}(p) - q(p)|}{|P|}$$

where q is a function that yields the true quality of each work. Figure 2 plots the percentage error reduction of CJ with respect to SAWA (computed as $(1 - \frac{MAE_{CJ}}{MAE_{SAWA}}) \cdot 100$) by aggregating the values obtained from 30 runs of each algorithm (each run samples all the distributions and thus generates different collective assessments). Note that CJ outperforms SAWA, as it is much more resilient to bad student assessors. As a matter of fact, as opposed to SAWA that

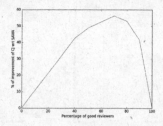

Fig. 2. Accuracy of opinions: percentage of error improvement of CJ over SAWA

treats all student assessors equally, CJ is designed to detect bad student assessors and diminish the importance of their opinions by the usage of the reputation measure. We observe that CJ's gains become larger than 20% and statistically significant for percentages of good student assessors between 20% and 80%.

Analysing the Accuracy of Rankings. Now we compare the accuracy of the rankings produced by CJ and SAWA with respect to the ranking resulting from the true quality of works. In order to compare two partial rankings, we largely rely on the work of [3], which provides sound mathematical principles to compare partial rankings. In particular, we use one of the four metrics presented in [3], the so-called *Kendall distance with penalty parameter p*, and we employ the normalised Kendall distance [4] with penalty factor $p = 0.5$.

We employed the partial rankings resulting from 30 runs of CJ and SAWA. We note by $\sigma_1^{CJ}, \ldots, \sigma_{30}^{CJ}$ the partial rankings produced by CJ by $\sigma_1^{SAWA}, \ldots, \sigma_{30}^{SAWA}$ the partial rankings produced by SAWA, and by σ^q the true ranking. Then, for each partial ranking computed by CJ and SAWA, we compute its normalised Kendall distance with respect to the true ranking. On the one hand, we assess the average Kendall distance of the rankings produced by CJ as $K_{CJ} = \frac{\sum_{i=1}^{30} \bar{K}^{(0.5)}(\sigma_i^{CJ}, \sigma^q)}{30}$. On the other hand, we assess the average Kendall distance of the rankings produced by SAWA as $K_{SAWA} = \frac{\sum_{i=1}^{30} \bar{K}^{(0.5)}(\sigma_i^{SAWA}, \sigma^q)}{30}$.

Figure 3 (left) plots the average Kendall distance of the rankings produced by CJ with respect to the true ranking, namely K_{CJ}, as the number of good student assessors increases. We observe that the distance between CJ rankings and the true ranking quickly decreases as the number of good student assessors increases. Notice that beyond 50% of good student assessors the distance drops below 0.1. That means that CJ can produce rather accurate rankings despite the presence of a large ratio of bad student assessors.

Figure 3 (right) shows the accuracy gain of CJ with respect to SAWA, for increasing percentages of good student assessors. We calculate such accuracy gain as $\frac{K_{SAWA} - K_{CJ}}{K_{SAWA}} \cdot 100$. We observe that the accuracy gain yield by CJ as the number of good student assessors grows, going beyond a 40% gain with 80% good student assessors. Similarly to experiment 6.2, the graph clearly shows that CJ performs significantly better even when the number of bad student assessors is high. We see that CJ has been able to discriminate poor assessments, while

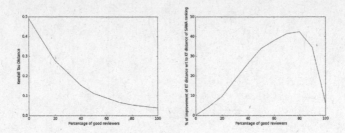

Fig. 3. (Left) Normalised Kendall ranking distance of CJ with respect to true rankings (Right) Accuracy gain of CJ with respect to SAWA

SAWA treats all student assessors equally. We observe also that CJ benefits larger from good student assessors than SAWA.

Analysing the Robustness Against Bad Student Assessors. As mentioned before, we model the opinion of good student assessors with a $Beta(\alpha, \beta)$ very positively skewed from which we sample the difference between the student assessor's opinion and the true quality. With $\alpha = 1$ and $\beta > 30$ the expert is frequently telling the true quality in her opinions (specially because we discretise the sampled values into our evaluation space—i.e. almost all the distribution mass is rounded to a distance of 0 with respect to the true quality). In Fig. 4 we plot the improvement of CJ with respect to SAWA for $\alpha = 1$, an increasing values of β (better student assessor behaviour), and a population with 50% good and 50% bad student assessors. We observe that the algorithm outperforms SAWA by 10% when the student assessor is frequently mistaken ($\beta = 5$). This shows that even when good student assessors give frequently inaccurate opinions, CJ is still able to capture them and increases the importance of their assessments. The improvement asymptotically grows to 51% with increasing quality of the student assessor behaviour.

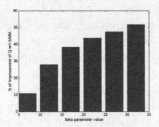

Fig. 4. Improvement of CJ over SAWA as assessors' quality increases

7   Conclusion

This work proposes two different models for tackling two different problems of aggregating peer assessments in online classrooms. The Collaborative Judgements (CJ) model, our first proposed model, requires that peers judge each other's assessments. This helps assess the reliability of student assessments: the weight used when aggregating assessments is based on the judgements that this assessment has received. The personalised automated assessment service (PAAS), our second model, modifies peer assessments to approximate the unknown teacher assessments. PAAS basically predicts how the teacher will assess an assignment, given how the fellow peers have assessed it (as opposed to calculating what the students think of this assignment).

Results from a real-world experiment (a small English classroom) have shown PAAS' improvements over collaborative filtering with respect to both: (1) decreasing the error in computed assessments, and (2) increasing the number of assignments that can be assessed. Whereas simulations have shown that CJ outperforms commonly used algorithms in academia, where reliability of assessments are based-on self-assessments (or self-confidence).

Concerning the effectiveness of PAAS, this naturally relies on the percentage of good student 'markers' in a classroom. A study of these values in real-world scenarios, for both small classrooms as well as MOOCs, would allow us to better assess the impact of PAAS in real-world settings, which we leave for future work. Nevertheless, the results presented earlier are promising already since they were based on students marking an average of 2.4 assignments, and the teacher marking 8.4% of the assignments. As for the CJ model, its effectiveness naturally depends on student reviewers being active in providing judgements. However, we believe this should not be a problem in real-life scenarios. For instance, in online conference management system, we already see reviewers being rated by authors, and as such, they can easily be rated by each other. Similarly, having student reviewers rating each other would be a non-demanding and straightforward task.

Last, but not least, the presented CJ and PAAS models lay the foundation for a future model, where we intend to combine both PAAS and CJ into a single model that takes into consideration judgements when weighing student assessments, as well as tune assessments to the point of view of the teacher. The aim is to build an automated assessment system that results from the collaboration of both students and teachers.

Acknowledgements. The second author is supported by an Industrial PhD scholarship from the Generalitat de Catalunya. Furthermore, this work is supported by the Gencat 2014 SGR 118 project (funded by the Generalitat de Catalunya), and the CollectiveMind and Collectiveware projects (funded by the Spanish Ministry of Economy and Competitiveness, under grant numbers TEC2013-49430-EXP and TIN2015-66863-C2-1-R, respectively).

References

1. de Alfaro, L., Shavlovsky, M.: Crowdgrader: crowdsourcing the evaluation of home-work assignments. Technical report. arXiv:1308.5273 (2013)
2. Debenham, J., Sierra, C.: Trust and honour in information-based agency. In: Proceedings of the Fiftth International Joint Conference on Autonomous Agents and Multi Agent Systems (AAMAS 2006), pp. 1225–1232. ACM (2006)
3. Fagin, R., Kumar, R., Mahdian, M., Sivakumar, D., Vee, E.: Comparing and aggregating rankings with ties. In: Proceedings of the Twenty-Third ACM SIGMOD-SIGACT-SIGART Symposium on Principles of Database Systems, pp. 47–58, PODS 2004, NY, USA. ACM, New York (2004)
4. Fagin, R., Kumar, R., Mahdian, M., Sivakumar, D., Vee, E.: Comparing partial rankings. SIAM J. Discret. Math. **20**(3), 628–648 (2006)
5. Hang, C.W., Singh, M.P.: Generalized framework for personalized recommendations in agent networks. Auton. Agents Multi-Agent Syst. (JAAMAS) **25**(3), 475–498 (2012)
6. Hill, T., Lewicki, P.: Statistics: Methods and Applications. StatSoft, Inc., Tulsa (2005)
7. Kamvar, S.D., Schlosser, M.T., Garcia-Molina, H.: The eigentrust algorithm for reputation management in P2P networks. In: Proceedings of the 12th International Conference on World Wide Web (WWW 2003), pp. 640–651. ACM (2003)
8. Lu, J., Zhang, Z.: Understanding the effectiveness of online peer assessment: a path model. J. Educ. Comput. Res. **46**(3), 313–333 (2012)
9. Osman, N., Sierra, C., McNeill, F., Pane, J., Debenham, J.: Trust and matching algorithms for selecting suitable agents. ACM Trans. Intell. Syst. Technol. **5**(1), 1–16 (2014)
10. Piech, C., Huang, J., Chen, Z., Do, C., Ng, A., Koller, D.: Tuned models of peer assessment in MOOCs. In: Proceedings of the 6th International Conference on Educational Data Mining (EDM 2013). International Educational Data Mining Society (2013)
11. Rubner, Y., Tomasi, C., Guibas, L.J.: A metric for distributions with applications to image databases. In: Proceedings of the Sixth International Conference on Computer Vision (ICCV 1998), pp. 59–66. IEEE Computer Society (1998)
12. Shardanand, U., Maes, P.: Social information filtering: algorithms for automating "word of mouth". In: Proceedings of the SIGCHI Conference on Human Factors in Computing Systems (CHI 1995), pp. 210–217. ACM Press/Addison-Wesley Publishing Co., New York (1995)
13. Sierra, C., Debenham, J.: An information-based model for trust. In: Proceedings of the Fourth International Joint Conference on Autonomous Agents and Multiagent Systems (AAMAS 2005), pp. 497–504. ACM, New York (2005)
14. Stepanyan, K., Mather, R., Jones, H., Lusuardi, C.: Student engagement with peer assessment: a review of pedagogical design and technologies. In: Spaniol, M., Li, Q., Klamma, R., Lau, R.W.H. (eds.) ICWL 2009. LNCS, vol. 5686, pp. 367–375. Springer, Heidelberg (2009). doi:10.1007/978-3-642-03426-8_44
15. Topping, K.: Peer assessment between students in colleges and universities. Rev. Educ. Res. **68**(3), 249–276 (1998)
16. Walsh, T.: The peerrank method for peer assessment. In: Schaub, T., Friedrich, G., O'Sullivan, B. (eds.) Proceedings of the 21st European Conference on Artificial Intelligence (ECAI 2014). Frontiers in Artificial Intelligence and Applications, vol. 263, pp. 909–914. IOS Press, Amsterdam (2014)

Argumentation Support Tool
with Modularization Function
and Its Evaluation

Yuki Katsura, Kei Nishina[✉], Shogo Okada, and Katsumi Nitta

Department of Computational Intelligence and Systems Science,
Tokyo Institute of Technology, 4259 Nagatsuta-cho, Midori-ku,
Yokohama, Kanagawa, Japan
{katsura_y,nishina}@ntt.dis.titech.ac.jp,
{okada,nitta}@dis.titech.ac.jp

Abstract. In a school, it is a matter of importance to educate students on discussion skills. On-the-job training (OJT) is an effective method for discussion education. To reduce the burden of the supervisor taking care of several discussion groups, a discussion support tool for use on a tablet PC is developed. Each student is assumed to participate in the discussion with the tablet PC and exchange messages through a computer network. This tool has an easy input interface by which a student inputs his message in the form of an argumentation diagram. Then, this message is converted into logical formulas, and furthermore, converted into an argumentation framework, which represents a logical structure of the discussion. The semantics of the argumentation framework is calculated and they are displayed on the screen to the student. This information helps students to understand the current status of the discussion and to select the next utterance. In addition to the basic functions, this tool has a modularization function which divides the complex arguments into modules and integrates semantics of each module. The effectiveness of the tool is evaluated by analyzing argumentation records.

Keywords: Argumentation theory · Argumentation framework · Argumentation support tool · Logical analysis of real complicated discussions · Reliability of argument · Modular structure

1 Introduction

In order to educate students on discussion skills in a school, on-the-job training (OJT) is conducted. The typical procedure of discussion training is as follows. At first, a supervisor explains the subject of discussion to students, then he divides students into several groups, and each group starts the discussion. During the discussion, the supervisor circulates around these groups, listens and observes their discussion, and gives advice. A discussion contains several types of speech acts such as *claim, concede, denial, argument, counter argument,* and so on.

© Springer International Publishing AG 2016
F. Koch et al. (Eds.): CARE 2016/SocialEdu 2016, CCIS 677, pp. 117–135, 2016.
DOI: 10.1007/978-3-319-52039-1_8

To give the proper advice, the supervisor has to recognize these speech acts in the students' utterances, and grasp the logical structure of arguments. Though OJT is a useful method for educating on discussion skills, as the supervisor has to take care of several groups at once, OJT by a single supervisor is difficult to give sufficient advice to everyone involved.

On the other hand, several on-line discussion support tools have been developed [1–7]. By using these tools, users can exchange text messages by way of a computer network. Some tools have a user interface which accepts users' input in the form of a diagram [1–3]. As a diagram shows the logical structure between messages visually, a diagram helps users to grasp the flow of topics, to recognize points of issue which should be discussed more, and to proceed in a discussion effectively. Consequently, these tools are expected to reduce the burden of the supervisor during OJT.

However, these tools have several problems when using them instead of supervisors. The first one is that they are lacking in the ability to give advice during discussion. From a diagram, a user may find several candidates of utterances to be selected next. However, a diagram doesn't have information about selecting which one is proper. The advice about selecting the next utterance is needed. The second one is that when the discussion theme is complex and contains a lot of sub topics, the diagram becomes huge and it is difficult to recognize the whole structure. To cope with a huge diagram, dividing the whole diagram into several sub-diagrams and to observe each sub-diagram separately is a promising way. The third one is that users tend to stick to one issue point which appears on the screen and not to move to another topics. Some mechanism which notifies users the existence of another issue points is necessary. The force one is that when a user participates in the discussion using a discussion support tool, they may hesitate to express their opinion by means of a lengthy and detailed explanation because they have to input messages as text data which is troublesome.

Our research is an effort to provide an on-line discussion support tool for educating students on discussion skills. This tool is designed to reduce some of above problems, by recognizing the logical structure of discussion and giving advice to users. The advice is provided by calculating semantics of argumentation and by showing similar scenes from old discussion records. Also this tool has a function to modularize a diagram into sub-diagrams.

2   Theoretical Background

Our discussion support tool is based on the Toulmin diagram [8] and the theory of Argumentation Framework (AF) [9]. Though the Toulmin diagram is appropriate to represent a structure of a single argument, there is no way to obtain the consequence of a set of arguments. On the other hand, the theory of AF has the semantics of a set of arguments.

The participants of the discussion input their messages in the form of a Toulmin diagram. The diagram is converted into a graph structure of AF, then the semantics of the discussion is obtained by theory of AF.

2.1   Toulmin Diagram

Stephen Toulmin, a British philosopher, insisted that for a good argument, it
needs to provide good justification for a claim. He proposed a model of argument
which contains six interrelated components such as *claim (conclusion), data,
warrant, backing, rebuttal,* and it mode (qualifier) [8].

Figure 1 is an example of Toulmin diagram which shows six components as
the justification of a claim "Tweety flies." When a user counter argues against
the opponent's argument, a user must specify whether the counter argument
attacks opponent's data, warrant or conclusion. Though the Toulmin diagram is
useful to make clear the logical structure of argument, the diagram is too detailed
for describing actual arguments from mathematical view and from practical view
because actual arguments often contain only the claim, the data and the rebuttal.
We call the Toulmin diagram which is composed of only the claim, the data and
the rebuttal as an "argument diagram" (AD, in short).

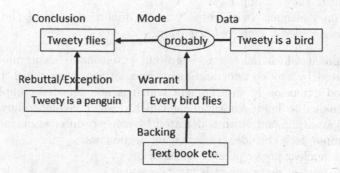

Fig. 1. Toulmin diagram

2.2   Argumentation Framework

The theory of Argumentation Framework [9] which is one of the fundamental
theories of the field of argumentation theory, and can judge which of arguments
are dialectically better in a discussion. This theory has been extended in various
ways to accommodate different kinds of abstraction about argumentation [10–
14]. An argumentation framework is a tuple $AF = (Args, attacks)$, where $Args$
is a set of arguments, and $attacks \subseteq Args \times Args$ is a binary attack relation
on $Args$. An attack from an argument $a \in Args$ to an argument $b \in Args$ is
expressed as $(a, b) \in attacks$. The *semantics* of AF is defined as follows:

- The set $S \subseteq Args$ is *conflict-free* iff $^\forall x, y \in S, (x, y) \notin attacks$.
- For any $x \in Args$, x is *acceptable* with respect to conflict-free $S \subseteq Args$ iff
  $^\forall y \in Args$ s.t. $(y, x) \in attacks$ implies $^\exists z \subset S$ s.t. $(z, y) \in attacks$.
- For conflict-free $S \subseteq Args$, S is *admissible* iff $\forall x \in S \; \forall y \notin S$ s.t. $(y, x) \in attacks$ implies $^\exists z \in S$ s.t. $(z, y) \in attacks$.

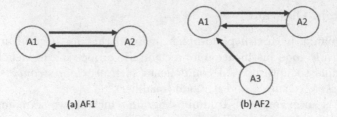

Fig. 2. Example of argumentation framework

- Let F_{AF} be a characteristic function which is defined as follows.
  $F_{AF} : 2^{Args} \rightarrow 2^{Args}$, and $F_{AF}(S) = \{a \in Args \mid a$ is acceptable w.r.t. $S\}$.
- $S \subseteq Args$ is a *complete extension* iff S is *conflict-free* and $F_{AF}(S) = S$.
- The smallest element (with respect to set inclusion) among the complete extensions is called a *grounded extension*. A grounded extension is the minimum fixed point of the function F_{AF}.
- The maximal element (with respect to set inclusion) among the complete extensions is called a *preferred extension*.

An argument which belongs to a ground extension is an argument which is not defeated by any counter argument, and an argument which belongs to any preferred extension is an argument which is not defeated completely and which has chance to hold. An argument which doesn't belong to any complete extension is an argument which is defeated by other counter argument.

For example, let's consider the following arguments.

   A1: A nuclear power plant is necessary.

   A2: A nuclear power plant is not necessary.

These arguments are represented by $AF1 = (\{A1, A2\}, \{(A1, A2), (A2, A1)\})$ (Fig. 2(a)). The set of complete extensions CEs, the grounded extension GE and the set of preferred extension PEs of AF1 are $CEs = \{\{\}, \{A1\}, \{A2\}\}$, $GE = \{\}$ and $PEs = \{\{A1\}, \{A2\}\}$ respectively. That means either $A1$ or $A2$ has a chance to be accepted equally.

Here, let's consider following argument A3 be added to AF1.

   A3: A nuclear power plant is not necessary because a solar power plant may supply sufficient energy.

Then, the new structure is represented by $AF2 = (\{A1, A2, A3\}, \{(A1, A2), (A2, A1), (A3, A1)\})$ (Fig. 2(b)). Semantics of AF2 become $CEs = \{\{A2, A3\}\}$, $GE = \{A2, A3\}$ and $PEs = \{\{A2, A3\}\}$ respectively. That means $A1$ is defeated and the set $\{A2, A3\}$ is accepted.

3   Argumentation Support Tool on Tablet PC

3.1   Overview of Argumentation Support Tool

Our argumentation support tool [15] is designed to be used in the course of discussion training (argumentation training) in the school. This tool is installed on a tablet PC, and each student is assumed to participate in the discussion using his (her) tablet PC. These PCs are connected to the argumentation server, and students can exchange messages (utterances) via this server (Fig. 3). The argumentation server stores old discussion records in the discussion database, and has a function to search similar discussion scenes (parts of scenario) by comparing the sequence of utterances in the discussion database.

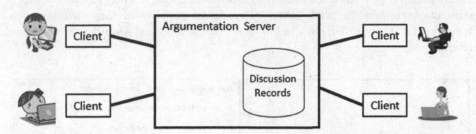

Fig. 3. On-line argumentation support system

This tool uses two types of diagrams - an argument diagram (AD) and an argumentation framework (AF). A participant of the discussion is assumed to input his message in the form of AD. This tool has a graphical interface which helps a participant to input the data and the conclusion.

Figure 4(a) is an example of AD. In this figure, one support link (a double shafted arrow) and two attack links (arrows) exist. There are two ways to obtain the conclusion (semantics) of AD which includes support links. One way is to interpret this AD as a bipolar argumentation framework BAF = (Args, attacks, supports) [18,19] where

Args = { "Tweety can fly", "Tweety can't fly", "I saw Tweety flied"},
attacks = {("Tweety can fly", "Tweety can't fly"),
        ("Tweety can't fly", "Tweety can fly")},
supports = {("I saw Tweety flied", "Tweety can fly")}.

The other way is to convert this AD into an argumentation framework AF = (Args, attacks) (Fig. 4(b)) where

Args = {"I saw Tweety flied, therefore Tweety can fly", "Tweety can't fly", "I saw Tweety flied" }
    attacks = {("I saw Tweety flied, therefore Tweety can fly", "Tweety can't fly")}.

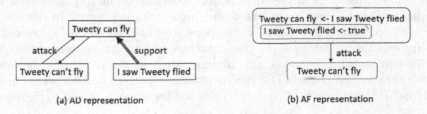

(a) AD representation   (b) AF representation

Fig. 4. AD and AF

We selected the second way because the semantics of AF is simpler than that of BAF. In the discussion, a lot of arguments are exchanged. Though an AD is a convenient form to describe an argument, if we describe a whole discussion in the form of AD, the diagram becomes huge which reduces the visibility of the whole structure. On the other hand, as an AF is simpler form than AD, an AF is proper form to describe the whole structure.

In a client system, a user interface appears on the screen (Fig. 5) by which students communicate with others. This figure consists of three windows - a window of AD (upper left), a window of AF (lower left) and a window of messages (right).

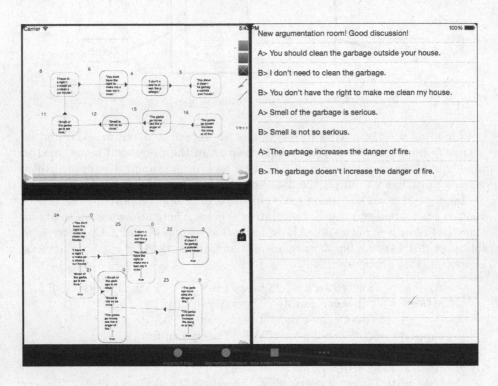

Fig. 5. Snapshot of the screen of the argumentation support tool

Figure 6 shows the architecture of our argumentation support tool. At first, users input utterances in the form of AD from the input interface, then the information of the diagram is sent to the argumentation server. In the server, the AD is converted into logical expressions. Logical expressions are stored in the argumentation database. In this database, old argumentation records are stored. During argumentation, the argumentation server recognizes the latest three utterances and searches for similar utterance pattern (similar scene) in the database. If the argumentation server finds similar scene, it is sent to the client.

The logical expressions are converted into AF and its graph structure is shown on the client's screen by the output interface. Then the semantics of AF is calculated and its semantic information is shown on the client's screen, too.

Details of components in Fig. 6 are described in Subsects. 3.2, 3.3, 3.4, and 3.5.

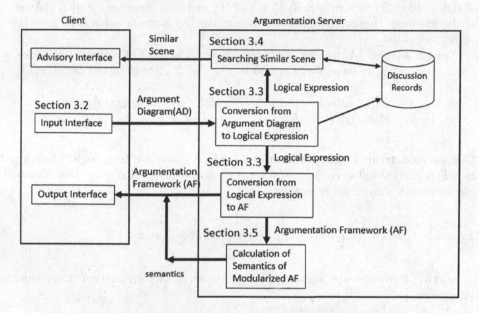

Fig. 6. Architecture of argumentation support system

3.2 Input Interface

The AD represents the logical structure of utterances consisting of Data nodes, Claim nodes and Support links, which indicate the reasoning from the contents of Data nodes to the Claim node, and Attack relation between the components of them.

Using the graphical user interface, the user creates new nodes on the screen manually, makes a link (a support link or an attack link) which combines nodes, and inputs his text message in the node. For example, let consider a node A whose content is "Tweety flies" exists on the screen. If a user wants to make a counter argument, he may create two nodes B and C, and make a support link from node C to node B and an attack link from node B and node A. Then, he inputs a message "Tweety doesn't fly" in node B, and a message "Tweety is a penguin" in node C.

Definition 1. *The argument diagram (AD) is a tuple, $(A, attacks, supports)$, where, A indicates a set of utterances, while attacks and supports indicates binary relations between utterances in A. A corresponds to nodes on the screen, while attacks and supports indicates two kinds of links between nodes.*

3.3   Conversion from AD to AF by Way of Logical Expression

Interpretation of AD as Logical Formula: As an AD is composed of a data, a conclusion and a rebuttal, it is converted into the logical formula.

Usually a formula is classified to R_s(A set of strict inference rules), R_d(A set of defeasible inference rules), K_p(A set of the ordinary premises) and K_n(A set of the axioms). However, we restrict that converted formula belongs to only R_d or K_p as follows.

Let an ADs be $(A, attacks, supports)$. Here, A is a set of messages of nodes. For any member of attacks and supports, R_d and K_p are obtained as follows.

– $\forall a, b \in A,\ (b, a) \in attacks$
   $\implies \{\neg a \Leftarrow b\} \in R_d,\ \{b\} \in K_p$

– $\forall a, b \in A,\ (b, a) \in supports$
   $\implies \{a \Leftarrow b\} \in R_d,\ \{b\} \in K_p$

Conversion from Logical Formula to AF: Conversion from logical formula to AF is carried out according to the conversion process of Aspic+ [16]. *Example* 1 shows a conversion example.

Example 1. $K_p = \{p, q\},\ K_n = \{\},\ R_s = \{\},\ R_d = \{\neg p \Leftarrow q\}$

Above formulas are converted into following argumentation framework (Fig. 7).

$$AF = (\{A_1, A_2, A_3\}, \{(A_3, A_1)\})$$
Here, $A_1 : \{p\},\ A_2 : \{q\},\ A_3 : \{\neg p \Leftarrow A_2\}.$

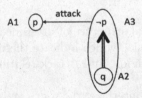

Fig. 7. Argumentation framework of Example 1

By showing this AF on the screen in the form of a graph structure, students can understand the overall logical structure of argumentation. However, if the AF contains a lot of arguments, the graph becomes too complex to understand at a glance. In such case, students can divide the AF into several modules by pointing pivot argument on the screen. Then, the AF graph is divided into two subgraphs at the designated node and each subgraph is treated in the different modules (see Sect. 3.5).

Semantics of AF: During discussion, every time an argumentation framework is updated, its semantics is calculated. After the complete extension, the grounded extension and the preferred extension are calculated, each argument is checked to see if it is included in the grounded extension or if it is included in the complete extension. If an argument is contained in the grounded extension, the color of its node becomes blue on the screen. If an argument is contained in the complete extension, its color becomes yellow, and if it isn't the complete extension, its color becomes red.

In the case of *Example* 1, the set of complete extensions CEs, the grounded Extension GE, and the set of preferred extensions PEs are followings.

$$CEs = PEs = \{\{A_2, A_3\}\}, GE = \{A_2, A_3\}$$

Therefore, the color of nodes A_2 and A_3 is blue, and the color of A_1 is red on the screen. Students can recognize the status of argument by its color, which is useful information needed to select the next utterance.

3.4 Searching Similar Scene

The argumentation server stores old discussion records (argumentation records) in the Discussion Database. Each discussion record is a sequence of logical formulas as Fig. 8. In this example, $P1$, $Q1$, $R1$, $S1$ and $T1$ are text data.

$$...$$

$id201 : P1 \Leftarrow Q1$	Q1 supports P1
$id202 : \neg Q1 \Leftarrow R1$	R1 attacks Q1
$id203 : \neg R1 \Leftarrow S1$	S1 attacks R1
$id204 : R1 \Leftarrow T1$	T1 supports R1

$$...$$

Fig. 8. Sequence of formula in the discussion database

During discussion, the server recognizes the sequence of arguments and searches for a similar sequence in the database. For example, if the latest three arguments of the current discussion are $id105$, $id106$ and $id107$ as Fig. 9, and if $P1$ and $P2$, $Q1$ and $Q2$, $R1$ and $R2$, and $S1$ and $S2$ are similar texts, then the argumentation server judges that the sequence from $id201$ and $id203$ is similar to the sequence from $id105$ and 107.

$$...$$
$$id105 : P2 \Leftarrow Q2$$
$$id106 : \neg Q2 \Leftarrow R2$$
$$id107 : \neg R2 \Leftarrow S2$$

Fig. 9. Sequence of formula of current discussion

Similarities between two texts are measured by the number of common key words. Let $\{w1, w2, ..., wn\}$ be a set of predefined key words. Then, each utterance is represented as a vector $V = (v1, v2, ..., vn)$ where vi is the number of appearance of wi in the utterance. The similarity between V1 and V2 is defined by the cosine similarity

$$\cos \theta = \frac{V1 \cdot V2}{\mid V1 \mid\mid V2 \mid}.$$

When a student wants advice for the next utterance at $id108$, he may search for similar scenes in the discussion database, and if he finds a sequence of Fig. 8, the utterance at $id204$ is one of candidates for the next utterance.

3.5   Modularization of Argumentation Framework

As an AF represents the logical structure of discussion as a graph structure, a student can understand the structure in a visually intuitive manner. Moreover, the AF theory defines strict semantics of the structure, which helps students to recognize if the discussion is dominant or not.

However, when the theme of a discussion is complex and contains a lot of sub issue points, students tends to stick to the discussion of the current sub issue point and not to move another. In such case, if primary sub issue points are indicated on the screen as an advice of a supervisor before hand, students will not leave these sub topics undiscussed. Moreover, when the theme of a discussion is complex, an AF may become very large. In such a case, students cannot grasp the overall logical structure at a glance and to calculate semantics becomes impossible because calculation cost of complete extensions is very expensive.

To solve these problems, dividing an AF into several sub-AFs and regarding them as local modules are promising approaches for visualizing and for calculating semantics. This modularization method needs a new argumentation theory which integrates semantics of each modules. We propose Modular Reliability-Based Argumentation Framework (MRAF) as one of the new argumentation theories which treats module structures.

There has already been several theoretical studies of AFs whose structure is of a modular structure which resembles our view about the support tool, such as Modular Assumption-Based Argumentation [12], Argumentation Context System [13], and hierarchical Extended Argumentation Framework [14]. However, their objectives of employing modular structure is different from ours. Their modularization theories are mainly based on PAF [17] or VAF [10] which are used to introduce relative priorities or relative ordering among values of arguments to AF theory. In the meta level module, they argue the relative priority, and in the object module, the semantics of the meta level module result is used to calculate the semantics of PAF or VAF. On the contrary, main objective of this research is to keep visibility of AF graph and to reduce the calculation time by dividing the overall AF graph into sub AF graphs.

Overview of MRAF: Basic idea of MRAF is as follows. Let the original AF be $AF = (Args, attacks)$, and it is divided into modules $(M_1, M_2, \ldots, M_n)$. Each module is a subset of AF ($AF_i = (Args_i, attacks_i)(i = 1, 2, \ldots, n)$). Here,

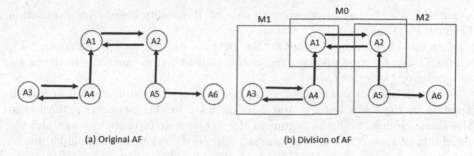

(a) Original AF   (b) Division of AF

Fig. 10. Example of modular argumentation framework

$Args = Args_1 \cup Args_2 \cup \ldots \cup Arg_n$, $attacks = attacks_1 \cup attacks_2 \cup \ldots \cup attacks_n$. We represent a set of all modules as Mod.

Among members of $Args$, some arguments are directly related to the conclusion of the discussion. Other arguments are used to support or attack such important arguments directly or indirectly. As the semantics of a module which contains important arguments is based on the semantics of a module which doesn't contain the important arguments, we say the former module refers to the latter one, or we say the former module is higher than the latter one (or the latter module is lower than then former one). As 'reference relation' is one way, if M_i refers to M_j, then M_j doesn't refer to M_i. And we assume that there is a unique module which is not referred to by any module, and another module is not to be referred to by more than two modules. If we represent a set of 'reference relation' as $refers : Mod \times Mod$, then $(Mod, refers)$ becomes a tree structure.

Let consider an AF $= (\{A_1, A_2, A_3, A_4, A_5, A_6\}, \{(A_1, A_2), (A_3, A_4), (A_4, A_3), (A_4, A_1), (A_5, A_2), (A_5, A_2)\}$ as Fig. 10(a). Among these arguments, let A_1 and A_2 be the most important arguments. Then, we can divide this AF into three modules as Fig. 10(b) in which MRAF is $(Mod, refers)$, where $Mod = \{M_0, M_1, M_2\}$, $refers = \{(M_0, M_1), (M_0, M_2)\}$, $AF_0 = (\{A_1, A_2\}, \{(A_1, A_2), (A_2, A_1)\})$, $AF_1 = (\{A_1, A_3, A_4\}, \{(A_3, A_4), (A_4, A_1), (A_4, A_3)\})$, and $AF_2 = (\{A_2, A_5, A_6\}, \{(A_5, A_2), (A_5, A_6)\})$.

Semantics of MRAF: When an AF is divided into modules (sub-AFs), the semantics of AF is different from that of sub-AFs. For example, in Fig. 10(a), semantics of AF is $CEs = \{\{A_1, A_3, A_5\}, \{A_5\}\}$, $GE = \{A_5\}$, $PEs = \{\{A_1, A_3, A_5\}\}$. And in Fig. 10(b), the semantics of AF_0 is $CE_0s = \{\{A_1\}, \{A_2\}, \{\}\}$, $GE_0 = \{\}$, $PE_0s = \{\{A_1\}, \{A_2\}\}$. And the semantics of A_1 is $CE_1s = \{\{A_1, A_3\}, \{A_4\}, \{\}\}$, $GE_1 = \{\}$, $PE_1s = \{\{A_1, A_3\}, \{A_4\}\}$. And the semantics of A_2 is $CE_2s = PE_2s = \{\{A_5\}\}$, $GE_2 = \{A_5\}$.

Here, we focus on the important arguments, A_1 and A_2. As A_1 is included in both of elements of CEs and CE_0s, there is no problem. However, A_2 is not included in any element of CEs and included in an element of CE_0s, which is conflict of semantics. In order to avoid the conflict, we redefine of the semantics of M_0 by introducing theory of Reliability-based Argumentation Framework (RAF).

Let an AF be $(Args, attacks)$. An RAF is defined as $(Arg, attacks, ST)$, where ST is a function mapping from an argument to any one element in the set of reliability $\{sk, cr, def, unc\}$.

The reliability of an argument is decided in the lower module. If the argument appears in the lower module and it is included in the grounded extension in the lower module, or if the argument doesn't appear in the lower module, the reliability of the argument becomes 'sk'. Else, if the argument is included in the complete extension of the lower module, the reliability becomes 'cr'. Else, if the argument isn't included in the complete extension, the reliability becomes 'def'. Else, the reliability becomes 'unc'.

In the example of Fig. 10(b), reliabilities of A_1 and A_2 are 'cr' and 'def', respectively. As the reliability of A_2 is 'def' means A_2 is defeated in the lower module, we ignore the existence of A_2 in the current module M_0. Consequently, only A_1 remains in M_0, and concerning A_1 and A_2, the semantics of M_0 coincide to that of AF.

This is the overview of semantics of MRAF based on RAF. We consider further about the semantics of RAF concerning A_1. If the reliability of A_1 is 'sk', then the semantics of M_0 is $CE_1s = PE_1s = \{\{A_1\}\}$ and $GE_1 = \{A_1\}$, which matches the semantics of the original AF. However, in this example, the reliability of A_1 is 'cr', which means A_1 may not hold in the lower module. From the optimistic view, GE_1 becomes $\{A_1\}$, and from the pessimistic view, GE_1 should be $\{\}$.

From these considerations, we employ three kinds of semantics in RAF such as Non-Def semantics, Optimistic semantics and Pessimistic semantics as follows.

- **RAF-Non-def** semantics of $RAF = (Args, attacks, ST)$ is the semantics of $AF' = (Args', attacks')$ where $Args' = Args/\{A \in Args \mid (A, def) \in ST\}$ and $attacks' = attacks/\{(A, B) \in attacks \mid (A, def) \in ST \; or \; (B, def) \in ST\}$ The complete extension, the grounded extension and the preferred extension of Arg' are called RAF-Non-Def complete extension, RAF-Non-Def grounded extension and RAF-Non-Def preferred extension, respectively.

- **RAF-Optimistic** semantics of RAF is also based on $AF' = (Args', attacks')$. The definition of $admissible$ is changed as follows.

> For conflict-free $S \subseteq Args'$, S is $admissible$ iff $\forall x \in S \; \forall y \notin S$ s.t. $(y, x) \in attacks$ and y's reliability is 'sk' implies $\exists z \in S$ s.t. $(z, y) \in attacks$.

The complete extension, the grounded extension and the preferred extension of Arg' using the above definition of $admissible$ are called RAF-Optimistic complete extension, RAF-Optimistic grounded extension and RAF-Optimistic preferred extension, respectively.

- **RAF-Pessimistic** semantics of RAF is also based on $AF' = (Args', attacks')$. The definition of $admissible$ is changed as follows.

> For conflict-free $S \subseteq Args'$, S is $admissible$ iff $\forall x \in S \; \forall y \notin S$ s.t. $(y, x) \in attacks$ and reliability of all members of S is 'sk' implies $\exists z \in S$ s.t. $(z, y) \in attacks$.

The complete extension, the grounded extension and the preferred extension of *Arg'* using the new definition of *admissible* are called RAF-Pessimistic complete extension, RAF-Pessimistic grounded extension and RAF-Pessimistic preferred extension, respectively.

The difference between Optimistic semantics and Pessimistic semantics is the difference of treatment of arguments whose reliability is 'cr' or 'unc'. In the Optimistic semantics, even if a set of arguments S is attacked by an argument from outside of S, if the reliability of the argument is 'cr' or 'unc', the attack is ignored to obtain the preferred extensions. In the example of Fig. 11(a), though an argument 'a' is attacked by 'b', the reliability of 'b' is 'cr'. Therefore, S is RAF-Optimistic preferred extension even if 'a' is not protected. On the contrary, in the Pessimistic semantics, only the arguments whose reliability is 'sk' is included in the grounded extension. In the example of Fig. 11(b), an argument 'a' is protected by 'c', but the reliability of 'c' is 'cr'. Therefore, S is not the RAF-Pessimisitc ground extension.

The reason why optimistic semantics and pessimistic semantics are employed is that this tool is designed for law school students. In the case of legal argumentation, as the burden of proof is on the plaintiffs, the plaintiffs will take the pessimistic view. On the contrary, as the role of the defendants is just to defeat the plaintiffs' arguments, the defendants will take the optimistic view.

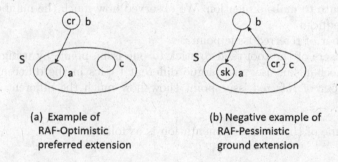

(a) Example of
RAF-Optimistic
preferred extension

(b) Negative example of
RAF-Pessimistic
ground extension

Fig. 11. RAF-Optimistic preferred extension and RAF-Pessimistic ground extension

4   Evaluation

In Sect. 1, we pointed out four problems of traditional diagram based discussion support tools.

1. Lacks in the ability to give advice.
2. A diagram tend to become huge.
3. Users tend to stick to one issue point.
4. Users may hesitate to express their opinions because inputting messages is troublesome.

To reduce these problems, in Sect. 3, we introduced an argumentation support tool, and in Sect. 4, we showed its modularization function.

For the first problem, we prepared a mechanism to calculate the semantics of argumentation and a module to search for similar scene from a case base. For the second and the third problem, we introduced the modularization mechanism by which users can divide the whole arguments into several sub topic arguments and can integrate their results. For the fourth problem, we have not developed any support mechanism.

To evaluate effectiveness of the argumentation support tool with modularization function, we made an experiment.

4.1   Experimental Setting

The main purpose of this experiment is to evaluate the effectiveness of modularization mechanism by comparing the following features of arguments in three cases - the argumentation in face-to-face, the argumentation using this tool without modularization mechanism, and the argumentation using this tool with modularization mechanism.

– The number of messages:
  To argue using this tool, participants have to input their utterances as text messages. As inputting text messages is very troublesome, the participants may hesitate to make a mention. We observed how much the number of messages is reduced.
– The number of referred issue points:
  Though users of the tool tend to stick to one issue point, by using modularization mechanism, user may argue different topics in the different module. The number of referred issue point show how much the different topics are discussed.

The theme of the mock argumentation is as follows.

Theme of Argumentation: Garbage House problem. An old man lives in a big house by himself. He has hoarded the garbage for a long time. Sometimes he scavenged in the public dump and brought trash in bulk to his house. Recently not only his house but also the sidewalk is overflowing with garbage. His garbage has caused several problems such as a rancid smell, producing worms, preventing pedestrians from walking past, and a small fire caused by a carelessly discarded cigarette butt. It is possible for the civil authorities to clear the garbage under compulsion based on the civil ordinance. But, if the old man isn't happy about it, he will no doubt start to gather the garbage again. Therefore, the official of the city government visits him and tries to persuade the old man to clear up his house and the sidewalk.

This garbage house problem includes several sub issue points as follows. Ideally, after these sub issue points are discussed, to clear the garbage by himself or by the civil government, or other solution is expected to be discussed.

- Value of Garbage: Among garbage, some bulk trash has property value. As the old man lives off a pension, he doesn't make sufficient money. Therefore, he wants to keep bulk trash in his house.
- Common Welfare: Because the garbage causes a vile smell, crows, insects and a small fire, environmental ecosystem of this zone is damaged. Is it going beyond the limits?
- Personal Rights: To hoard garbage in his house comes under the issue of individual freedom. No one should violate fundamental human rights. Does the civil government have the rights to force the old man to clear up the house based on legal grounds?
- Trash in the Dump: Bulk trash in the public dump are properties of the civil government. Therefore, to take them to his house is possible thievery.
- Care of Life The old man doesn't have good relations with his neighbors. As he feels lonely, he may gather garbage in his house. Therefore, after cleaning up the house, taking care of his life is necessary.

We gathered 22 graduate students of Tokyo Institute of Technology. They are around 23 years old, and their major is in the computer science. They don't have any knowledge about the law concerning the garbage house problem.

We divided them into 11 pairs. Then, for every pair, one student was allocated the role of the old man, and the other student was allocated the role of the civil servant. Then 11 pairs were divided into three groups. The first group was asked to argue in face-to-face. The second and the third groups were asked to argue using the discussion support tool. While the second group started the discussion from the initial screen on which no information exists, the third group started from the screen which had already been divided into six modules consisting of one top module and five modules each of which corresponds to one sub issue point.

We assigned four pairs to the first group, another five pairs to the second group and the other two pairs to the third group.

After discussiontheme and five sub issue points, we gave them 15 min to consider the strategy of discussion, and we started the discussion. The discussion time is limited to around 40 min. When the discussion doesn't finish, the discussion time is extended about 10 min.

As one or two argumentations were performed in a day, the total experiment was performed in two weeks.

From the discussion records of the first group, we extracted the AF manually and compared it to the those of the second group and the third group.

4.2 Result

In the 10 argumentation records, for each issue points, the typical sub topics are as follows.

- Value of Garbage: "By selling trash, he may get money.", "Some trash is object of memory.", "Some trash is recyclable.", "To sell the trash, segregation of trash is necessary", and so on.

- Common Welfare: "Garbage outside the house prevents pedestrian from passing by.", "Garbage outside the house increases the danger of a small fire.", "As the smell is not so serious, neighbors should have patience.", "Cats are lovely.", "To treat homeless cats is civil government's responsibility.", "The responsibility of a small fire is not me but the person who threw litter the cigarette." and so on.
- Personal Rights: "No one has the right to take objects from my house.", "My property inside my house is protected by the Japanese Constitution", and so on.
- Trash in Dump: "Trash in the public dump is the property of the city.", "Trash which I brought is not so much, and it is not such a serious problem.", and so on.
- Care of Life: "Neighbors has prejudice against me.", "Civil service is not sufficient.", "To keep good relationship with neighbors is important.", "To clean the house is good for health." and so on.

We observed what sub topics appear in each argumentation record, and its result is summarized as Fig. 12. The average numbers of sub topics which were mentioned in the argumentation are shown in this figure.

Topic Number	Issue Point	Group1 (Face-to-face)	Group2 (Tool without Module)	Group 3 (Tool with Module)
0	Clear Garbage	10.5	11.2	14.0
1	Value of Garbage	6.5	4.2	6.0
2	Common Welfare	5.0	6.0	7.5
3	Personal Right	13.5	11.8	10.5
4	Trash in the Dump	4.0	2.4	4.0
5	Care of Life	3.5	2.4	4.0
	Total	43.0	38.0	46.0
	Number of Utterance	272.5	34.2	51.0

Fig. 12. Experimental result

At first, we focus on the number of utterances. While the average number of the group 1 (face-to-face argumentation) is 272.5, those of group 2 (using tool without module) and group 3 (using tool with module) are 34.2 and 51.0. We estimate the reason why utterances of group 2 and group 3 are not so many is that students hesitated to input the messages using the input interface because it takes much time.

However, the numbers of sub topics which students mentioned are 43.0, 38.0 and 46.0, respectively, and there isn't big difference between three groups. This is because the group 1 includes a lot of redundant utterances in the argumentation records. For example, Fig. 13 shows a part of argumentation of group 1. Though 12 utterances appear in this figure, this part just mentions the claims from neighbors. Generally, in the case of face-to-face argumentation, a lot of utterance

Utterance ID	Utterance
A08	Concerning my trash, what kind of claims did you receive?
B09	They complained there was a vile smell, insects were produced, and so on.
A10	Did they say the reason of a vile smell and insects was my trash?
B11	And they compained crows and cats gathered to your house..
A12	But, cats and crows are very lovely, aren't they?.
B13	Yes.
A14	I don't know why they dislike cats and crows. Though they are noisy, they are pretty.
B15	I agree.
A16	And also they should not hate insects. We can see insects, crows and cats anywhere in this town. Is it right?
B17	Yes, it is.
A18	All right.
B19	But, neighbors' environment of daily life is surely damaged by your trash. It is beyond their limitation.

Fig. 13. Argumentation record

appear. However, a lot of very short messages or simple question are included in utterances, which are redundant messages.

Then, we observe the numbers of sub topics in detail. The numbers of sub topics of 'Value of Garbage' of Group 2 is 4.2, which is less than those of Croup 1 and Group 3. And, the numbers of sub topics of 'Trash in the Dump' and 'Care of Life' of Group 2 are both 2.4, which is also less than those of Group 1 and Group 3. The reason is that two argumentation in Group 2 records didn't mention sub topics of these two issue points at all because they stick to another issue point and to skip some issue points.

Though our experiment is still in the early stage, we summarize its result as follows.

– Usually, by using a diagram-based tool, users tend to stick to one topic, and sometimes skip important topic untouched. However, in our tool, by using modularization function, users argued all important topics without missing any of them. We prepared 6 modules at the beginning discussion, which became good advice for users.
Before the discussion of the top module, discussions of another modules have been finished already. Therefore, users can discuss in the top module by confirming the results of discussion of sub topic, and consequently the discussion of the top module became economical and effective.
– In our system, users have to input his message with a support link or an attack link. This means users have to represent their message logically, which is not easy for ordinal users. We sometimes observed users make the wrong link from the logical view. If users' input is wrong, the system can't calculate semantics of argumentation correctly.

5   Conclusion

We introduced an argumentation support tool based on the theory of AF. This tool helps users by supplying the environment for on-line discussion, by visualizing logical structure of arguments, by calculating semantics and by searching similar scene in old records. The feature of our tool is the modularization function. By dividing a whole discussion into several modules, users can discuss the complex theme without missing important sub topics. Generally, argumentation by exchanging text messages is not effective compared to the face-to-face argumentation because inputting text message takes much time. However, our experiment shows the quality of argumentation is less effective than face-to-face argumentation because noisy utterance is not allowed in the support tool.

To use our tool to the practical education, we found several problems. First one is that as users' utterances are not so logical in many cases, they sometimes make wrong link between irrelevant messages. In such case, the obtained semantics is not correct. Users need practice before using this tool. Furthermore, a mechanism which extracts logical structure from the English sentence will help for users to use this tool. Second one is that users cannot input detail message in our system because it takes much time. Therefore, we should consider some education method which uses both the face-to-face argumentation and the argumentation using the support tool. To solve these problems, another user interface and a novel education method using the tool should be developed.

References

1. Reed, C., Rowe, G.: Araucaria: software for argument analysis, diagramming and representation. Int. J. Artif. Intell. Tools **13**(4), 961–979 (2004)
2. Pinkwart, N., Aleven, V., Ashley, K., Lynch, C.: Evaluating legal argument instruction with graphical representations using largo. In: Frontiers In Artificial Intelligence And Applications vol. 158, p. 101. IOS Press (2007)
3. Pinkwart, N., Lynch, C., Ashley, K., Aleven, V.: Re-evaluating LARGO in the Classroom: Are Diagrams Better Than Text for Teaching Argumentation Skills? In: Woolf, B.P., Aïmeur, E., Nkambou, R., Lajoie, S. (eds.) ITS 2008. LNCS, vol. 5091, pp. 90–100. Springer, Heidelberg (2008). doi:10.1007/978-3-540-69132-7_14
4. Aleven, V., Ashley, K.D.: Evaluating a learning environment for case-based argumentation skills. In: Proceedings of the 6th International Conference on Artificial Intelligence and Law, pp. 170–179. ACM (1997)
5. Aleven, V.: An intelligent learning environment for case-based argumentation. Technol. Instr. Cogn. Learn. **4**(2), 191–241 (2006)
6. Ravenscroft, A., Pilkington, R.M.: Investigation by design: developing dialogue models to support reasoning and conceptual change. Int. J. Artif. Intell. Educ. **11**(1), 273–298 (2000)
7. Muntjewerff, A.J., Breuker, J.A.: Evaluating PROSA, a system to train solving legal cases. In: Proceedings of AIED, pp. 278–285 (2001)
8. Toulmin, S.: The Uses of Argument. Cambridge University Press, Cam bridge (1958)
9. Dung, P.M.: On the acceptability of arguments and its fundamental role in non-monotonic reasoning, logic programming and n-person games. Artif. Intell. **77**(2), 321–357 (1995)
10. Bench-Capon, T.J.M.: Persuasion in practical argument using value-based argumentation frameworks. J. Log. Comput. **13**(3), 429–448 (2003)

11. Dung, P.M., Kowalski, R.A., Toni, F.: Assumption-based argumentation. In: Simari, G., Rahwan, I. (eds.) Argumentation in Artificial Intelligence, pp. 199–218. Springer, New York (2009)

12. Dung, P.M., Thang, P.M., Hung, N.D.: Modular argumentation for modelling legal doctrines of performance relief. Argum. Comput. **1**(1), 47–69 (2010)

13. Brewka, G., Eiter, T.: Argumentation context systems: a framework for abstract group argumentation. In: Erdem, E., Lin, F., Schaub, T. (eds.) LPNMR 2009. LNCS (LNAI), vol. 5753, pp. 44–57. Springer, Heidelberg (2009). doi:10.1007/978-3-642-04238-6_7

14. Modgil, S.: Reasoning about preferences in argumentation frameworks. Artif. Intell. **173**(9), 901–934 (2009)

15. Katsura, Y., Okada, S., Nitta, K.: Dynamic argumentation support tool using argument diagram. In: 29th Annual Conference of the Japanese Society for Artificial Intelligence, pp. 1–4. The Japanese Society for Artificial Intelligence (2015)

16. Prakken, H.: An overview of formal models of argumentation and their application in philosophy. Stud. Log. **4**(1), 65–86 (2011)

17. Li, H., Oren, N., Norman, T.J.: Probabilistic argumentation frameworks. In: Modgil, S., Oren, N., Toni, F. (eds.) TAFA 2011. LNCS (LNAI), vol. 7132, pp. 1–16. Springer, Heidelberg (2012). doi:10.1007/978-3-642-29184-5_1

18. Amgoud, L., Cayrol, C., Lagasquie, M.-C., Livet, P.: On bipolarity in argumentation frameworks. Int. J. Intell. Sys. **23**, 1–32 (2008)

19. Boella, G., Gabbay, D.M., Van Der Torre, L., Villata, S.: Support in Abstract Argumentation. In: Proceedings of COMMA, pp. 111–122 (2010)

Gamification Design Framework to Support Multi-Agent Systems Theory Classes

J. Baldeón[1,2(✉)], M. Lopez-Sanchez[1], I. Rodríguez[1], and A. Puig[1]

[1] WAI Research Group, Department of Mathematics and Computer Science,
IMUB and UBICS Research Institutes, University of Barcelona,
Gran via, 585, 08007 Barcelona, Spain
{johan.baldeon,maite_lopez,inmarodriguez,annapuig}@ub.edu
[2] Avatar Group, Informatic Section, Engineering Department,
Pontificia Universidad Católica del Perú, Av. Universitaria 1801, Lima, Peru
http://www.ub.edu/wai

Abstract. Nowadays, gamification, or the use of game elements in serious activities, is applied to enhance engagement and to improve user's outcomes. On another note, the teaching of core concepts about Multi-Agent Systems (MAS) - such as distribution, autonomy, and interaction - is mostly performed by means of traditional theory classroom dynamics. Our claim is that MAS theory classes could be enhanced with gamified activities so that students can experience theoretical concepts in fun hands-on activities. Nevertheless, the design of the gamified classes requires the support of a suitable Gamification Design Framework (GDF) oriented to learning. This work analyses different GDFs and proposes an extension of one of the most widely used. This extension provides further support because it considers social computing in education when proposing an additional design stage along with alternative technologies such as ARS (Audience Response Systems) and LSP (Lego Serious Play). Furthermore, we illustrate its applicability by means of a case study of gamified activities in a multi-agent systems classroom.

Keywords: Gamification · Teaching MAS · LSP · ARS · LEGA

1 Introduction

Gamification, or the use of game design elements and game mechanics in non-game contexts [10], is currently applied in different contexts both to increase engagement and to promote certain learning behaviours on users [11].

Nevertheless, the actual design and deployment of gamified activities can become quite challenging [25]. A Gamification Design Framework (GDF) provides a useful guidance for gamification designers in their design processes since it considers the definition of different phases and goals as well as the identification of users, gamification elements, and their relationships.

Some researchers theorize that gamification could also be used in education as a tool to increase student engagement and to drive desirable learning behaviours on them [24]. When gamification is applied to the educational context

© Springer International Publishing AG 2016
F. Koch et al. (Eds.): CARE 2016/SocialEdu 2016, CCIS 677, pp. 136–155, 2016.
DOI: 10.1007/978-3-319-52039-1_9

to engage students, motivate actions, promote learning and solve problems, it is called Gamification of Learning (GoL) [20]. GoL must consider the specific characteristics of the educational context such as students (players), intended learning outcomes, educational levels and educational approaches.

Concretely, in this research, we address the gamification of learning Multi-Agent Systems (MAS). Most often, students experience MAS learning individually, joying a unidirectional teacher-student communication, and immersed in a traditional classroom environment and methodology. In this context, students experience theory classes – which happen to include many abstract concepts [4] – as boring, and thus, they simply do not engage and fail to attend (skip) classes. As a result, theory classes suffer from low attendance rates. A way to address these issues is by means of role-playing, where teachers and students can interact continuously, work collaboratively, act as agents that (distributively) interact and promote an emergent behaviour [2].

In this scenario, both existing knowledge and skills could be put into practice, keeping in mind that this experiential approach would ensure that teaching ideas, principles, and concepts have a lasting value [8]. Therefore, if session activities could include emulating MAS applications in this collaborative setting, it would consolidate learned concepts and would also enhance students experience [39]. Moreover, these activities would exploit transversal skills such as teamwork, social applications, collective thinking, argumentation and social intelligence [5]. Furthermore, if we gamify these activities, students would become more engaged and motivated.

This work proposes an extension of a Gamification Design Framework and its adaptation to education in order to gamify the learning of Multi-Agent Systems (MAS) theory concepts. This extension is two-fold. On the one hand, it considers the inclusion of the *end game* as a relevant element within the framework. On the other hand, it considers the addition of two external supporting systems, Lego Serious Play (LSP) [15] and Audience Response System (ARS) [21], that help to put into practice the design framework. LSP is included to brainstorm about how to improve theory classes. This brainstorming is conducted by building MAS metaphorical models using Lego bricks. Game-Based ARS allows to involve all students in a classroom, enhancing their learning feedback and interactivity within the class. Due to its collaborative nature, both LSP and ARS systems support social computing in education.

Additionally, we illustrate the applicability of our proposal through a case study of an undergraduate MAS class, where students revisit MAS theoretical concepts and design a specific MAS. When working collaboratively, MAS principles become somehow mapped into an experiential and immersive design, where students have autonomy to design and play agent roles themselves. Moreover, in this context, student interaction also becomes key to orchestrating the overall designed system.

Thus, the contribution of this work is twofold: (1) An extension of the Gamification Model Canvas framework; and (2) The gamification of an educational serious activity (i.e., a MAS class) to assess the value of this extension proposal.

2 Background and Related Work

This section starts by introducing those basic concepts that are key to pursuit the gamification of Multi-Agent Systems theory classes. Subsequent subsections detail them. Last subsection discusses some alternative gamification research works.

2.1 Teaching MAS

Although there are activities specifically conceived to introduce complex (dynamic) systems to high-school students or even to school children [22], Multi-Agent Systems is usually considered to be a rather specialized subject taught in last courses of Computer Science degrees, Artificial Intelligence masters or even Social Simulation doctoral courses.

This work focuses on an introductory MAS course in higher education, where students should get familiar with the main basic concepts of Multi-Agent Systems: agent definition, properties and related concepts (such as autonomy, roles, or situatedness); agent communication (i.e., indirect communication through the environment, direct communication through messages, protocols); coordination (cooperation, competition, task accomplishment, and the like); groups of agents (e.g., teams or coalitions); and organizations (social structures or institutions). Rather naturally, all these concepts can be translated into practical assignments orchestrated through laboratory sessions, where students work in pairs. Nevertheless, when introducing these concepts in theory classes, teacher's discourse can become quite abstract, which causes students to have difficulties in grasping them and, consequently, students often lose their interest. This, when combined with the fact that most students work part-time and tend to be quite selective regarding the classes they actually attend, lowers attendance rates in a significant manner.

Therefore, low attendance rates of undergraduate theory classes become a serious concern. This is especially the case when the term arrives to its end and the overall course workload becomes higher.

2.2 Gamification of Learning

Huotari and Hamari [17] define gamification as the process of enhancing services with affordances for gameful experiences, using game-based mechanics, aesthetics, and game thinking to engage people, motivate action, promote learning, and solve problems. Specifically, Gamification of Learning is known as an educational approach to motivate students to learn by using game elements within learning environments [20].

Gamifying effectively an activity is not as straightforward as to use points, medals, and badges to engage users. It should be a process carefully designed because of the inherent complexity of intervening elements (goals, users, context and resources, game elements, etc.). Therefore, gamification frameworks become a useful guidance for designers [31]. Several frameworks have been proposed in the literature applicable to different contexts or to specific sectors [7,9,12,14,27, 28,42].

Honey identifies various types of activities for teaching and learning as brainstorming, problem-solving, group discussion, puzzles, competitions, role-play, observing activities, think about how to apply learning in the real world, etc. This work borrows two well-known methodologies that facilitate brainstorming and problem-solving activities: Lego Serious Play (LSP) and Audience Response System (ARS).

LEGO Serious Play (LSP). LEGO Serious Play (LSP) is a methodology that lets people brainstorm and discuss complex ideas by means of storytelling activities accompanied with represented metaphors using LEGO bricks [23]. The central idea behind the LSP methodology is: "When you build in the world, you build in your mind" [36]. This refers to mental models that are used to make sense of the world, whether they represent a work environment, computer programming concepts, or personal beliefs. According to Papert's *constructionism* [34], touching, manipulating, and creating physical objects with our hands activates a richer kind of learning.

LEGO Serious Play allows articulating complex and tacit knowledge, extending the concept of "thinking with objects". Moreover, LSP participants usually understand that their models will not look very realistic and will have little meaning without providing their own stories. This helps the participants focus on building models with rich metaphorical meaning without worrying about their artistic abilities [15].

In LSP, LEGO models act as a starting point for discussion. Students open up and start brainstorming ideas together, exploring and finding unexpected solutions to the presented problems. LSP rules are based on a build-share-reflect sequence, where the facilitator gives a challenge related to the problem and participants build LEGO models, sharing stories about them, and reflecting on their understanding of the problem.

Audience Response System (ARS). Audience Response Systems (ARS) are technologies used to gather responses and give feedback to an audience in real-time [30,35,38]. ARS can be used in the classroom as an active learning tool. When using an ARS, the teacher launches (asks publicly) questions to the students, students answer them individually and receive immediate feedback so that they can assess their level of understanding.

Kay and LeSage [21] have mentioned there has been a widespread use of Audience Response Systems in higher education, and according to Pettit et al. [35], students show positive attitudes about the use of ARS, and they happen to be more attentive and engaged when ARS is used during lectures. However, some studies have concluded that the only use of ARS can tire students. Therefore, ARS seems to be more suitable when combined with other types of learning activities [35].

An example of Audience Response System is Kahoot! [6]. It allows the creation of interactive quizzes to be answered in real-time from any device by an unlimited number of students (*players*). It is a gamified ARS where students can earn points for answering questions correctly and on time. These points allow students to win prizes. Moreover, top ranked students appear in a classroom scoreboard. Overall, Kahoot! creates a social, fun, and game-like learning environment.

2.3 Related Work

The popularity of gamification in the education field has increased in the last years. Many experiences have introduced gamification into elementary, high school, and even higher education settings, obtaining uneven results in educational attainment and motivation [37]. Usually, unfruitful results can be due to the fact that gamification is being applied by merely adding game rewards to an existing set of learning activities, instead of using gamification design frameworks to make activities more attractive and engaging.

Game designers state that the core of a game for learning should be aligned with those competencies students are aimed to acquire [20]. This should be taken into account in order to guarantee the success of a gamified class. Actually, the effective gamification of courses is still a challenge. This is especially the case in the higher education context [19], where students must assimilate high-level concepts in a short period of time.

To the best of our knowledge, there are few GDFs focused on education:

FRAGGLE [32] is a framework based on the use of the Agile methodologies for the design of gamified learning experiences on higher education in order to obtain a fast Minimum Viable Product (MVP) ready for testing. The framework applies techniques all the way down to the lowest levels of abstraction through its step-by-step process. Moreover, the creation phase of the framework defines game mechanics and game activities according to player prototypes (defined by gender, learning experience, origin, etc.) and the different stages of the game (discovery, on-boarding, mid-game and end-game).

Lee Sheldon, in his book 'The multiplayer classroom' [40], presents a guide to gamify the classroom from game design syllabi to playing games, showing techniques to create multiplayer games on any subject that would engage students by using formats found in video games.

Furthermore, there are few gamified and game-based experiences for teaching and learning multi-agent systems [2,13,29,39,41]. Some of them are encouraging experiences related to teaching MAS concepts. For example, Sakellariou et al. [39] have used a multi-agent programmable modeling environment to increase active learning, where students enjoyed and the level of satisfaction increased. Melo et al. [29] have integrated a first-person shooter in the curriculum of course Autonomous Agents and Multi-Agent Systems, achieving motivated students. Fasli and Michalakopoulos [13] have integrated a simulation game in their graduate course on Agent Technology for E-commerce to teach students the principles of electronic markets and strategic interaction, and they get to engage, have challenges and fun. Soh [41] introduced a game-based technique to his Multi-Agent Systems class in four game days, where student teams competed against themselves in games related to MAS issues, achieving motivated students and they learned about MAS. Barreteau et al. [2] included role playing games in teaching the content of an MAS, where players understood the basis, were motivated and had fun. As in all these previous experiences, the Multi-Agent Systems subject that constitutes our case study already includes such hands-on activities in the lab sessions. Nevertheless, this work focuses our work in gamifying the acquisition of theory concepts.

In other experiences about the effectiveness of brainstorming driven by Lego Serious Play, Kurkovsky [23] gamified the process of formulating and refining use cases in software development. In general, students who used LSP attained a higher level of skills in the areas of comprehension, application, and analysis. Moreover, the quality of software projects submitted at the end of the course improved, and student engagement increased significantly.

Related to the use of Gamification Design Frameworks, there are few educational experiences that applied them. Li et al. [26] applied MDA framework (standing for Mechanics, Dynamics, and Aesthetics) to introduce Computer Science in a course. Hunicke et al. [16] encouraged students to increase participation in social and learning activities by using PeerSpace, an online social network for collaborative learning. As for Ibanez et al. [18], their students achieved higher understanding and engagement in programming in the context of a C-programming language gamified course. Its design was based on Nicholson's theoretical framework [33]. In this engaging experience, most students continued working even after earning the maximum amount of grade points. They also continued mastering unexplored C-programming topics.

Pointing out the encouraging results attained in these experiences, we propose to use Lego Serious Play, Audience Response Systems and Gamification Model Canvas framework (detailed below) to gamify classes of multi-agent systems, a subject that implies the introduction of theoretical abstract concepts, which may become tiresome and dull to follow.

3   Gamification Model Canvas - GMC

The Gamification Model Canvas (GMC) [12] is a Gamification Design Framework (GDF) that constitutes an agile, flexible and systematic instrument that helps designers to find play-based solutions to develop behaviours in non-game environments. It is based on the MDA game design framework [16] – focused on the Mechanics, Dynamics and Aesthetics included in games –, and on the Business Model Canvas, a tool to design a business model[1].

The Gamification Model Canvas presents the gamification design as an iterative and incremental process that involves nine key stages. These stages correspond to the definition of the main game components described below (and depicted as white boxes in Fig. 1).

1. *Revenues:* The first stage is the definition of the economic or social return that the gamified solution can provide (or enhance).

---

[1] http://www.businessmodelgeneration.com/canvas.

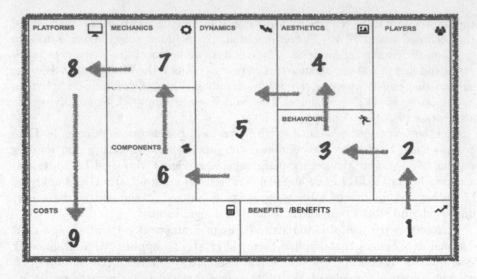

Fig. 1. Gamification model canvas.

2. *Players:* This phase focuses on who are the users, how are they, and what are their expectations. They can be considered *newbies, masters* or *designers*[2], and each profile involves different Bartle and Marczewski's gamification user types [3,28]. The *newbie* profile is an early user of the system and could be *killer, self-seeker, consumer,* or *exploiter.* The *master* is a regular user who needs more meaningful incentives to become an expert or designer user and could be *explorer, achiever* or *socializer.* The *designer* is a very committed user who helps the system and needs self-realization opportunities to develop himself and could be *philanthropist, free spirit* or *disruptor.*

3. *Behaviours:* In this stage, the gamification designer defines the main activities to be performed by players taking into account the player profiles, player types and the expected revenues, stated in the previous phases. Some examples of such activities are: visit a website; read content; answer a survey; buy something; create something from scratch; or investigate some topic.

4. *Aesthetics:* Next, it is necessary to describe those emotional responses evoked in players that can draw out during their playing experiences. For instance, the satisfaction to overcome a challenge –when the game is presented as an obstacle course–, or the feelings of fellowship and group membership — in case the game constitutes a social framework. Naturally, the selection of the desired aesthetics are directly correlated with the player's types selected previously.

5. *Dynamics:* Once aesthetics become clear, dynamics develop the run-time components that support or invoke these emotional responses. For example, fellowship aesthetics can be facilitated by means of dynamics that allow sharing information within a group via chat or by collaborative tasks that cannot be

---

[2] http://gecon.es/gamification-model-canvas-framework-evolution-2.

achieved by single players. Other aspects such as identity, status, scarcity, or altruism have also to be described at this stage.

6. *Components:* The sixth stage is devoted to the definition those lower-level elements involved in the creation of dynamics and feedback that will allow to create the game rules. Some widely-used components are points, badges, levels, missions, or avatars.

7. *Mechanics:* This is the most critical stage of the framework, since it is about the specification of the rules of the game. Thus, mechanics include actions, behaviours and control mechanisms afforded to the player within a game context. Mechanics relay on the selected components in previous stage for creating the desired game dynamics.

8. *Platforms:* In this step, the environment on which to implement game mechanics should be defined. In general, gamification can be achieved either by means of physical components or through virtual spaces, so platforms can range from fully equipped physical classrooms to sites on the Internet.

9. *Costs:* Finally, it is important to describe –and be aware of– the required investment to fully develop the gamified activity. Investment can come in the form of time as well as of physical and human resources.

The Gamification Model Canvas (GMC) framework has been applied only in business contexts rather than in academic ones. In the following section, we present the proposed extensions to this GMC framework.

4   Proposal

As the introduction states, the contribution of this work is twofold:

- First, in this section we propose an extension of the Gamification Model Canvas (GMC) framework previously introduced.
- Second, the value of this extension proposal is illustrated by applying it to gamify an educational serious activity (i.e., a MAS class).

Specifically, as Fig. 2 shows highlighted in blue (grey in grayscale print), we propose extensions of the GMC at two different levels. On the one hand, at an inner level, we propose the inclusion of a new relevant element within the framework: the END GAME stage, — so that it results in a framework composed by 10 elements. On the other hand, at an outer level, we consider the addition of external supporting systems (LSP and ARS) that help to put into practice the design framework.

4.1   End Game: A New Element in GMC

Each iteration in the Gamification Model Canvas (GMC) helps to further define and validate the hypothesis associated to those elements of the model defined in previous stages. Specifically, the *mechanics* element, which is core in the gamification process, is the component that requires more iterations and refinements.

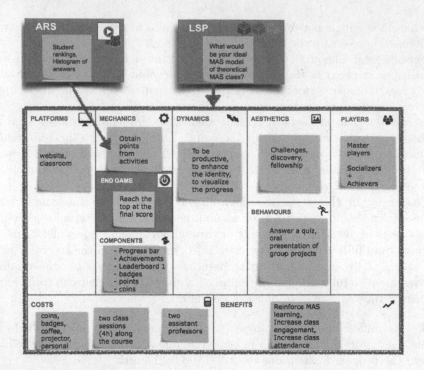

Fig. 2. Design of the gamification experience applying the extended GMC. (Color figure online)

This is the case even if the rest of elements are well designed, since the complexity of designing game mechanics is intrinsically high. In fact, some initiatives plan to provide tools to aid gamification designers with the transformation of selected components in the GMC workflow into specific mechanics suitable for the gamification process at hand.

Moreover, Mora et al. [31] point out that specific hypothesis referred to the logics of the game, such as game on-boarding or end game rules, do not appear explicitly in any element of the GMC framework. Certainly, although one may argue that some of these rules could be defined during the subsequent refinement steps of the *mechanics* element, its design becomes unavoidably complex when combining all actions, behaviours and components to define all the rules of the gamified activity. Therefore, we argue that isolating the specific rules of the end of the game would help in the modularity of the overall design process.

Thus, we propose to extend the GMC framework with a new element named *end game* (see blue box, or grey box in grayscale print, in Fig. 2). This element integrates different actions and behaviours to create specific game dynamics that will reach the end of the game. These dynamics will lead to a final state of victory or goal accomplishment which, most often, will stretch players to the limits of their abilities in their pursuing of this final (desirable) state. In the case of a learning serious activity, our claim is that students will make further progress in their skills and knowledge acquisition. To become a top user –with the highest score in a competitive environment– or to become the most popular player – with greater peer recognition in a collaborative context– are some examples of end-game rules.

4.2 GMC Extensions

As we consider *revenues*, *players*, *aesthetics* and *mechanics* rough elements in the GMC framework, we propose to extend it with two external systems that may help designers when defining these elements. Figure 2 depicts this extended GMC framework.

On the one hand, we advocate for using tools that involve users in the corroboration of *revenues* (we also refer to them as *benefits*); user profile (*player*) refinement; and that let them provide suitable and creative solutions (*aesthetics* and *mechanics*). The LSP is one representative example of these tools. In fact, Fig. 2 shows the LSP newly added box related (through an arrow) to the whole GMC box, to illustrate that LSP enriches many different components.

On the other hand, *mechanics* can be deployed by using ARS (Fig. 2 depicts the addition of the ARS box into the *mechanics* component). For example, ARS quizzes create a competitive atmosphere, including timed responses, real-time feedback, and points. Additionally, ARS Surveys, which lack of any competitive aspect, can be used for getting feedback from learners, being more suitable for group discussions.

5 Case Study

In order to explore the application of our extended GMC framework, we performed a case study of teaching Multi-Agent Systems, an optional subject in the fourth-year of a Computer Engineering degree. It has 6 ECTS (European Credit Transfer System), students attend two 2-hour-long in-class activities per week: one 2-hour slot corresponds to a theory class; and the other one is a practical session conducted in a computer laboratory.

As for class attendance, a total number of 26 students were enrolled in the course. Nevertheless, just a few of them (less than 20%) attended all theory classes. In fact, none of the theory classes did surpass fifty percent attendance. Additionally, when attending, the majority of students did not actively participate in class discussions. Therefore, our gamification goals (i.e., *benefits*) are to increase both class engagement and attendance, as well as to reinforce MAS learning, considering that concepts introduced in MAS theory classes are often abstract and difficult to grasp.

5.1 Design

The design of the gamification was conducted by a team formed by a game designer coach, the teacher of the MAS subject, and two collaborator teachers who also acted as assistants during the gamified sessions.

As the starting point of the design process, we involved a group of students in a brainstorming session to corroborate our diagnosis of the problem and our definition of the solution (i.e. gamification goals). We also aimed at knowing our users better, collecting therefore their opinions, values and ideas. To do so, we scheduled a Lego Serious Play (LSP) activity (see the LSP box at the top of Fig. 2) with eight voluntary students distributed in two heterogeneous groups of four students each (see left picture in Fig. 3).

Upon coach's requests, students built and shared with their group peers several models of different complexity: (i) a basic animal model; (ii) a model about a multi-agent systems (MAS) application in the real world; (iii) a model of a novel MAS model that could improve the world; and finally, (iv) a model of their ideal class to learn MAS topics. The former model (i) was simple because it was just intended to warm up students in building and sharing (i.e., explaining to peers) models. On the contrary, second and third MAS models where aimed at consolidating multi-agent system concepts. Finally, (iv) –the process of building the ideal class model– constituted the actual targeted brainstorming session. It is worth mentioning that individual models from (iii) and (iv) also involved a subsequent integration of the four models in the group into a single one, which required student's agreement (see right picture in Fig. 3).

Fig. 3. LSP Activity. Left: One group of four students building their models. Right: One example of a resulting aggregated MAS model.

The session concluded with students answering a survey that gathered their opinions about the LSP activity and current dynamics of (non-gamified) MAS theory classes. In the light of the results, all students agreed on the fact that the activity of modelling a MAS application with Lego bricks had helped them conceptualize and reinforce concepts of the subject. They also claimed that they had learned from the MAS application proposals made by their fellows. They imagined their ideal class as an engaging and collaborative activity with the teacher giving support to groups of students, who interact among themselves and apply theoretical concepts to real applications. It is noteworthy that during the LSP activity they had fun and felt committed and motivated.

These results helped us to confirm the suitability of the gamification project. Moreover, some students' suggestions about their ideal class inspired our class gamification design, which is depicted in Fig. 2 and detailed in the following.

The *revenues* (*benefits*) we expected to achieve with the gamified class are: reinforce MAS learning; increase class engagement; and increase class attendance.

Related to *players*, students could be considered as *master players* in GMC framework because they are familiar with the basic concepts of MAS. Furthermore, the design team agreed that user types were socializers and achievers.

As students usually have difficulties with the first contact with MAS concepts, and also to be continuously engaged during the class, our proposal of *behaviours* to develop in the players is to increase attendance and participation in MAS classroom sessions by means of several quizzes with real-time feedback along the class and oral presentations of group projects.

The *aesthetics* –desirable emotional responses evoked in students– we considered are: to overcome a challenge, explore MAS concepts, and fellowship.

As for *dynamics*, we chose to: be productive or contribute to reinforcing concepts for all class students, enhance the group identity and progression within the classroom, and visualize the progress of each student inside the gamified MAS session.

Components we used are leaderboards, progress bars, achievements, badges, coins, and points.

The *mechanics* we defined revolve around point rankings. First, students answer an interactive quiz –performed by means of an ARS– and obtain individual points. The student at the top of the ranking earns a badge, and each student adds his points to a paper scoreboard. Afterwards, students design an MAS project consisting of several activities that include the build-share-reflect sequence from LSP. Along this sequence, students share proposals and get rewards: physical coins that correspond to a number of points on the scoreboard. Badges are also awarded for most valued (voted) projects. Additionally, a shared coffee break was included to promote group identity.

The *end game* consists in, firstly, choosing (and rewarding) the three students with the higher scores (that is, the number of points accumulated along the performed activities) and, secondly, declaring the absolute winner.

Regarding *platforms* where to apply gamification, we required using both the physical classroom environment –together with its typical resources– as well as an Audience Response System (ARS) website.

Finally, some *costs* are identified to be necessary to get some of the resources required to develop the gamification project. These are: coins; badges; class projector; and personnel.

Next section explains the actual execution of these *mechanics* and *end game* as well as the usage of *platforms* and incurred *costs*.

5.2   Gamified Class

We conducted a two-hour-long theory class with 24 students which were familiar with the subject, and thus, they could be considered as *master players*. The session was first introduced by recalling our gamification goal (i.e., expected *benefit*) and describing its outline: reviewing theory concepts and designing a Multi-Agent System.

agent coordination

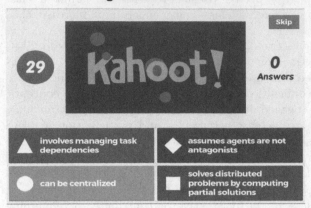
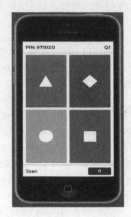

Fig. 4. Left: Example quiz question posted on the class projection screen. Students are requested to choose one among four possible answers identified by: red/triangle; blue/diamond; yellow/circle; or green/square. Number provided answers and number of remaining seconds are also displayed. Right: Answering user interface. (Color figure online)

Theory Concepts Review. The class started by reviewing theory concepts for half an hour. This activity was designed to consolidate MAS concepts by means of an Audience Response System (ARS) that induced the 'answer a quiz' *behaviour* with 'individual challenge' *aesthetics*.

Specifically, students participated in an interactive quiz we created at Kahoot! [6] web *platform*. It consisted of 5 consecutive theory questions posted on the class projection screen. Left image in Fig. 4 shows the first question. Students answered (and received feedback) by means of their mobile phones. Right image in Fig. 4 depicts the colour-and-shape-code user-friendly interface that students are provided to select their individual answer. As for feedback, Fig. 5 shows alternative student feedback. On the one hand, on the left, a cross-marked red (or dark grey in grayscale print) screen is provided to inform that the time for providing the answer expired (i.e., there was a time-up). Similarly, cross-marked red (or dark grey in grayscale print) screen on the right indicates an incorrect answer. As a result, no points are awarded in any case and the correct answer is provided for both cases. On the other hand, the tick-marked green (or grey in grayscale print) screen in the centre of Fig. 5 indicates the answer is correct as well as the number of awarded points. Students were awarded up to 1000 *points*[3] if they answered each question correctly and within a 30 s time-up period, so that the quicker they answered, the most points they got. Subsequently, for each question/answer cycle, the class projection screen showed a histogram of aggregated answers indicating how many students had chosen each option. When figures showed that some concepts were not clear enough, the teacher opened a discussion about most common errors (see left image in Fig. 6).

---

[3] For the sake of readability, we also use italics to highlight previously designed components from Fig. 2.

Fig. 5. Mobile phone interface for alternative types of feedback.

Fig. 6. Left: Histogram of students' answers — and teacher opening a discussion on issues that require clarification. Right: Quiz overall scoreboard.

The *mechanics* of this Audience Response System (ARS) incorporated different ways of providing immediate feedback to students. On the one hand, as Fig. 5 shows, each mobile phone showed individual achievements: if the answer was correct or wrong, the awarded points, and current position in the class ranking. On the other hand, the class projection screen showed student rankings after each question (see right image in Fig. 6). Notice, however, that just top-ranked students are shown, and thus, tactfully, positions remain non-public for the remaining students. Afterwards, at the end of the quiz, the winner got a badge and all students were asked to write their total awarded points in a paper *scoreboard* (see right image in Fig. 7). It is worth mentioning that we had provided beforehand this scoreboard for including subsequent activity scores, and thus, it also acted as a *progress bar*.

From here onwards we devoted most of the session to experience with the design of a Multi-Agent System (MAS).

Fig. 7. Left: Sharing market designs within a group of 4 pairs of students —all of them trading the same product. Right: The winner student. He holds a badge and his paper scoreboard appears on his desk.

MAS Design. During this second part of the session, the teacher first presented subsequent parts of a Multi-Agent Based Simulation research project, and then we encouraged the students to collaboratively design related examples of MAS – so we induced an MAS design *behaviour*.

Simweb is a former European research project that aimed at defining and studying alternative market models for the distribution of electronic contents – such as music or pieces of news. It involved the definition of a market as an MAS including both market stakeholders as well as those products being traded. Thus, it required characterising: (i) buyer and provider agent roles and associated behaviours, and (ii) product ontologies. Different actions and strategies were defined for each role: "imitation", "innovation", or "reputation leadership" constituted alternative provider strategies; whereas "buy cheapest offers", "satisfy requests exactly", or "be loyal to provider" were some buyer strategies. Additionally, products were defined in terms of its attributes (not just price but also other features such as product characteristics or delivery time) and associated value domains (i.e., attributes' possible values). These definitions were key to define provider product offers as well as buyer preferences over the products of their interest.

Students were asked to design a MAS market collaboratively, a market where the buyer and provided agents traded different products. Initially, we grouped students in pairs and assigned them one from 3 different products (a party organizing service, a drone, and an electronic book) as well as one of the various provider and buyer strategies mentioned before. Each pair had a specific product, buyer and provider strategies assigned such that there were 12 different pair assignments but 4 pairs traded the same product — so that they could form 3 bigger groups afterward. When working collaboratively, MAS principles were somehow mapped into an experiential and immersive design, where each student had autonomy to design and play one agent (i.e., its behaviour) but student interaction was key to agree on the overall system orchestration (i.e., common product definition and interaction).

MAS market design was partitioned in two phases, each following a (i) design -(ii) share -(iii) reward sequence similar to the one from Lego Serious Play (LSP). Each phase stage had a 3-to-5-min time limitation in order to kept students focused on their tasks. The first phase required students to define the product to trade and both provider's specific offers and buyer's preferences about this product. Whereas in the second, students specified the agent interaction protocol and executed (i.e., played) the system so that agent decision making –based on buyer satisfaction with respect to offered products– become apparent. For each phase: (i) design was done in pairs; then (ii) each pair shared their design with those 3 other pairs trading the same product; and finally, (iii) students awarded each others' work by awarding physical *coins* that were initially equally distributed. Specifically, each pair agreed on the design they liked the most and awarded this other pair by giving 2 of their coins (one coin from and for each student). Left image in Fig. 7 depicts one group of 4 pairs of students sharing their designs.

The complexity of the task together with the time limitation led us to a quite demanding activity. Therefore, a shared coffee break was introduced in between to relax students a bit. During this break students had an opportunity to socialize in a more relaxed atmosphere and to *enhance the group identity*.

Overall, considering the activity from a gamification point of view, our final goal was to increase the mastery (i.e., knowledge) of 'master' players, but students were also considered as both 'socializers' and 'achievers' players since they worked collaboratively to achieve their design task. Furthermore, the *aesthetics* were that of 'discovery' and 'fellowship' and main *dynamics* pursued students to be productive while learning to design an MAS market.

Students obtained points from different activities so that the *End game* was defined by accounting for the students that reached the top at the final *score*. Thus, the *mechanics* consisted in:

1. Sharing: The pair having most coins within each group explained their market design to the rest of the class. As a result, 3 pairs explained market examples that traded different products.
2. Reward: Classmates voted for the preferred one. Each member of the winner pair won a badge.
3. Teacher's feedback: The teacher provided final remarks on MAS design such as model visualization or MAS execution indicators.
4. Ranking: Students updated their paper *scoreboards* by computing their total number of points and by considering that both *coins* and *badges* accounted for 1000 *points* each.
5. Winner and price assignment: top-three-scored students raised their subject grades proportionally. The overall winner (depicted in the right hand side of Fig. 7) was also acclaimed by classmates.

6   Results

Based on data gathered from surveys filled by students after the gamified class, we present here the following results (see Fig. 8):

- 96% of students considered that their knowledge or skills in multi-agent systems (MAS) concepts had increased after the hands-on activities included in the gamified MAS class.

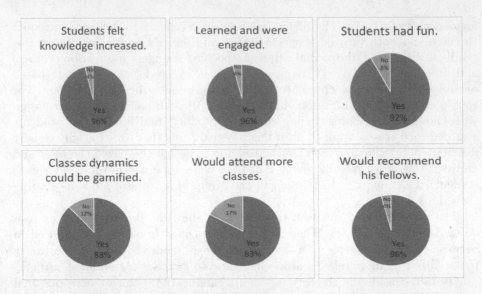

Fig. 8. Survey results regarding students' opinion about the gamified MAS class designed according to the extended GMC framework.

- 96% of students indicated that tools used in class (such as interactive game, participatory activities, group work, or awards) had helped them to be engaged, motivated, and also to reinforce and further learn MAS concepts.
- 92% of students had fun during the gamified theory session.
- 88% of students believed that classes should include gamified dynamics.
- 83% of students would attend more classes, in case they were gamified.
- 96% of students would recommend their fellows to attend gamified sessions.

Analysing these results, we can conclude that the vast majority of students perceived knowledge acquisition during the session. We can also observe that students were a bit more engaged and motivated than took pleasure. It could be due to the fact that some of them did not follow the activities comfortably due to an overloaded agenda, as they themselves mentioned. Then, as a lesson learned, we could say that gamified activities must be carefully designed to facilitate participation and engagement of students in class.

Related to students' opinions about the use of gamification in theory classes and if they would attend classes more frequently, the reason of the decrease of values until 88 and 83% respectively may result from (i) the preferences of some students of "learning by example", which demands from them a less cognitive effort (they play a passive role) in contrast to their active role during gamified classes, (ii) and the overlapping of class and work timetables. Recall that this is a subject intended for last year undergraduate students, so that many of them work and study simultaneously. Additionally, it should be noted that the majority students had fun with Audience Response System (ARS) quiz and found it interesting. Nevertheless, some others did not liked the competitive aspect of gamification.

7 Conclusions and Future Work

This work presents a methodology to improve traditional classroom dynamics and knowledge acquisition. Specifically, it aims at promoting student's performance, in-class participation, and attendance. This methodology is based on the Gamification Model Canvas framework but extends it to include Multi-Agent Systems principles, as well as those of Lego Serious Play and Audience Response System, so that its application in current academic contexts become most suitable.

We have developed a use case consisting of the design and implementation of a gamified class in an undergraduate subject of Multi-Agent Systems. Results show that 96% of students believed that activities and tools used in the gamified class had helped them to consolidate and deepen their knowledge. Students also reported to be engaged and motivated during that class. As future work, we expect to be able to further evaluate the proposal extending this experience to next year MAS course as well as to other undergraduate subjects. We plan to conduct these new experiences in such a way that allows us to statistically compare traditional with gamified classes so to better assess the contribution of our proposal. Furthermore, since current Gamification Design Frameworks do not explicitly consider educational aspects –such as intended learning outcomes, learning styles and activities, or academic evaluation–, our research group has proposed a Learner-centered Gamification Design Framework (LEGA) [1] that aligns both educational and gamification approaches. Thus, we plan to combine the extensions proposed in this work together with this new framework to advance the state of the art in the area of Gamification of Learning.

Acknowledgments. We thank projects TIN2012–38876–C02–02, 2014SGR623, TIN2015–66863–C2–1–R (MINECO/FEDER), Carolina Foundation, and contribution of members Avatar Group of the Pontificia Universidad Católica del Perú for supporting the development of this research.

References

1. Baldeón, J., Rodríguez, I., Puig, A.: LEGA: a LEarner-centered GAmification design framework. In: Proceedings of the 17th International Conference on HCI. ACM (2016)
2. Barreteau, O., Bousquet, F., Attonaty, J.M.: Role-playing games for opening the black box of multi-agent systems: method and lessons of its application to senegal river valley irrigated systems. J. Artif. Soc. Soc. Simul. 4(2), 5 (2001)
3. Bartle, R.: Hearts, clubs, diamonds, spades: players who suit MUDs. J. MUD Res. 1(1), 19 (1996)
4. Beer, M.: Multi-agent Systems for Education and Interactive Entertainment: Design, Use and Experience: Design. IGI Global, Hershey (2010)
5. Bellanca, J.A.: 21st Century Skills: Rethinking How Students Learn. Solution Tree Press, Bloomington (2011)
6. Brand, J., Brooker, J., Versvik, M.: Kahoot! (2016). https://getkahoot.com/

7. Burke, B.: Gamify: How Gamification Motivates People to Do Extraordinary Things. Bibliomotion Inc., Brookline (2014)
8. Casasola, E., De, V., Cliffe, O., Padget, J.: Teaching MAS in the UK and in Latin America. Innov. Teach. Learn. Inf. CS (2005)
9. Chou, Y.K.: Actionable Gamification: Beyond Points, Badges, and Leaderboards. CreateSpace Independent Publishing Platform (2015)
10. Deterding, S., Dixon, D., Khaled, R., Nacke, L.: From game design elements to gamefulness: defining gamification. In: International Academic MindTrek Conference: Envisioning Future Media Environments, pp. 9–15. ACM (2011)
11. Domínguez, A., Saenz-de Navarrete, J., De-Marcos, L., Fernández-Sanz, L., Pagés, C., Martínez-Herráiz, J.J.: Gamifying learning experiences practical implications and outcomes. Comput. Educ. **63**, 380–392 (2013)
12. Escribano, F., Moretón, J., Jiménez, S.: Gamification Model Canvas Framework Evolution (2016). http://gecon.es/gamification-model-canvas-framework-evolution-1
13. Fasli, M., Michalakopoulos, M.: Teaching e-markets through simulation games. In: AAMAS 2005 Teaching MAS Workshop (2005)
14. Francisco-Aparicio, A., Gutiérrez-Vela, F.L., Isla-Montes, J.L., Sanchez, J.L.G.: Gamification: analysis and application. In: Penichet, V.M.R., Peñalver, A., Gallud, J.A. (eds.) New Trends in Interaction, Virtual Reality and Modeling, pp. 113–126. Springer, Heidelberg (2013)
15. Gauntlett, D.: Creative Explorations: New Approaches to Identities and Audiences. Routledge, Abingdon (2007)
16. Hunicke, R., LeBlanc, M., Zubek, R.: MDA: a formal approach to game design and game research. In: AAAI Workshop on Challenges in Game AI, vol. 4 (2004)
17. Huotari, K., Hamari, J.: Defining gamification: a service marketing perspective. In: Proceeding of the 16th International Academic MindTrek Conference, pp. 17–22. ACM (2012)
18. Ibanez, M.B., Di-Serio, A., Delgado-Kloos, C.: Gamification for engaging computer science students in learning activities: a case study. IEEE Trans. Learn. Technol. **7**(3), 291–301 (2014)
19. Iosup, A., Epema, D.: An experience report on using gamification in technical higher education. In: Proceeding of the 45th ACM Technical Symposium on Computer Science Education, pp. 27–32. ACM (2014)
20. Kapp, K.M.: The Gamification of Learning and Instruction: Game-Based Methods and Strategies for Training and Education. Wiley, Hoboken (2012)
21. Kay, R.H., LeSage, A.: Examining the benefits and challenges of using ARS: a review of the literature. Comput. Educ. **53**(3), 819–827 (2009)
22. Klopfer, E., Scheintaub, H., Huang, W., Wendel, D.: Starlogo TNG: making agent based modeling accessible and appealing to novices. In: Komosinski, M., Adamatzky, A. (eds.) Artificial Life Models in Software, pp. 151–182. Springer, Heidelberg (2009)
23. Kurkovsky, S.: Teaching software engineering with lego serious play: conference workshop. J. Comput. Sci. Coll. **30**(6), 13–15 (2015)
24. Lee, J.J., Hammer, J.: Gamification in education: what, how, why bother? Acad. Exch. Q. **15**(2), 146 (2011)
25. Levy, H.P.: Five key trends in Gartner's 2015 digital marketing hype cycle (2015). http://www.gartner.com/smarterwithgartner/five-key-trends-in-gartners-2015-digital-marketing-hype-cycle

26. Li, C., Dong, Z., Untch, R.H., Chasteen, M.: Engaging computer science students through gamification in an online social network based collaborative learning environment. J. Inf. Educ. Technol. **3**(1), 72–77 (2013)
27. Marache-Francisco, C., Brangier, E.: Process of gamification from the consideration of gamification to its practical implementation. In: Proceeding of the CENTRIC 2013, pp. 126–131. IARIA (2013)
28. Marczewski, A.C.: Even Ninja Monkeys Like to Play. CreateSpace Independent Publishing Platform (2015)
29. de Melo, C., Prada, R., Raimundo, G., Pardal, J.P., Pinto, H.S., Paiva, A.: Mainstream games in the multi-agent classroom. In: Proceeding of the IEEE/WIC/ACM International Conference on Intelligent Agent Technology, pp. 757–761. IEEE Computer Society (2006)
30. Miller, R.G., Ashar, B.H., Getz, K.J.: Evaluation of an audience response system for the continuing education of health professionals. J. Contin. Educ. Health Prof. **23**(2), 109–115 (2003)
31. Mora, A., Riera, D., González, C., Arnedo-Moreno, J.: A literature review of gamification design frameworks. In: 2015 7th International Conference on Games and Virtual Worlds for Serious Applications (VS-Games), pp. 1–8. IEEE (2015)
32. Mora, A., Zaharias, P., González, C., Arnedo-Moreno, J.: FRAGGLE: a FRamework for AGile Gamification of Learning Experiences. In: De Gloria, A., Veltkamp, R. (eds.) GALA 2015. LNCS, vol. 9599, pp. 530–539. Springer, Heidelberg (2016). doi:10.1007/978-3-319-40216-1_57
33. Nicholson, S.: A user-centered theoretical framework for meaningful gamification. In: Proceedings of GLS 8.0 Games+Learning+Society Conference, pp. 223–229 (2012)
34. Papert, S., Harel, I.: Situating constructionism. Constructionism **36**, 1–11 (1991)
35. Pettit, R.K., McCoy, L., Kinney, M.B., Schwartz, F.N.: Student perceptions of gamified audience response system interactions in large group lectures and via lecture capture technology. BMC Med. Educ. **15**(1), 92 (2015)
36. Rasmussen, R.: When you build in the world, you build in your mind. Des. Manag. Rev. **17**(3), 56–63 (2006)
37. Richter, G., Raban, D.R., Rafaeli, S.: Studying gamification: the effect of rewards and incentives on motivation. In: Reiners, T., Wood, L.C. (eds.) Gamification in Education and Business, pp. 21–46. Springer, Heidelberg (2015)
38. Robertson, L.J.: Twelve tips for using a computerised interactive audience response system. Med. Teach. **22**(3), 237–239 (2000)
39. Sakellariou, I., Kefalas, P., Stamatopoulou, I.: Teaching intelligent agents using NetLogo. In: ACM-IFIP IEEIII (2008)
40. Sheldon, L.: The Multiplayer Classroom: Designing Coursework as a Game. Cengage Learning, Boston (2011)
41. Soh, L.K.: Using game days to teach a multiagent system class. SIGCSE Bull. **36**(1), 219–223 (2004)
42. Werbach, K., Hunter, D.: For the Win: How Game Thinking Can Revolutionize Your Business. Wharton Digital Press, Philadelphia (2012)

The Role of Agent-Based Simulation in Education

Andrew Koster[1](✉), Fernando Koch[2], Nicolas Assumpção[3], and Tiago Primo[4]

[1] Artificial Intelligence Research Institute (IIIA-CSIC),
Universitat Autònoma de Barcelona, Barcelona, Spain
andrew@iiia.csic.es
[2] Korea University, Seoul, Republic of Korea
fkoch@acm.org
[3] Instituto de Pesquisas Eldorado, Campinas, SP, Brazil
nicolasriccieri@yahoo.com.br
[4] SAMSUNG Research Institute, Campinas, SP, Brazil
tiago.t@samsung.com

Abstract. Agent-Based Modelling and Simulation (ABMS) is a research methodology for studying complex systems that has been used with success in many social sciences. However, it has so far not been applied in education research. We describe some of the challenges for applying ABMS in the area of education, and discuss some of the potential benefits. We describe our proof-of-concept model that uses data collected from tablet-based classroom education to model how students interact with the content dependent on their engagement level and other properties, how we are calibrating that model, and how it can be validated.

1 Introduction

Agent-Based Modelling and Simulation (ABMS) is a methodology for studying complex systems, and is employed in diverse fields such as economics [30], social sciences [9], biology [13] and transport engineering [3]. [17] describe ABMS as being "particularly suitable for the analysis of complex adaptive systems and emergent phenomena". Despite pedagogy studying what can clearly be described as a complex system [5,15,16], ABMS has, to our knowledge, not been applied in studying education.

There are a number of possible reasons for this, but in our opinion the most prominent one is that to apply ABMS, one needs a lot of available data, and a sufficient understanding of intermediate constructs and how they can be extracted from the data. This type of research is performed in the twin fields of Learning Analytics and Educational Data Mining, which have only recently reached sufficient maturity for ABMS to be a valid approach in researching various aspects of education. In this work, we aim to promote ABMS as a methodology for pedagogical research; in particular when studying classroom environments. We will give an overview of the state-of-the-art in ABMS, and describe some ways in which it could be applied to education research. Moreover, we will present a

© Springer International Publishing AG 2016
F. Koch et al. (Eds.): CARE 2016/SocialEdu 2016, CCIS 677, pp. 156–167, 2016.
DOI: 10.1007/978-3-319-52039-1_10

proof-of-concept ABMS for modelling a classroom education environment, and how we can use it in both the research and practice of education.

2 Background

Agent-Based Modelling and Simulation (ABMS) is a computational research methodology to study complex phenomena. In particular, an *agent* in this methodology is an autonomous (computational) individual that acts within an *environment*. The aim is (usually) to model the agents and their interactions, and study the resulting emergent properties of the system. It has long been known that very simple systems can portray complex behaviour. Probably the most well-known example of this is Conway's game of life [10], in which a cellular automaton with four simple rules can, dependent on the starting scenario, have such complex behaviour that people are still discovering new patterns.

ABMS can be seen as the natural extension of such cellular automata, in that it considers the system as being distributed: rather than the system having a single state, each entity (agent) has a state, and agents decide individually (and asynchronously) on their next action, rather than the system as a whole moving from state to state. Nevertheless, they have in common that both ABMS and cellular automata are bottom-up (aka micro) models, where the behaviour of the system emerges from the behaviour of individuals, as opposed to macro models, which aim to (usually mathematically) describe the system as a whole without worrying about individuals. Because ABMS allows for distinct types of agents within the system, it is rapidly gaining popularity in biology and social science research, where describing the entire system in a set of mathematical equations is often too complex to be of much use, if possible at all, whereas it is possible to build sufficiently realistic models of individuals and how they interact with each other, and study properties of the system that emerge from the behaviour of many individuals.

For the development of an ABM, it is necessary to be able to calibrate and validate it [4]. The former refers to the process of tuning the model to best correspond to real data. In particular, this requires that there is detailed data on individuals' behaviour in order to calibrate the agent models, data on their interactions, in order to calibrate the interaction models, and finally, data on the emergent properties of the system in order to validate the model. The validation of an ABM, or any model for that matter, is a complicated issue and there is ongoing research on how best to approach this [14,24], but without doubt, it is only possible with sufficient real data against which to validate.

Up until very recently, such data was not available for the field of education. However, over the last decade, many areas of education have been making increasing use of technology: (i) on the administrative side to keep track of students, their grades, attendance rates, etc. (ii) at the course level, where Learning Management Systems (LMS) applications help teachers distribute course material, collect assignments and perform many of the day-to-day tasks of administering a course; and (iii) at the class level, mostly in the form of Massive Open Online Courses (MOOC), where teachers provide a digital course for students to follow worldwide (usually completely separate from the normal curriculum). All such applications generate, and store, detailed data at the level they are designed for. An administration system will store a history of students and classes throughout time, whereas an LMS tracks students through a course, in combination with the material each student accessed, and created, throughout the course. Finally, MOOCs and other systems within a class collect detailed usage data for each student, logging each action a user takes throughout the class. The use of such data to perform data-driven analysis of pedagogical measures is a development of the last few years.

In particular, *Learning Analytics* is defined as: "the measurement, collection, analysis and reporting of data about learners and their contexts, for purposes of understanding and optimising learning and the environments in which it occurs." —Siemens [29]. Learning Analytics and Educational Data Mining are both relatively young, but fast-growing areas of research that focus on finding algorithmic methods for quantifying various metrics that can model a student's learning process. There is a large overlap in the two areas, both in goals and in methodologies, with the differences between the areas being mostly in the philosophical and historical roots of the fields [28]. However, as Gašević et al. [11] point out, in accordance with our own findings, "there has been a dearth of empirical studies that have sought to evaluate the impact and transferability of this initial work across domains and context", and "instructors expressed their preferences of learning analytics features that offer insights into learning processes and identify student gaps in understanding over simple performance measures". Eberle et al. [8] discuss 12 grand challenge problems for Technology-Enhanced Learning. Among these challenges, we distinguish the similar themes: they identify challenges on how to model students using continuous temporal data, and how to use the data in providing appropriate feedback to empower teachers. In short, while there is a significant amount of work [7, 25–27] into descriptive and predictive measures, what is missing is how different measures can be combined into a theoretically sound, data-driven model of student learning.

We propose that Agent-Based Modelling for Education can address this question.

3   ABMS for Education

The integration of cognitive theory and agent-based approaches in technology-enhanced learning has so far been the particular domain of Intelligent Tutoring Systems (ITS) [12]. In this approach, the focus is on individual learning, and the student is helped by an artificial tutor. Cognitive theories are employed to model user knowledge, and a diverse range of AI techniques, including intelligent agents and recommender systems are used to decide how the tutor should act, what learning object to present to the user, etc. An example of a modern ITS approach is SimStudent [22], which uses machine learning techniques to update a rule-based agent system to adapt to students' needs. A similar approach is presented by López Bedoya et al. [21], which uses a combination of computational techniques to plan, and replan coursework based on heterogeneous characteristics of the students. Such systems serve a different purpose from what we propose: rather than attempting to model students as socio-cognitive systems in order to understand them, these systems model students as parameters for adaptive computational tutors.

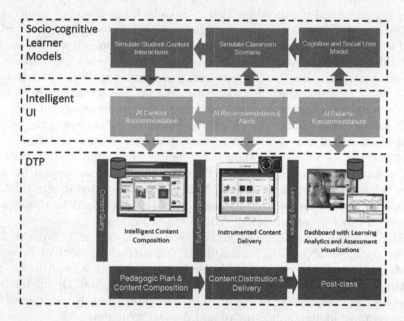

Fig. 1. Overview of components of a digital teaching platform with intelligence models

Figure 1 gives the outline of components in a contemporary system for technology-enhanced learning and outlines what kind of models can help improve our understanding at each stage of education. We see that at the individual level, the modelling follows a cognitive modelling approach [1], and the aim, as best as possible, is to model the psychology of learning, and understand such concepts as creativity, learning styles, engagement and performance. This usually treats students as individuals in isolation, relying for instance on data from MOOCs where students can mostly be considered to be working through a course alone; interacting only with the content and not (much) with their fellow students or the educator. A system comprised of multiple agents like this could model a classroom. In this model, in addition to individual properties, the social interactions come into play. We distinguish between implicit and explicit social interactions. Implicit interactions are those that arise from individual actions that predicate a response. For instance, the teacher changes pages, and expects the students to follow suit. Explicit social interactions are those actions that are directly aimed at a social goal, such as discussing an item, asking a question, solving an exercise together. MOOCs and LMS systems attempt to capture many such interactions, although it is often impossible to do so: if interactions happen outside the system, the data is usually not available. The emergent properties from such a system can also be studied at two levels: firstly, the interactions can have an effect on individual students, and secondly we can study properties of the classroom, both as aggregates over the individuals, like average performance or engagement, and properties that only arise at the level of a classroom, such as sociability. Finally, we can study how such systems are situated in the environment; the environment is generally described as everything that is modelled, but is not an agent. In the education scenario this is the course material and the possibilities for students and educator to interact with it, but also external parameters, such as noise level, light level, temperature, time of day and day of week, etc. With regards to the content, the data that is most easily manipulated by a computational model is the metadata, which describes properties of the actual course material, such as whether it is textual, a video, or interactive content, what subject(s) the content is related to, and for what level it is intended. By modelling the content, and other aspects of the environment, one can answer other types of questions, such as whether the same exact class at a different time of day would have led to better overall performance? Or what effect switching textual content for video content might have. This is the use of ABMS we have started to study, and we present our proof-of-concept class simulator in the next Section. However, we can think of other potential uses of ABMS for education.

ABMS can also be applied at a higher level of abstraction, in order to assist in policy decisions about educational institutions, teaching methodologies and content. Students might be modeled as having to decide what institute to study at, taking into account the policies and teaching philosophies. Or the institutes themselves can be modeled as agents. The modelling of such macro-level phenomena requires more administrative and demographic data.

A different, but complementary, approach for using ABMS in education is to use the ABMS as an educational tool for modelling other systems (e.g. a biological ecosystem). While that is not the use of ABMS we are interested in this work, it may nevertheless be insightful to give students control over an ABMS simulating their own situation, and allow them to experiment with what types of interventions might improve their own, their class's or their school's performance.

4   Proof-of-Concept Model of a Classroom

We built the proof-of-concept Classroom Simulator to model a classroom in which the students are following the teacher during a lecture. We model students interactions' based on different educational contents and teacher characteristics, however we do not take explicit social interactions into account. In simulating a classroom, the model is composed of three different steps: (I) Initialization, (II) Generate Signals, (III) Content Analysis and optimization. This aims to simulate the actual data that is *output* by a tablet-based digital teaching platform that we developed [18] for use in classrooms. This system generates detailed usage logs for each student, and the teacher. The idea of the model is to be able to generate such usage logs artificially, and simulate some specific types of interventions.

In particular, we aim at modelling teacher-oriented interventions, such as changing the type of material or teaching style. The simulator focuses on a subset of the log data, specifically those related to navigation through the content.

Step (I), generates the variation of students signals' based on the characteristic of the teacher, the content and a class profile. Input in this step are the duration of a class, the educational content profile, the students' profile and the teacher profile. The educational content profile is the number of different contents, their difficulty, their type (image, video, text or assessment) and their order. The teacher profile is related to this content: how orderly he goes through the material and what types of content he spends more time on. Students' profiles are generated stochastically, by drawing random samples from a class profile. The class profile defines the number of students, and normal distributions for engagement (the amount of time a student spends working on the same content as the teacher), activity (the number of actions per time step), and orderliness (whether they navigate through the content linearly from start to finish, or a haphazardly fashion that jumps between contents and navigates backwards) of the students. Furthermore, we simulate eye tracking time series data about whether an individual student is looking at, or away from the tablet at every time stamp. All of these parameters can also be extracted from the real usage logs generated by our tablet-based system. In addition to these profiles, a set of rules are generated (also adding random noise in the generation process) based roughly on the *possible* values each of the different parameters might take for each student, and the states these create within the system, the next state for any student. An example of such a rule, for a student, is the following:

IF

> the student has the profile of being highly engaged, medium active and highly orderly;
> the student's recent history of actions are that he or she is looking towards the tablet, and has been studying the first content (a difficult video) for at least 10 time steps;
> and the teacher is looking at the second content (an image)

THEN

> the student will change pages to the second content.

Rules for the teacher are simpler, as they only take the teacher's actions into account, whereas we assume that students are influenced by what the teacher is doing (while the reverse is also possible, we disregard that form of feedback at this stage). Even so, for both the students and the teacher, there is the possibility for combinatorial explosion in creating the rules, so we instead generate them randomly without overlap until a sufficient (parameter of the model) number have been generated.

In Step (II), the class is simulated. All students, and the teacher, are initialized on page 0. For each time step, the teacher and each student is evaluated: for each agent the list of rules are run through, and a distance from the agent's state to the state described in the precondition of the rule is computed. The rule with the minimum distance is selected, and if this distance is lower than a threshold, the rule is executed and the agent transitions to a new state. The output of the simulation is a log of the events that occur during the simulation run.

In Step (III), we can *calibrate* (and also *validate*) the model by analysing the simulated log with regards to student engagement, orderliness and activity, and see if these correspond to the student profiles generated in Step (I). The calibration can be done by many different optimization algorithms, but in particular, we believe Genetic Algorithms (GA) are appropriate, with as fitness criterion a distance measure between the generated student profiles, and the input student profiles. We start by generating different class, teacher and material profiles and generate a population of rule sets. The rules are evaluated through simulation, and then a subsequent population of rules is generated. The best rule set is selected. This rule set can then be tested with *real* data: compute the engagement, orderliness and activity level of a real classroom based on the logs from a session of use of the tablet-based education platform. Then use the rule set to generate an artificial log (which could also be compared to the *real* log for additional validation), and based on the artificial log, compute the different profiles again. We can then see how far they differ.

4.1   Implementation

In order to test this idea, we have implemented the simulation above. In order to test our initial assumptions, we generate a random set of student agents, and a single teacher agent. The students are generated from the class profile in Table 1.

Table 1. Class profile used to generate student agents

#students	Activity	Orderliness	eye tracking	at tablet
5	$80(\sigma = 5)$	$80(\sigma = 5)$	$80(\sigma = 5)$	$50(\sigma = 5)$
10	$30(\sigma = 10)$	$40(\sigma = 10)$	$40(\sigma = 10)$	$90(\sigma = 5)$

In this table, we see that there are two different *profiles* for students in the class, with the first profile used to generate 5 students, and the second to generate 10. Each student agent's behaviour is governed by its profile, generated at random from the Gaussian distributions with the parameters as in the table. For instance, this can result in a student with profile 1 having an activity level of 85.25, an orderliness of 83.5, "eye tracking" parameter of 82.0, and "at tablet" parameter of 49.25. Each of these values governs different aspects of the agent's behavior. A high activity level means that the agent is more likely to click, change pages, or perform other activities, at each time stamp. An agent with high orderliness is likely to work through the material sequentially, whereas a low orderliness indicates a propensity to jump around in the material haphazardly. The "eye tracking" and "at tablet" parameters together govern what the student looks at. "Eye tracking" gives the percentage of time that a student spends looking at either the tablet, or the teacher (as opposed to elsewhere), while "at tablet" is used to divide that time between the tablet and the teacher.

The teacher agent has a similar profile, but there is no need for eye tracking, so it only consists of activity level and orderliness. Finally, we generate a material profile, which specifies a set of learning objects, and their order and organization by chapters. Each learning object is modeled with a type of object and its difficulty level.

Independently of the class, teacher and material profiles, the main engine of the simulator is the rule-based system for each agent. All student agents use the same rules (or plans), and the teacher agent has a separate set. Because we do not know how to model such rules, we calibrate the rules with a genetic algorithm (GA). As stated in the previous section, the rules are used to define each agent's behaviour, given the state of the world: what learning object the agent is at (and for how long), what learning object the teacher is at (and for how long), the characteristics of both learning objects, whether it is currently looking at the tablet or the teacher, and the intrinsic parameters defined in the agent's profile). The agent matches the plan rule that is nearest to its current state, and that rule specifies the parameters for the stochastic method of choosing the next state. In our GA, the initial population consists of 200 models (individuals), for each of which we generate a random set of 650 rules for students and a further 150 for the teacher (or approximately 800 rules out of a possible $2exp13$). We then run each model to generate the events, which in turn are analysed and result in 15 student profiles and a teacher profile. The fitness of this profile is simply how near it is to the original profile (using Euclidean distance).

For creating the next generation we use an elitist approach: the 20% best models of each generation are copied over as is, with a 1% chance for mutation. Furthermore, these serve as the basis for crossover (random pairs are selected) which creates a further 20% of the next population. The remaining 60% is generated randomly. To perform crossover we pick two parents randomly, and for each rule, either parent has an equal chance to contribute theirs (and if one parent has more rules than the other, these are also all copied over). Our mutation operator works as follows: there is a chance a set of rules is mutated, in which case one rule (chosen randomly) is generated again randomly. For further information on genetic algorithms and these operators we refer to Mitchell's work [23].

4.2 Experiments

We implemented the simulator and genetic algorithm (GA) as described above in Python. The rules, class profile, teacher profile and material profile are all represented in JSON format. Subsequently we ran the GA for 200 generations, but the results plateaued after 40 generations. To compare whether crossover and mutation were contributing anything over random search, we also ran the algorithm with a selection of 40%, and no crossover or mutation. We then compare the top 40% of each generation; the results are in Fig. 2.

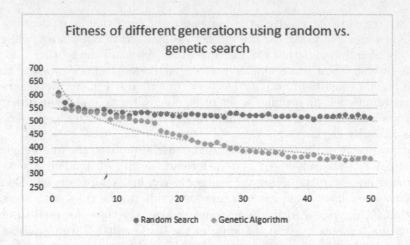

Fig. 2. For each generation, a comparison between pure random search, and the GA with crossover and mutation. The dotted lines are the trend lines (logarithmic for the GA, and linear for the random search)

We see that the GA improves the performance significantly over a standard random search, indicating that our crossover and mutation operators work. Nevertheless, the error still seems high, even in the best case. However, that is if we expect the simulation process to predict the exact same set of students (and thus have a distance of 0). What we actually aim for is to simulate at a class level, and thus what we expect is that the process results in a set of students from the same class profile. The expected distance[1] between two sets of agents generated using the profiles of the table above, is 232. The best model in the last generation from the GA has a score of 272, or in percentages, it is 17% away from this optimal score. Whereas the best result from the random search has a score of 385, or 66% away from the optimal score. This indicates that our GA is on the right track, and we can probably improve it, by fine tuning the parameters.

In order to validate the result, we also have to test how well the simulation works on real data. For this, we test the 20 best results of our last generation on real data collected in field trials of the Digital Teaching Platform [18,19]. However, the real data is logs of actions in the tablet-based system, and not the resulting profiles. As such, we should compare the simulated logs with the real one. In order to do this, we extract the class, material and teacher profiles from the real log data, and use this profile in each of the 20 models. This generates a log

---

[1] For each student, the expected distance is the expected distance between two samples from the same normal distribution (as defined by the class profile), which is: $\sqrt{\sum_{p \in parameters} 4\sigma_p^2/\pi}$, with σ_p^2 the variance of the distribution for parameter p. Summing this distance over all students gives us the expected distance between two sets of student agents generated from the same class profile.

of actions, which we can compare to the original log. However, this comparison is not trivial. Our first impression is that the simulated log and the real log are very different. For starters, the simulated log contains over 100,000 actions, whereas the real log contains only 8,000. This also results in the Levenshtein (edit) distance (the minimal number of insertions, deletions and substitutions to make two strings equal) [20] between the two logs being approximately the same as the length of the simulated log, and thus not a useful measure. Instead, we look at the frequency of event types, and the χ^2 distance measure [6] between them. This results in an average distance of 0.27, which is a more useful measure: it shows that while the number of events are different, the general frequency of events is fairly similar. As a measure of similarity between logs, we therefore suggest to use the geometric mean of the edit distance between the actual logs and the χ^2 difference between their histograms.

Future work is to adapt the simulator using a two-step GA to evolve a model that is both calibrated (in the sense outlined in the first experiment) and valid (using the distance measure we just discussed).

5 Discussion

Agent-Based Modelling and Simulation is a powerful tool for doing research into complex systems, such as education, and while it has so far not been used in this field, we believe the data is now available to take advantage of this methodology. Moreover, data-driven research into education is a fast-growing field of research, and ABMS can take advantage of increasingly sophisticated quantitative metrics of education to incorporate into the agent models. Once agent-based models are sufficiently robust, they can even help validate these metrics, by quantifying how much explanatory power they add in the model, in comparison to the added complexity. This can be an invariable tool in quantitative research into education, by helping to hone in on what metrics best explain and predict student learning, and present such information to the students, teachers, parents and other stakeholders. Moreover, simulations can be designed to test what type of interventions work best.

Our own agent-based model, although still in an early stage, is intended in such a capacity. The model as described thus far is a first step, and we have specific extensions planned to better take advantage of the unique possibilities of agent-based approaches: the rules that are created to differentiate between agents' behaviour do not take social interactions into account, and the student profile does not take motivational factors or learning styles into account. Moreover, we are still working on creating a valid model based on the data we gather, but the potential is clear: we can take real class profiles and test how they perform using a different content profile. If the students are more engaged than their input profile suggested, this is an indication that perhaps that type of content works better with that class. We can design experiments to test such hypotheses and use a methodology like *design-based research* [2] to iteratively improve the model and test its predictions.

Acknowledgements. This research was implemented with support from Samsung Research Institute Brazil, project "Integrated Ecosystem of Digital Education". Fernando Koch, Andrew Koster and Nicolas Assumpção were working with Samsung Research Institute Brazil during the time of the implementation of this project. Fernando Koch received a CNPq Productivity in Technology and Innovation Award, process CNPq 307275/2015-9. Andrew Koster is a Marie Sklodowska-Curie COFUND Fellow in the P-Sphere project, funded by the European Unions Horizon 2020 research and innovation programme under grant agreement No. 665919. Andrew Koster also thanks the Generalitat de Catalunya (Grant: 2014 SGR 118).

References

1. Anderson, B.: Computational neuroscience and cognitive modelling: a student's introduction to methods and procedures. Sage (2014)
2. Bakker, A., van Eerde, D.: An introduction to design-based research with an example from statistics education. In: Approaches to Qualitative Research in Mathematics Education, pp. 429–466. Springer, Dordrecht (2015)
3. Bazzan, A.L., Klügl, F.: A review on agent-based technology for traffic and transportation. Knowl. Eng. Rev. **29**(03), 375–403 (2014)
4. Bonabeau, E.: Agent-based modeling: methods and techniques for simulating human systems. Proc. Nat. Acad. Sci. **99**(suppl 3), 7280–7287 (2002)
5. Burns, A., Knox, J.: Classrooms as complex adaptive systems: a relational model. TESL-EJ **15**(1), 1–25 (2011)
6. Chardy, P., Glemarec, M., Laurec, A.: Application of inertia methods of benthic marine ecology: practical implications of the basic options. Estuar. Coast. Mar. Sci. **4**, 179–205 (1976)
7. Chrysafiadi, K., Virvou, M.: Student modeling approaches: a literature review for the last decade. Expert Syst. Appl. **40**(11), 4715–4729 (2013)
8. Eberle, J., Lund, K., Tchounikine, P., Fischer, F.: Grand challenge problems in technology-enhanced learning II: MOOCs and beyond. In: Perspectives for Research, Practice, and Policy Making Developed at the Alpine Rendez-Vous in Villard-de-Lans. Springer (2016)
9. Epstein, J.M.: Generative Social Science: Studies in Agent-Based Computational Modeling. Princeton University Press, Princeton (2006)
10. Gardner, M.: Mathematical games: the fantastic combinations of john conway's new solitaire game "life". Sci. Am. **223**, 120–123 (1970)
11. Gašević, D., Dawson, S., Siemens, G.: Lets not forget: learning analytics are about learning. TechTrends **59**(1), 64–71 (2015)
12. Greer, J.E., McCalla, G.I.: Student Modelling: The Key to Individualized Knowledge-Based Instruction. Computer and Systems Sciences, vol. 125. Springer, Heidelberg (1994)
13. Grimm, V., Berger, U., Bastiansen, F., Eliassen, S., Ginot, V., Giske, J., Goss-Custard, J., Grand, T., Heinz, S.K., Huse, G., et al.: A standard protocol for describing individual-based and agent-based models. Ecol. Model. **198**(1), 115–126 (2006)
14. Herd, B., Miles, S., McBurney, P., Luck, M.: MC^{2}MABS: a monte carlo model checker for multiagent-based simulations. In: Gaudou, B., Sichman, S.J. (eds.) MABS 2015. LNCS, vol. 9568, pp. 37–54. Springer, Cham (2016)

15. Jordan, M., Schallert, D.L., Cheng, A., Park, Y., Lee, H., Chen, Y., Chang, Y.: Seeking self-organization in classroom computer-mediated discussion through a complex adaptive systems lens. In: Yearbook of the National Reading Conference, vol. 56, pp. 39–53 (2007)

16. Keshavarz, N., Nutbeam, D., Rowling, L., Khavarpour, F.: Schools as social complex adaptive systems: a new way to understand the challenges of introducing the health promoting schools concept. Soc. Sci. Med. **70**(10), 1467–1474 (2010)

17. Klügl, F., Bazzan, A.L.: Agent-based modeling and simulation. AI Mag. **33**(3), 29 (2012)

18. Koster, A., Primo, T., Koch, F., Oliveira, A., Chung, H.: Towards an educator-centred digital teaching platform: the ground conditions for a data-driven approach. In: Proceedings of the 15th IEEE Conference on Advanced Learning Technologies (ICALT), Hualien, Taiwan, pp. 74–75. IEEE (2015)

19. Koster, A., Zilse, R., Primo, T., Oliveira, Á., Souza, M., Azevedo, D., Maciel, F., Koch, F.: Towards a digital teaching platform in Brazil: findings from UX experiments. In: Zaphiris, P., Ioannou, A. (eds.) LCT 2016. LNCS, vol. 9753, pp. 685–694. Springer, Cham (2016). doi:10.1007/978-3-319-39483-1_62

20. Levenshtein, V.I.: Binary codes capable of correcting deletions, insertions and reversals. Sov. Phys. Dokl. **10**(8), 707–710 (1966). Original in Russian in Dokl. Akad. Nauk SSSR 163, 4, 845–848 (1965)

21. López Bedoya, K.L., Duque Méndez, N.D., Brochero Bueno, D.: Replanificación de actividades en cursos virtuales personalizados con árboles de decisión, lógica difusa y colonias de hormigas. Avances en Sistemas e Informática **8**(1), 71–84 (2011)

22. Matsuda, N., Yarzebinski, E., Keiser, V., Raizada, R., Cohen, W.W., Stylianides, G.J., Koedinger, K.R.: Cognitive anatomy of tutor learning: lessons learned with simstudent. J. Educ. Psychol. **105**(4), 1152–1163 (2013)

23. Mitchell, M.: An Introduction to Genetic Algorithms. MIT press, Cambridge (1998)

24. Niazi, M.A., Hussain, A., Kolberg, M.: Verification and validation of agent based simulations using the VOMAS (virtual overlay multi-agent system) approach. In: Proceedings of the Second Multi-Agent Logics, Languages, and Organisations Federated Workshops (MALLOW), Turin, Italy, CEUR-WS (2009)

25. Papamitsiou, Z., Economides, A.A.: Learning analytics and educational data mining in practice: a systematic literature review of empirical evidence. J. Educ. Technol. Soc. **17**(4), 49–64 (2014)

26. Peña-Ayala, A.: Educational data mining: a survey and a data mining-based analysis of recent works. Expert Syst. Appl. **41**(4), 1432–1462 (2014)

27. Romero, C., Ventura, S.: Educational data mining: a review of the state of the art. IEEE Trans. Syst. Man Cybern. Part C Appl. Rev. **40**(6), 601–618 (2010)

28. Siemens, G., Baker, R.S.J.: Learning analytics and educational data mining: towards communication and collaboration. In: Proceedings of the 2nd International Conference on Learning Analytics and Knowledge, pp. 252–254. ACM (2012)

29. Siemens, G., Long, P.: Penetrating the fog: analytics in learning and education. EDUCAUSE Rev. **46**(5), 30 (2011)

30. Tesfatsion, L., Judd, K.L.: Handbook of computational economics: agent-based computational economics, vol. 2. Elsevier (2006)

Author Index

Printed in the United States
By Bookmasters